Growing
and Using
HERBS

Growing and Using HERBS

Andi Clevely and Katherine Richmond

SELECT
EDITIONS

This edition published by Sebastian Kelly
2 Rectory Road, Oxford OX4 1BW

Produced by Anness Publishing Limited
Hermes House, 88-89 Blackfriars Road, London SE1 8HA

A CIP catalogue record for this book is available at the British Library

ISBN 1-84081-173-0

Publisher: Joanna Lorenz
Project Editor: Penelope Cream
Photographers: John Freeman and Michelle Garrett
Consultant: Anthony Gardiner
Home Economist: Liz Trigg

Also published as *The Complete Book of Herbs*

Printed and bound in Singapore

© Anness Publishing Limited 1994, 1999
1 3 5 7 9 10 8 6 4 2

The publisher and authors would like to extend special thanks to
Anthony Gardiner for his unfailing enthusiasm and expert advice;
to Warren and Jenny Prestwich at R & G Stevens, and Lucas Green Nurseries,
for their generosity and warm hospitality; to Simon and Judith Hopkinson
and their staff at Hollington Nurseries and Rosemary Titterington at
Iden Croft Herbs for all their kind help and advice.

CONTENTS

Introduction

Juniperus lycia

The history of herbs is as long as the story of mankind, for people have used these plants since earliest times. Wars have been fought and lands conquered for the sake of plants, and even today we continue to depend on exotic species for many of our newest medicines and chemicals.

Today herbs are so pervasive that we take them for granted and barely give them a thought except when cooking or gardening – in contrast to the past when people had a more intimate relationship with the plants around them.

In medieval Europe, country people had always gathered wild harvests of useful plants, but it was in the monastic herb gardens that plants of known virtue were transplanted and organized in beds and borders, and their usefulness studied. This was then catalogued in such early works as the tenth-century book of 'simples' (herbal medicines) sent to Britain by the Patriarch of Jerusalem, and the major treatise on herbs written by a thirteenth-century Franciscan monk, Bartholomaeus Anglicus. Berries, seeds and barks from distant parts of the world were dried and imported as spices to increase the range of flavours and fragrances available to the few who could afford them.

Values change as settled societies become wealthy and less involved in the daily struggle for survival. Before

long herbs were being cultivated in Europe, not just for their availability when needed but also to be enjoyed as amenity plants. This growing appreciation of what is now termed their 'garden merits' seemed to coincide with a gradual decline in their practical use.

In the nineteenth century, prepared medicines, dyes and cosmetics had become widely available, and better methods of food preservation and distribution meant there was no need to use strong herbs and spices to disguise the flavour of rank meat and stale fish. Old herbal wisdom became suspect as primitive and unreliable, so that today in Western societies, herbalism has become synonymous with cranky superstition.

Below: *Illuminations of herbs and flowers were commonly used to decorate medieval Books of Hours.*

Left: *An elegantly spiralling clipped yew, flanked by the leafy stems of angelica.*

NATURAL SWEETENERS

Plants add an almost infinite variety of flavours to food, but only a few contribute obvious sweetness, even though the common names of many herbs include the description 'sweet'. For commercial production sugar cane is an important crop in the tropics, while sugar beet is grown in temperate regions. Tree saps can be evaporated to a syrup for use as sweeteners, notably the sugar maple (Acer saccharatum) *of North America, although walnut trees were recommended during the Second World War in Britain as a source of syrup. The best herb for this purpose is European sweet cicely,* Myrrhis odorata, *whose leaves can be substituted for some of the sugar needed in acid fruit recipes. In recent years* Lippia dulcis, *a relative of lemon verbena, was identified as the plant the Aztecs called 'sweet herb' and has been found to contain hernandulcin, a substance that is a thousand times sweeter than sucrose.*

Happily, changing fashion is restoring herbs to their former importance. Alternative medicine has rediscovered some of the skills of phytotherapy (the use of medicinal plants), and the ancient pedigree of healing herbs. Concern for the precarious status of many wild species, especially those that grow exclusively in threatened tropical rainforests, has highlighted the unique properties that might be lost with their extinction. An interest in international cuisines has made us familiar with the flavours of oriental lemon grass, leaf coriander from the eastern Mediterranean, and South American

Left: *An intricate herbal border in the fifteenth-century* Siege of Tripoli *by Guillelmus of Tyre.*

maté, the restorative tea brewed from the leaves of a holly, *Ilex paraguayensis.*

Histories of herbs and herb gardens used to be written from a European viewpoint, ignoring the important fact that global human dependence on plants is

Far Left: *An example of the popular Victorian art of arranging pressed herbs and flowers.*

Left: *Nicholas Culpeper, the great seventeenth-century herbalist, who produced the* Theatrum Botanicum *in 1640.*

Below: *Heartsease and wild strawberry are among the decorative motifs adorning this Book of Hours by Simon Marmion, c. 1480.*

characteristic of all societies in tune with their surroundings, yet Kuna Indians in Panama reserve parts of their forests as sanctuaries in which their healers can gather the medicinal herbs so important to their way of life; the Antasaka and other coastal tribes of Madagascar exploit forest plants for all their clothing, medicines, food and building materials; fishermen on the island of Socotra throw wood chips from the Adenium tree into pools to sedate fish for an easy catch; Arab horsemen treat their mounts with a whole pharmacopoeia of herbs developed by medieval Arabian physicians; and European Romanies still gather wild garlic and wayside herbs as they have done since their migrations began long ago.

Most modern gardeners need to relearn this instinctive affinity with herbs, but growing them in the garden will inevitably lead to an understanding of their qualities. None of us can grow them all, for the choice is vast and increasing as new species and their properties are discovered.

GROWING HERBS

Herbs as Garden Plants

There are many definitions of a herb, none altogether satisfactory. To the botanist it is a plant that dies down to ground level at the end of the growing season; medicinally the word refers to any plant that can assist in the prevention or treatment of illness; while in the kitchen it means a part of a plant that is used in the preparation of food.

Arctium lappa

Paradoxically many gardeners grow only a limited choice of herbs for use, planting others according to their ornamental merits. An essential collection might contain parsley, sage, thyme and mint, with rosemary, lavender or marjoram as optional extras.

How far to explore the treasury of herbs depends on your available space, and on the type of climate and terrain enjoyed by your garden. Plants of tropical origin need warm walls or greenhouse protection in temperate regions, while Mediterranean herbs and shrubs with grey or white leaves prefer dry, sunny places similar to their natural habitats. There are herbs for moist dappled shade, parched banks or the boggy margins of pools, for rock gardens, window boxes and patio pots, climbers to train on arches and trellises, and prostrate leafy mats for embellishing the edges of paths and tops of walls.

Many herbs have varieties and cultivars with coloured and variegated foliage, and these can be planted to create a satisfying tapestry of contrasting shades. They are usually a little less vigorous than the normal types from which they were bred. The plainer forms might not rival modern hybrid

EARLY HERBALS

The earliest books about herbs are a fascinating subject for collection and study. Apart from their obvious curiosity value, they are evidence of the beliefs and understandings of particular eras, and chart changing attitudes to plants, the ways in which they act, and their importance in diets, medicine and daily household life, as well as contemporary issues of astrology, alchemy and divination. The earliest scientific works were Theophrastus' Enquiry into Plants *and* Growth of Plants *(c. 300 BC). Seminal texts of the Middle Ages were Avicenna's* Canon Medicinae *(c. 1020) and the Anglo-Saxon* Leech Book of Bald *(c. 950).*

Left: *Even a small herb garden can supply a wide range of aromatic, edible and medicinal material for everyday use.*

Right: *Herbs are so diverse in shape and colour that they deserve a garden to themselves, although it need not be classically formal and restrained, as this kitchen herb garden reveals.*

USEFUL UMBELLIFERS

Fennel is a typical umbelliferous herb, with a branching stem system and flattened umbels – heads of little flowers – which are followed by long, aromatic seeds. Many other members of the Umbelliferae family are useful plants, including herbs such as European sweet cicely (Myrrhis odorata), parsley, chervil and angelica, vegetables such as carrots and parsnips, and medicinal herbs such as asafoetida. Unfortunately, some close relatives are extremely toxic – poisonous hemlock is perhaps the most notorious, but there are also others – so it is unwise to gather umbellifers from the wild without accurate identification.

flowers and shrubs for brilliance of colour, but their worth lies in their effectiveness as teas, tonics and ointments, for their fragrance, and for the complex flavours they impart to other foods. They are also easier to tend than most choice ornamentals.

USEFUL WEEDS

The nineteenth-century American writer Ralph Waldo Emerson defined a weed as 'a plant whose virtues have not yet been discovered', which is fairer than the common assumption that weeds are unwelcome plants. All plants should be judged by the same criteria, and if they have a pleasing appearance and known virtues they merit room in the herb garden. Wild chamomile, for example, used to be known as the 'plants' physician' for its ability to revive ailing plants nearby, while alliums such as wild garlic and Welsh onions are companion plants for roses, which seem healthier in their presence. Common comfrey has pretty purple flowers, and can be harvested as a compost activator and remedy for skin ailments, while even the ubiquitous chickweed is a valuable salad ingredient with some tonic properties.

There is little difference between garden weeds and wild flowers other than where they grow. Many wayside plants deserve to be grown in gardens,

being attractive enough to stand beside cultivated plants, and able to guard them from the threat of pollution and loss of habitat.

HERBS AND WILDLIFE

Bees, butterflies and other wild creatures depend on an enormous selection of plants for their survival. Herbs are ideal conservation plants because their strong perfumes and simple flowers attract browsing insects. In particular, bees love the sweet-scented blooms of thyme, sage, lavender, bergamot, mint, hyssop and rosemary, and it is no coincidence that a beehive was often the centrepiece of medieval herb gardens. Not only butterflies but also hoverflies, whose larvae are voracious allies in controlling pests, enjoy open single flowers or herbs with flat heads of blossom, such as sedum, catmint, sweet rocket and purple loosestrife.

A Place in the Garden

Chironia centaurium

Visiting herb gardens is the best way to decide on which plants to choose and where to grow them. If they are primarily intended for use, it may be enough to gather your favourite kinds in a small accessible bed, which might be a cook's garden of basic culinary herbs, a formally arranged medicinal border, or a relaxed collection of dye herbs in cottage garden style. Some of the more colourful herbs can be planted among ornamental flowers rather than kept separate in a distinct herb garden, while culinary varieties blend happily with kitchen garden crops.

Whatever your intentions, the cultural needs and habits of your plants must come first. It is no good trying to grow a majestic woodland herb such as angelica or lovage in a small, neat bed, for it will dominate the other plants and look hopelessly out of scale. Strictly geometrical designs must be created from evergreen perennials with similar heights and growth rates if the pattern is not to lose its clean outlines or disappear in winter.

Remember, too, that some herbs are very choosy about the soil and aspect they need, whereas others are almost infinitely adaptable – rosemary, for example, thrives almost anywhere, except in cold winters, and may be clipped as an informal flowering hedge or into simple evergreen topiary. A tall variety such as 'Fastigiatus' ('Miss Jessop's Variety') left to grow naturally will grace any shrub border and even support a small clematis for

variety; semi-prostrate 'Severn Sea' is perfect for cascading over a bank; while 'Tuscan Blue' or 'Majorca' with neater growth and brighter flowers are ideal as multi-purpose culinary, medic-

Below: *Whether your garden is a large expanse of soil and shrubs or a small front patch in front of a city house, herbs can be happily combined to produce an attractive display – space need not be a limiting factor in a herb garden.*

ROYAL PRECEDENT

Far from being a modern phenomenon, collecting aromatic herbs can be traced back as far as ancient Egyptian times. Around 1500 BC, Queen Hatshepsut ordered the mass felling of fig trees in her kingdom to build rafts that were poled up the River Nile for hundreds of miles in search of exotic trees and aromatic herbs for the royal gardens. Sennacherib, son of Sargon II of Assyria, constructed magnificent gardens and planted them with myrrh and other aromatic shrubs collected from the lands of the Hittites. Once gathered they were treasured for their great value, and widely used, traded or offered – the Queen of Sheba, for example, is recorded as taking a present of balsam seeds to King Solomon, and King Gentius of Illyria in the second century AD was renowned for his healing exploits with the roots of *Gentiana lutea*, which was named after him.

inal and ornamental container shrubs for a prominent position on the patio.

FITTING IN THE PLANTS

Unless you plan to assemble a comprehensive herb collection immediately, perhaps arranged in classically formal beds, it is best to begin with the few herbs you know you will use constantly, and add others later. Your own needs and preferences must decide which herbs to select, while experience will reveal whether they thrive in the chosen situation. A start could be

Below: *A robust flamboyant climber with ornamental leaves and interesting 'cones' in autumn, the hop plant earns a place in the less formal herb garden as an edible, medicinal and aromatic plant.*

made with essential culinary herbs, planted together in the vegetable garden, leaving until later the option of expanding the collection and moving plants to a dedicated site elsewhere. Most simply, individual herbs may be tucked into existing beds and borders to make their gently colourful contributions, providing an effective foil for brilliant herbaceous plants.

Herbs are irresistibly collectable, however, and finding room for later acquisitions is often a problem, especially in a small garden. A score or so of essential varieties will grow comfortably in a bed about 3 x 1 m/10 x 3 ft, especially if annuals and invasive kinds are confined to containers. Enclosing the bed with a tapestry hedge of evergreens that tolerate clipping permits the addition of hyssop, germander, lavender and similar herbs, while at their base dwarf prostrate kinds (such as pennyroyal, thrift and woolly thyme) can be allowed to billow over the edge of the path. Instead of hedging, you could surround the garden with rustic fencing to support a rose

Above: *Aromatic herbs such as thyme and lavender arranged around the house as dried flowers or pot-pourri make inexpensive and efficient air fresheners, combining the ancient tradition of strewing herbs with modern principles of aromatherapy.*

such as 'Zéphirine Drouhin', which is early to flower and one of the last to finish. Fastigiate (slim and upright) or standard shrub varieties can be added to the bed as an extra tier above ground-level plants.

If your ambitions extend further, you may want to consider planting a larger border or separate herb garden. Collections in botanic gardens are often arranged systematically according to use or family, and these will give you an idea of the amount of room needed. Less congenial parts of the garden may be ideal for larger numbers of herbs – a dry bank, for example, is the perfect site for a collection of thymes, an arrangement of decorative pots in a courtyard might house some of the many available kinds of mint in partial shade or basil in full sun, while a simple heap of rubble and soil could be transformed into a herbal rock garden of mat-forming varieties and dwarf shrubs.

Different Types of Herb Garden

Herbs have always been an important ingredient of domestic country gardens, where they were grown almost exclusively for their practical uses. It is only comparatively recently that the cottage garden has been appreciated and become fashionable. Classic cottage garden herbs include the essential culinary species, perhaps with the addition of coriander, garlic and one or two specimens of southernwood or curry plant to brush in passing. On the whole, the authentic range of cottage herbs was fairly conservative.

Veratrum viride

Most herbs can be grown informally, even 'muddled up' with other plants as the garden designer Vita Sackville-West (1892-1962) preferred them to be, although this should not mean total neglect. Like any other plant, herbs become straggly and unkempt if left to themselves or if they seed themselves too liberally among their neighbours, and it is important to keep them in their place by pruning, division, dead-heading or harvesting as necessary.

Some species blend remarkably well into a flowering border, especially more robust kinds such as angelica, foxglove, and bronze fennel which partners prettily the broad leaves of irises and the rich autumn shades of helenium, dwarf sunflowers or rudbeckias. Rue, santolina and lemon balm succeed in the middle of borders, while sage, marjoram, violets and lady's mantle are compact plants for growing near the front.

Annual and biennial herbs can be sown *in situ* or transplanted from elsewhere to fill space in beds and borders. Try sowing pinches of dill, borage, parsley and marigold seeds in pots for emergency use where gaps appear, and add young marjoram, savory and feverfew plants to edgings of pinks and other low perennials. Container-grown mints such as *Mentha* x *gentilis* (ginger mint) and *M. suaveolens* 'Variegata' (pineapple mint) may be plunged into the soil, with the pots buried up to their rims, to fill gaps with their decorative seasonal foliage.

FORMAL GARDENS

Herbs lend themselves most to a formal layout, as they have done since, in Tudor times, gardeners translated embroidery and plaster ceiling patterns into floral designs for the garden. The discipline imposed by a geometrical arrangement of beds and paths has its advantages: the plants are easy to reach for maintenance and harvest, their numerous and complementary shades and shapes are particularly suitable for combining in artistic patterns, and symmetry is satisfying for its own sake.

Designs can be simple and intimate: the familiar fan or cartwheel, for example, with wedge-shaped beds radiating from a common centre, or a chequerboard arrangement of alternate paving slabs and square beds, perhaps with small vegetables and salad herbs to

Above: *Even a simple area of stone setts can be transformed into a miniature herb pavement when the joints are planted with prostrate mints, thymes, marjoram and similar mat-forming species.*

Left: *The clean classical outlines of dwarf hedges and evergreen topiary echo the restraint and balanced patterns of a formal herb garden.*

create a French-style *potager;* these are often the most effective, especially in small gardens. Where there is space, larger and more complex gardens are traditional, with beds of herbs surrounded by clipped dwarf hedges of germander, santolina, hyssop or box, either as strict frames for herb parterres or woven and intertwined to produce the classic knot garden.

Precision is essential for ambitious designs to succeed, as is frequent maintenance to keep the hedges trim. Within the chosen framework, herbs can be planted informally in whatever way pleases the eye, arranging them systematically so that culinary herbs are kept separate from medicinal species, for example, or in traditional style, using large numbers of a few

compatible herbs to create a form of carpet bedding.

THE WILD HERB GARDEN

The opposite of the strict parterre, a wild herb garden combines informality with the pleasures of re-creating a natural environment and providing a haven for wildlife. The ground needs to be prepared in the same way as for conventional herb borders, because there will be room only for chosen plants and not for some of the more invasive wild species. Arrange naturally meandering paths, together with one or two places to sit in peace and, if possible, a pool for moisture-loving herbs and aquatic wildlife. There is no need to level the ground – in fact, banks, hollows and gentle undulations add to the garden's

Above: *Many herbs have a natural exuberance that makes them ideal for herbaceous borders and wild gardens. These informal beds border a cool turf path beside which a strategically placed pedestal fountain plays.*

charm. Choose seeds of herbal wild flowers, grasses and woodland herbs such as angelica, woodruff, campion and lovage (some specialist seedsmen will blend a mixture to your requirements), and sow at the appropriate time. Add ferns, and a few suitable shrubs and trees such as elder, crab apple or quince. The only maintenance necessary will be routine cutting back to restrain vigorous species, the removal of unwelcome species, and occasional propagation of older perennials.

The Ornamental Herb Garden

Although individual herbs may look their best when in flower or in early spring as the young foliage unfolds, a decorative herb garden can be expected to give pleasure at every season, and year-round interest should be taken into account when drawing up garden plans. Include hardy evergreen species to balance the seasonal changes and to provide winter colour and continuity from one year to the next: variegated and coloured forms remain brilliant highlights on the darkest days.

Bryonia cretica

Herbaceous herbs die down to the ground as the season closes, leaving areas of bare ground, so be sure to disperse evergreens to provide plenty of attractive ground cover in spite of winter gaps in your design.

Some perennial herbs take time to get started in spring, but early colour is provided by groups and drifts of bulbs such as winter aconites, snowdrops and early crocuses. Hardy annuals sown in pots or in a frame in autumn flower earlier than those sown outdoors, and they can be hardened off for transplanting where there is space in the herb garden. Later sowings of annuals provide a succession of colour throughout the season.

Height is an essential consideration in any design, for many herbs are small to medium-sized plants and on their own may give a herb garden a disappointing uniformity. A feature such as a sundial, statue or large urn can relieve the flatness, although you should always consider the scale of the garden and the suitability of any ornaments – they must neither dominate nor spoil the overall impact of the design. A central feature is traditional, or you could embellish corners and turns in paths with smaller features – but guard against triviality, for it is easy to destroy the elegance of a herb garden with banal additions.

Topiary is another classic means of providing height, and several herbal plants adapt readily to formal

Left: *An inspired choice of striking colours and leaf forms will produce a memorable display, and proves that herbs are not only useful and practical plants, but also as decorative as any summer bedding.*

clipping. Common yew, holly, rosemary and bay where hardy, lavender and larger forms of box are ideal for bold designs that will catch the eye all the year round. Trained plants such as honeysuckle on pillars and standard or weeping roses are all suitable for hedges, and need little attention apart from annual pruning and tying in to supporting frames. On a larger scale, arches clad with climbers, tunnels of trained fruit, vines or hops, and even substantial pergolas of brick and timber can be used to frame paths or emphasize paved areas. For shade, some of the more ornamental trees with herbal connotations can be planted – elder, almond, cherry, quince, juniper or walnut, for example, according to the space available.

At least one seat is essential for prolonged peaceful enjoyment of the herb garden, especially in the evening when colours and scents are most intense. Position it where you are likely to sit most often, perhaps at the far end or facing your favourite view. There is a wide choice of styles and materials for garden seats, from elegantly wrought iron to simple rustic timber, or you can construct a bank from mounded earth, covering it with turf, thyme or chamomile around a stone or timber slab for all-weather seating; add a few plants of heartsease (wild pansy) and primrose for Shakespearean authenticity. Plant one or two aromatic herbs nearby to scent the area, and for intimacy train fragrant roses and honeysuckle on a framework arching over the seat to form a secluded arbour.

BUILDING A HERB WHEEL

1 Mark out the planned area, using a peg and taut line to ensure a perfect circle, before removing the turf and some of the topsoil. Ideally, the subsoil should also be loosened.

2 Position the edging materials, here house bricks arranged at an oblique angle and tapped firmly into place, but special-purpose edging tiles would be more frost-resistant.

3 Quarter the circle with two courses of sound bricks to allow access and create four separate beds.

4 Break up the excavated topsoil and refill the four quadrants almost to the surface of the brick paths.

5 Plant pot-grown herbs of your choice, watering them beforehand and allowing enough room for expansion as they grow.

6 Water in the plants if necessary, and then mulch with gravel or chippings to retain moisture and suppress weeds.

Herbs for Colour

It is sometimes claimed that herbs are not sufficiently varied to create an interesting garden by themselves, but this is not so. Even if only green varieties are used, rather than variegated forms, there are so many leaf shapes and contrasting plant habits in an infinity of green shades that a satisfying composition can be made from basic species alone.

Malva sylvestris

Green is, after all, a colour like any other, and green forms are particularly welcome in winter when evergreen herbs supply colour while all around seems dormant, as noted by Thomas Hyll in 1563 in *The Art of Gardening*, where he advised that knot gardens should be 'set with winter savory and thyme, for these endure all the winter through greene'.

Above: *Formal geometrical designs are best planted in blocks of contrasting colours and leaf shapes for the greatest impact, using sculptural highlights such as simple topiary to relieve any uniformity.*

Achieving a riot of brilliant colour with herbs is not easy. Most are subtly coloured, low-key plants, which helps explain the healing sense of refreshment and wellbeing in a herb garden. Vibrant, exciting colours are only found in a few flowers and leaves – peonies and poppies, nasturtiums, golden elders and the ruby Pasque flower, for example. Many variegated leaves have a brilliance of their own, however, especially if grown in full sun. Always assess plants before you buy them, because some forms, gold variations in particular, can be confused with normal plants suffering from a mosaic virus.

Colour needs to be used with discretion in the herb garden, where strident exuberance is usually out of place. Carefully position single specimens of brightly coloured plants as important accents or to mark entrances, exits and changes in the layout – remember that a dominant colour only works by contrast with its surroundings, and the more subdued plants should predominate for maximum effect. They may be paler, for example a sea of silver santolinas, set off with a few bobbing red poppies; or more sombre, such as the dark foliage of a yew hedge as a background for bright yellow mullein.

The low-toned colours of most herbs work best in simple designs, such as the contrast between woven green box and grey lavender hedges in a knot garden, or variations on monochrome planting made popular by the

NOTABLE HERB FLOWERS

- borage – rich blue, for salads and summer drinks
- lavender – soft purple, for scent and pot-pourri
- nasturtiums – vivid reds and yellows, for coloured garnishes
- violets – purple, for medicines and crystallized as decoration
- elderflowers – white and fragrant, for wines, cordials, and

flavouring fruit dishes
- pot marigolds or calendulas – vivid orange, for salads, pot-pourri and food colouring
- rose petals – red roses of scented varieties, for colour and fragrance, wines and perfume
- woodruff – tiny and white, imparts scent of hay and vanilla when warm

garden designer Gertrude Jekyll (1843-1932), who created cool blue and grey borders and sunny yellow gardens. True blues are hard to find among herbs, though there are blue-flowered species such as chicory, borage, flax, hyssop, lavender and sea holly. However, there are many subtle shades of lilac and violet which harmonize with the greys and silvers of lavender, artemisia and rue. Yellows and golds are easier to mass, for these colours form the majority of variegations. Most herbs have forms with white leaves or flowers (cultivar names such as 'Alba', 'Alba Plena' and 'Albovariegata' are indications of these), and a white garden, at the same time cool and reviving, is perhaps the most popular of single-colour themes.

Herbs in the red, purple and brown part of the spectrum are hardest to use effectively. Depending on the quality of light and surrounding plants, they can look rich and sumptuous, or merely lacklustre. Deep red forms make excellent groundwork and specimen plants: crimson or purple bugle, for example, beneath the soft green of lady's mantle, or red

Above left: *Planted in drifts, flowering herbs such as wall germander can erupt into a startling carpet of colour that will be alive with bees in summer.*

Right: *A branch of wild marjoram in full bloom reveals an intensity of colour to rival any decorative shrub.*

Above right: *Ornamental forms of edible herbs add a decorative bonus to the salad garden: French sorrel (*Rumex scutatus*), for example, has the same tangy flavour as ordinary sorrel, but also creates a carpet of ground-cover foliage.*

sage (*Salvia officinalis* 'Purpurescens') standing out against a carpet of pale golden marjoram. Remember, though, that reds change as the day progresses and in full sun can reach out towards you, whereas evening twilight makes them recede almost to the point of invisibility.

FOLIAGE BEDS

When designing herb beds and borders, do not sacrifice leaf shape to colour, for the two qualities work together and can blend to make a stun-

ning impact. The many thistle-like herbs are spectacularly eye-catching, creating dramatic stands of green, grey or silver foliage and robust stems: holy thistles, cardoons, globe artichokes, sea holly and milk thistles are all plants of great presence. Ferns, too, form a group with wide design potential, especially as a number of them have intricately varied forms with ruffled, divided or filigree detail. Their shades vary, and they tolerate moist shade, offering scope for planting schemes in corners where little else will flourish.

Herbs for Fragrance

Until the reign of King George IV (1820-30) English monarchs appointed Strewers of Herbs to precede them in procession and scatter dried aromatic herbs such as rosemary, thyme and rue to ward off diseases. The appointment of these royal 'strewing ladies', as they were popularly known, was a legacy from the times of the medieval plagues, which were thought to be caused by foul air. Dried herbs and essential oils were incorporated into pot-pourris, snuff, fumigants and scented waters, in the belief that fragrance would deter both infections and insects; and judges still carry posies of sweet herbs to shield themselves from the rest of humanity in the courtroom.

Anthemis nobilis

Research has shown that there is some substance to medieval ideas of hygiene. While most plants attract insects, others actively repel them. Others have an antiseptic effect, for example the gums exuded by some trees to heal wounds in their bark. These varied effects of fragrance have become part of the great tradition of herbal use, but in garden terms perfume is usually regarded as one of the pleasant qualities of desirable plants, especially herbs. Plant fragrances are hard to describe precisely. They are traditionally classified, simply by nose, in groups such as camphoraceous, fruity or hay-scented. Some scents, most notably those of open flowers (roses and gardenias, for example), are released as a reaction to sunshine – most of the Mediterranean herbs protect themselves from prolonged heat by surrounding their foliage with a defensive cloud of volatile oils.

Night-flowering plants often have heavy scents, and plants such as honeysuckle, nicotiana and evening primrose should be grown near an open window or beside a seat where you can enjoy their fragrance on a still evening. Plants that flower in winter also need planting close at hand for appreciation in all weathers. Disperse others according to the strength of their fragrance: the heady scent of *Lilium regale* can fill large areas and reach you from far away, whereas other plants need close approach to be enjoyed, and should therefore be placed within easy reach.

Left: *The smoky blue foliage of rue has a sharply resinous pungency, and a reputation for causing skin irritations if carelessly handled.*

WASTE FRAGRANCE

Although the fragrance of herbs is the main reason for their cultivation, in many cases the scent represents nothing more than the waste products of the plant's normal metabolism. Substances such as geraniol (the principal scent of roses), or the thymol and eucalyptol in thyme, are essential oils formed within the plant, and then stored in cells near the leaf surfaces. Pressure or movement, such as that of a browsing animal or of a strong breeze, or even the heat in sunlight, all cause the release of these chemicals to defend or shield the plant from injury. It is the release or evaporation of these waste materials that delights us when we walk on a thyme lawn or stand on a warm day downwind from a bush of rosemary.

***Drying lavender: 1** Heads of lavender flowers gathered at the peak of their perfection. Timing is important, and for full fragrance the flowers should be gathered when fully opened, whereas for medicinal use the critical time is often just before flowering.*

2 Spread out the complete flowering shoots to dry, in the sun or in shade according to species, or in warmth indoors in a cool season (lavender is best dried in a shady room). Turn the flowers frequently to ensure that all parts are dried.

3 The complete flowering shoots can be used intact, or individual blooms can be stripped off when dry for use in pot-pourri, herb bags and sachets. Keep different varieties separate, as their perfumes will be subtly different.

Leaf scents tend to be released when the foliage is bruised or brushed in passing, and most culinary herbs fall into this category, as well as aromatic trees and shrubs such as eucalyptus, rosemary, southernwood and the resinous conifers. Plant them strategically beside seats, at corners in paths or flanking gateways. Many of these species also make excellent hedges, and in earlier times it was the custom to spread freshly washed clothes on hedges to absorb a little of their fragrance while they dried.

Drying herbs often enhances their scent, sometimes releasing it from otherwise insignificant herbs – the delicious hayfield fragrance of sweet woodruff only reaches its full intensity days after the plant is cut and hung to dry, for example. Essential oils and tinctures are prepared from many herbs for use in aromatherapy or as Bach homeopathic flower remedies, where particular fragrances have been found to heal disorders and change moods. In the garden, plants can have the similar effect of raising your spirits or soothing tension, so be sure to plant your favourite scented herbs where they are accessible when needed.

Above: *The most important feature of pot-pourri is its fragrance, so ingredients such as thyme and lavender must be dried thoroughly to concentrate the volatile oils.*

Right: *Carpeting herbs such as chamomile, thyme and pennyroyal are ideal ground cover plants for informal lawns, which give off a heady scent when walked upon.*

Herbs for Clipping

Gratiola officinalis

The more you clip a woody perennial, the denser the foliage becomes: this is the principle behind hedge trimming, topiary and mowing lawns. Really a form of pruning, trimming off the end of a stem usually encourages the development of two or more side shoots, and the best species for hedges and lawns are those that respond to clipping by producing the densest regrowth.

Compact plants such as rosemary, lavender, santolina, southernwood, germander, hyssop, yew and, of course, box are traditional for herb garden hedges ranging in height from 15 cm/6 in around small beds to 2 m/ 6 ft 6 in in grander schemes. Their chief function is to enclose, divide or define herb borders, conferring a sense of order and control, but they can be used to create the playful patterns of classic knot gardens and are often decorative in their own right, especially when kept neatly disciplined – this requires only one, perhaps two, trims a year in the case of box and yew, but vigorous plants such as privet and lonicera need clipping every month during the growing season.

Lavender is a particular favourite for a herb hedge and will yield a generous supply of flowers and leaves for drying. Use a compact cultivar rather than the loose-growing English and trailing forms, and clip it to shape in spring without cutting into the old wood; leave it to flower and then trim it again, harvesting the fading blooms for use. In warm gardens, santolina's intricate silver foliage is a useful foil for green plants, and if it is trimmed close in mid-spring it will retain its neat shape, although the yellow button-shaped flowers will be sacrificed.

Frequently clipped hedges make special demands on the soil, and the site should therefore be well dug beforehand, at the same time adding plenty of compost or decayed manure to sustain fast growth. Clear perennial weeds as you work, for these are hard to remove afterwards, and always plant in single rather than staggered rows to allow access for weeding in the early years before the hedge is established. Water the hedge thoroughly in dry weather during its first year or two, and feed it annually because you want to encourage rapid development in both height and density, together with prompt revival after clipping, which must start at an early age.

Topiary needs the same kind of thoughtful preparation and care, for it is no more than a whimsical form of hedge training and clipping. Used for ornament since Roman times, it can have a dramatic impact, especially where specimens are given positions of prominence – a mop-head bay in the centre of a herb garden, box finials to embellish the corners of beds, or rosemary obelisks as sentinels beside gateways and paths, for example. Feed and water topiary regularly, and clip it frequently with scissors to maintain the shape. Use plants sparingly and with discretion: you are creating a herb garden, not an exhibition of topiary, and they should serve only as decorative highlights.

HERB LAWNS

Prostrate herbs are suitable for growing densely to create fragrant lawns that can be kept neat, preferably after flowering in most cases, by clipping with shears or mowing with the mower

HERBS FOR POTTED TOPIARY

- germander
- mintbush (*Prostanthera rotundifolia*)
- rosemary
- scented-leaf pelargoniums (especially *P. crispum*)
- manuka (*Leptospermum scoparium*)
- myrtle – especially *Myrtus communis* 'Microphylla'
- santolina (including *S. virens*)
- Victorian rosemary

blades set high. They are not as hard-wearing as turf and therefore should be made in corners of their own or where traffic is not heavy, but they have a special timeless charm and surround you with fragrance when you tread on them.

A lawn made of chamomile is traditional – use a non-flowering clone such as 'Treneague' – and it has the advantage of remaining green long after drought has scorched ordinary turf. It can be difficult to keep weed-free, however, requires shearing rather than mowing, and after only a few years usually needs remaking; it is better planted in mortar joints between paving slabs where it is more easily maintained. Thyme (single or contrasting variegated cultivars) and mint-scented pennyroyal are far more satisfactory lawn herbs, producing thick mats of growth that once established suppress most weeds, and both bear heavy flushes of attractive flowers as a bonus.

To make a herb lawn, the ground needs thorough preparation in the same way as a seedbed, with a top dressing of general fertilizer raked in just before planting. Plant your lawn in

Above left: *Even while young and still growing, hedging herbs, such as santolina, need clipping to induce bushy growth.*

Above right: *A taut line acts as a guide and helps ensure consistent height and width along the hedge.*

spring or autumn, setting chamomile plants about 10 cm/4 in apart, other species at 30 cm/12 in spacings, and water it well until it is established. Chamomile spreads faster if it is occasionally rolled (Shakespeare's Falstaff noticed, 'The more it is trodden on the better it grows'). Remove any weeds promptly before they get a hold, especially in the early stages while there is still bare soil to colonize.

Above: *Many grey and silver herbs, such as santolina, can be kept neat and compact if clipped in spring and prevented from flowering by a further trim in summer.*

Left: *The traditional knot garden, with its contrasting threads of hedging plants, takes several seasons before it is established, and the small plants from which it develops need frequent clipping to transform them into dense hedges.*

Herbs as Flowering Plants

Visually the flowering season is a pinnacle of delight in the herb garden. Although herbs cannot compete with the gaudiness of summer bedding plants, their soft and subtle flower hues contribute a cottage garden innocence, altogether in keeping with their sensuous simplicity. Many of the flowers are useful in their own right, for their fragrance and colour in pot-pourri, their medicinal uses in cosmetics and tisanes, or simply for eating in salads and adding to cool summer drinks.

Althaea officiualis

It is a mistake to assume that herbs are grown primarily for their leaves, and that allowing them to bloom exhausts their energies or dilutes their active properties. The removal of flowers is only occasionally necessary: strictly formal hedges lose their precise geometry if allowed to bloom, and annuals such as basil will deteriorate rapidly after flowering. Prolific self-seeders, such as fennel and angelica, need dead-heading for restraint, or you can cut out the flowering stems at an earlier stage.

Many herbs have a rich tradition of religious or national symbolism: the chrysanthemum in China and Japan, for example, and jasmine in Arab

ENCOURAGING HONEY BEES

If you keep honey bees yourself or find that large numbers regularly visit your garden, planting some of their favourite flowers (not necessarily the same as those frequented by bumble bees) will increase the honey flow or entice them to stay and fertilize your fruit and vegetable crops.

- basil
- borage
- clover
- crocus
- hollyhock
- ivy
- lemon balm
- marjoram
- mustard
- rosemary
- savory
- bergamot
- bugle
- comfrey
- dandelion
- hyssop
- lavender
- mallow
- mint
- pulmonaria
- sage
- thyme

cultures, and as early as the second century AD the Greek *Dream Book of Artimedorus* catalogued the meanings attached to flowers. A large number were sacred to the Virgin Mary – hence the profusion of common names prefixed with 'Mary', 'lady', and 'Our Lady's' – and these were often gathered in medieval St Mary Gardens.

Left: *Feverfew, like other members of the Compositae family such as chamomile and tansy, has pretty daisy-like flowers which are as medicinally useful as its leaves.*

Elizabethan floral alphabets and the Victorian love of creating bouquets of flowers to send floral messages are all part of this enduring tradition. Even herbal weeds and wild flowers had their significance: chickweed meant you wanted to make a rendezvous, buttercups promised prosperity and sorrel affection, while the course of love could be charted with foxglove for treachery and hops for injustice, followed inevitably by evening primrose for uncertainty, lily of the valley for restored joy and finally rosemary for remembrance.

HERBS FOR SEEDS

Flowering leads ultimately to seeding, an important part of the herbal calendar, as many plants are cultivated for their seeds, sometimes exclusively: caraway, coriander, cumin, dill, fenugreek, mustard, poppy and sesame are all staple seed producers. Where large quantities are needed, plants are best grown as utility crops in the kitchen garden, perennials gathered in a sunny corner and annuals sown in rows between the vegetables, for few seeding herbs look very decorative, and you will probably want to prevent accidental seeding among other herbs. Always choose a warm position for them, to help seeds ripen and dry on the plants.

USEFUL GARDEN FLOWERS

In addition to familiar herbs with attractive blooms, there are plants that are normally grown for ornament in flower beds and borders, but which have traditional herbal uses, and these provide valuable extra colour in the herb garden. Larger species, such as eucalyptus, elder, broom, hollyhock and mullein, all contribute height as well as colour. For the middle of borders, you can integrate blue cornflowers, sea holly, greater celandine (beware of self-seeding), peonies, columbines and hydrangeas, while the edges of beds are ideal for low-growing plants such as thrift, candytuft, violets and garden pinks.

HERB TEA

1 Many flowering herbs can be used to make herbal teas and tisanes. Collect the flowerheads in summer and allow them to dry. Store them in sealed containers so that they keep well. To make a tea, place 1 tbsp dried flowers or petals per person in a teapot or jug and fill with boiling water.

2 Leave the infusion to steep for 5-8 minutes. When the flavour is strong enough, pour slowly through a strainer.

Left: *The prolific heads of arching borage flowers self-seed freely and guarantee plenty of seedlings for the next year. The ample crop of blooms can also be floated in summer drinks, face-upwards to display their immaculate shape and intense violet-blue colour.*

Salad Herbs

People have gathered herbs for thousands of years, not just in their search for natural remedies, but also to supplement their diet with nutritious wild plants. Lettuce, cabbage and carrots are all derived from wild ancestors that sometimes bear little obvious resemblance to their modern descendants. Few people today would want to depend on these primitive plants for their food, but numerous wild flowers, herbs and even weeds remain popular as salad ingredients, while some are still used occasionally as leaf vegetables or pot herbs for cooking.

Daucus carota

Early salads, or 'sallets' as they were known, seem wildly eclectic in comparison with today's cautious list of limited ingredients, and it is only recently that we are beginning once more to include the vast larder of herbal flavours. In the late seventeenth century, John Evelyn was already complaining about the impoverished imagination of contemporary cooks, compared with the Latin races 'who gather anything almost that is tender to the very tops of nettles, so as every Hedge affords a sallet (not unagreeable), and seasoned with Vinegar Salt and Oil, which gives it both the relish and the name of Salad…'.

It must be added that gathering wild herbs indiscriminately has its very real dangers, as Evelyn observed when he reminded us that 'Sad experience shows how many fatal mistakes have been made by those who took hemlock for aconite, cow weed for Chervil, Dog's Mercury for Spinach, whose dire effects have been many times sudden death and the cause of mortal accidents…'.

The best way to avoid 'mortal accidents' is to grow salad herbs in the garden where their identity is known. Even then it is wise to use only moderate amounts, for many are pungent or strongly flavoured and are added sparingly for a hint of stimulating flavour, while the most benign herb can have unforeseen effects if taken in large

Above: *Sorrel is particularly welcome in early spring, when it supplies tasty and nutritious leaves long before conventional salad ingredients are ready. Lamb's lettuce is another useful hardy leaf herb.*

Left: *Garlic chives, like other alliums, are valuable members of the salad herb garden, combining culinary usefulness with all the charm of delicate wild flowers.*

quantities: over-consumption of parsley, for example, has been known to cause liver damage.

Nevertheless, a leaf taken from here and there, together with a few coloured edible flowers, will add interest and piquancy to a plain salad, and there is every reason to revive the flair and variety of older traditions. Growing your favourite salad ingredients together in a separate bed will create an attractive miniature garden that can be harvested easily, for it need only take a few minutes to gather leaves of various lettuces, burnet, dandelion, fennel, lovage, lemon balm, common daisy and pulmonaria, together with flowers such as marigolds, cowslips, violets, nasturtiums and bugloss for a connoisseur's salad. Chinese cabbage is an ideal substitute for lettuce in oriental salads, especially when mixed with authentic herbs such as sesame seeds, ginger, lemon grass, mugwort and mallow.

NATURAL SEEDBEDS

Chervil and parsley, both popular salad herbs, can be grown as self-perpetuating crops, producing their own self-sown seedlings for subsequent use. Simply transfer a single parsley plant to a clear part of a nursery bed, where you can continue using its foliage until it flowers in its second year from sowing. Keep the soil clear around the base of the plant as the seeds ripen, and you will find these fall and produce a bed of seedlings to transplant for future supplies. Chervil behaves in the same way, although as an annual it self-seeds within a single season. It is best sown broadcast in patches, where later generations of seedlings can remain to form a constantly regenerating bed.

HOP SHOOTS

Apart from their important commercial use as a flavouring and preservative in brewing, hops have medicinal and culinary value, and are also grown as ornamental climbers where space allows. The twining annual stems can reach 6 m/20 ft or more on strong supports of posts and wires, their handsome foliage and decorative female 'cones' making them ideal companions for climbing roses to divide larger gardens. From the dormant crowns more shoots emerge in spring than will be needed, so thin them when they are about 15-20 cm/6-8 in tall, leaving four to six of the strongest, and steam or poach the surplus shoots as an alternative to asparagus.

Above: *Many familiar flowering annuals make useful additions to a herb collection: nasturtiums not only add a splash of colour to the garden, but their leaves are edible, the pleasantly flavoured flowers can be used to brighten up salads, and the seeds, when pickled, taste very similar to capers.*

Herbs for Seasoning

National cuisines have evolved over many centuries and even now include strong echoes of former customs. The choice of seasoning herbs is no exception. Certain flavours are instantly attributable to regional cookery: sumac, cardamom and sesame in the Middle East, Mediterranean olives, garlic and dill in northern Europe, saffron in North Africa and chillies in Mexico, lemon grass in South-East Asia, ginger and star anise in China, and a multitude of Indian seasonings such as coriander, fenugreek, nigella and turmeric.

Coriandrum
sativum

Modern cooks add herbs to a dish for flavouring rather than for medicinal or preservative purposes, but earlier generations used them from necessity. A medieval peasant, for example, often could not afford to feed his livestock through the winter and so would slaughter animals in autumn and keep the meat as best he could. In the days before refrigeration, stored produce gradually deteriorated, and strong flavours, easily provided by herbs, were needed to disguise stale ingredients in a dish.

Apart from the historical reasons for adding them, herbs all serve some further purpose, whether it is to stimulate the appetite, aid digestion or stop the food from going off.

Horseradish is a pungent seasoning with typical antibiotic properties, used for centuries in Europe to preserve meat and disguise 'off' flavours, although the sauce prepared from its roots is now more usually regarded as an optional condiment with roast beef. The plant, which resembles an over-enthusiastic dock, belongs in the safety of the kitchen garden, where it

can be grown as an annual root crop or as a perennial in a confined space to restrain its natural invasiveness. Here, too, you should grow coriander, whether for its seeds or spicy leaves; the sturdy annual fenugreek, undistinguished in appearance but essential for curries, and the various kinds of mustard with their medicinal, seasoning and carminative uses.

DIGESTIVE AIDS

Seasonings primarily satisfy the palate, while carminatives aid later digestion. Several herbs, all important candidates for the culinary herb garden, possess volatile oils that are helpful in preventing wind or stimulating the

MINT ROOT CUTTINGS

1 Mint beds need regular renewal, which is easily done by taking healthy young roots, trimming them into short sections and pressing these into trays of moist compost.

2 Cover the cuttings with a layer of compost, and they will soon start to grow – those prepared in early autumn can provide young shoots for winter use.

Above: *Many culinary herbs blend perfectly together; for bouquets garnis gather the various ingredients at the same time and mix together in small bunches, as they are easier to assemble while fresh.*

secretion of digestive juices, and many people like to include one or two of these at the table. Dill is perhaps best known because of its popularity in the form of dill water or 'gripe water', but caraway, coriander, fennel and aniseed are also effective carminatives, either separately or mixed in equal proportions. The seeds are the part used, so make a point of leaving them to flower for harvesting at the end of the season.

MAINTAINING SUPPLIES

Since gardeners tend to grow herbs mainly for seasoning, it is well worth trying to plan a continuous supply. Most culinary herbs can be preserved by drying or some other method, but in most cases the fresh product has a better flavour. Some kinds can be potted up in autumn or sown in late summer to reach their peak during the winter, and these will often provide useful crops on a kitchen window sill. A warm greenhouse or conservatory is a more congenial home out of season for potted herbs because they receive more light there, but you can also keep many hardy kinds growing in a cold frame by reserving a sequence of pots there until needed. A permanent collection of perennials may be planted in a soil-based frame, while a portable frame can be placed over a specially planted bed in the autumn. Protect individual plants with cloches or smaller covers, and wrap these with old mats or several sheets of bubble plastic in the event of frost.

HERB OILS

1 Herb oils can be used to add flavour to cooked dishes, salad dressings or marinades. Use one large bunch of herb leaves and 1 litre/1¾ pints of olive oil. Take a large bunch of a leafy seasoning herb such as mint or basil and separate the leaves from the stems. Tear the leaves into rough strips and discard the stems.

2 Using a pestle and mortar, pound the leaves with a little of the olive oil to release the flavour, gradually adding more leaves as the first few begin to break up.

3 Half fill a sterilized bottle with olive oil and half of the herb leaves. Add a generous pinch of rock salt and fill the bottle with the remaining oil and leaves. Seal firmly and leave to stand for two weeks, tipping the bottle upside down occasionally to ensure the flavours mix.

Left: *Gather culinary herbs for preserving on a warm, dry day, selecting clean, healthy pieces which can then be tied for drying in bundles, on their own or combined in bouquets.*

Above: *Herbs gathered fresh from the garden provide an instant assortment of flavours. Short sprigs can be snipped using scissors or clippers; use quickly or keep in a jar of water on a window sill for a few hours.*

Right: *Seasoning herbs such as bay, chives, rosemary and parsley are easy to grow and have an excellent flavour when fresh. Try experimenting with different culinary combinations when planning a new herb bed.*

Herbs for Healing

Cedronella triphylla

Herbs have long held an important place in the treatment of ailments, and herbal remedies are still popular. Today, the pace of research is accelerating rapidly throughout the world, using various scientific skills to evaluate plants and native traditions in the search for new remedies.

Homer wrote of healing roots, one of the earliest records of the use of medicinal plants in Europe, but Chinese manuals and Indian Ayurvedic texts pre-date this by centuries. Much early herbal medicine was based on superstition: the 'Doctrine of Signatures', for example, stated that a herb would treat that part of the body which it most resembled. European settlers arriving in North America found that the Indian inhabitants had their own version of the doctrine, and would associate yellow herbs with jaundice or red ones with blood disorders.

Most herbal remedies were compounds extracted and blended by apothecaries from several plants, each of which was known on its own as a 'simple'. Apothecaries realized that there were differences in purity and potency between substances found in similar species, and that the effects also depended on factors such as the site where they were gathered, or the time of the month or year. In an attempt to standardize quality, the first secular gardens of simples were established in Pisa, Padua, and thereafter throughout Europe and elsewhere – the first such garden in North America was planted by Dr John Bartram in Philadelphia in 1782. They were organized along the lines of earlier monastic hospital gardens, and were generally known as 'Physic Gardens'. It was here that systematic study of plants began in earnest, combining the disciplines of botany and medicine.

Very often scientific discoveries are based on established local use. Romanies, peasants and rainforest tribesmen alike have needed to be accurate botanists for their very survival. These people have understood the healing capabilities of plants in skilled hands, but they have also appreciated the potential dangers of misuse: rue was chosen by Mohammed, for example, as the most blessed of all herbs and it is central to many Arab and Chinese therapies, but it contains a number of active princi-

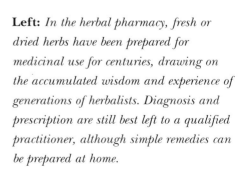

Left: *In the herbal pharmacy, fresh or dried herbs have been prepared for medicinal use for centuries, drawing on the accumulated wisdom and experience of generations of herbalists. Diagnosis and prescription are still best left to a qualified practitioner, although simple remedies can be prepared at home.*

HERB BALM

1 A herb balm can soothe aching muscles and so aid relaxation. Weigh out 25 g/1 oz fresh lavender and rosemary stems, mixed.

2 Place the herbs in a small pan set over a bain-marie. Add ³/₄ litre/1 pint olive or sunflower oil. Cover with a light lid and simmer for 2 hours, adding more water as necessary.

3 Allow to cool slightly then strain the liquid into a clean bowl.

4 Leave the liquid to cool and then pour into a sterilized jar or bottle and seal. Apply sparingly.

where allergic reactions or side effects are possible – even garlic, widely regarded as an infallible panacea, may reduce blood pressure and so cancel the impact of drugs taken for cardiac disorders. All the plants are complex factories producing diverse chemicals, some of them fragrances to attract pollinating insects, others toxins to deter predators, and any one of these substances may be harmful in particular circumstances.

NATURAL INSECTICIDES

Many plants produce natural insecticides as part of their defence systems, and some of these are widely used as prepared powders and liquids in the garden. Derris, or rotenone, a popular insecticide approved for organic use, is extracted from the powdered roots of a Malaysian shrub known as tuba root (*Derris elliptica*).

Sometimes particular species are grown as companion plants to protect crops nearby from attack.

Various *Tagetes* species have been found to repel whitefly and other pests when grown in greenhouses, and scientific experiments now confirm that their flowers emit volatile chemicals into the surrounding air for protection. As these have proved toxic to the mosquitoes that carry malaria and yellow fever, it is hoped that a new generation of insecticides can be developed for their control.

ples which often cause sensitivity to light, and people often develop skin rashes after contact with the plant.

Herbs interact in complex ways with our body chemistry, and their power to heal is formidable. Compared with synthetic drugs their actions may seem very mild, but you should not underestimate the dangers of self-medication on the assumption that herbs are harmless. Many traditional remedies are based on fantasy, guesswork and suggestion, while even the most reputable herbs are selective in their effects, working for one patient but not another.

Only a trained practitioner is qualified to diagnose an ailment, and then to suggest a personal prescription after fully assessing your individual needs. The medical benefits of herbs are no longer in doubt, and many are generally quite safe, provided that they are not misused or taken in circumstances

Right: *It is not just the visible flowers and leaves of herbs that are valuable. Very often the fresh or dried roots, such as those of comfrey, contain the highest concentrations of active ingredients.*

Herbs for Dyeing

Anyone who has gathered wild blackberries in autumn or pinched out sideshoots from tomato plants will readily appreciate the possibilities of using plant stains to dye animal skins and woven material. Until chemical dyes were introduced, roots, bark, flowers and leaves were the chief sources of colour, often made permanent by the addition of mordants – fixing chemicals – from mineral-rich earths and other sources. The shades obtained are rarely vivid, but mellow, subtle, and full of the lustrous beauty of the plants themselves.

Urtica dioica

Ancient China, India and other Asian countries developed sophisticated skills in dyeing, but similar techniques have always been used by tribespeople around the world, who adapted plant materials for painting on bark, to ornament clothing or decorate the skin in preparation for religious ceremonies or warfare, and even for disguise – Romanies once artificially tanned their faces with juices obtained from a favourite herb, *Lycopus europaeus* or gipsywort. The early Britons were described by Julius Caesar as 'blue and terrible' after they had dyed their skin with woad to make their appearance more alarming, while in ancient Egypt the plant was also used to colour imperial garments.

Dyeing with herbs remains a popular and pleasant craft, although large amounts of material are often needed, and colours tend to fade gently unless made fast with chemical mordants such as alum, tin, iron or chrome. Results vary according to the strength of the dye, the length of time that the wool (the easiest material to colour) is left immersed, and the parts of a plant that are used: the leaves of privet, for example, give yellow shades, whereas the berries impart a muted blue-green hue.

Some plants can be gathered from the wild, but in view of the amounts needed there is the risk of over-

Above: *Woad, or dyer's rocket, is cultivated in many countries for its distinctive blue dye.*

Left: *Manufacture of indigo dye paste from a species of* Indigofera *in southwest China.*

harvesting species that may not be abundant, and it is often better to grow your own supplies of the more useful kinds in a special dye border. This can be an attractive feature, for many of the plants are popular garden ornamentals whose flowers or fruits are the parts used, so that geraniums, dahlias, rudbeckia and mulberries can earn a place as dye plants in the herb garden. Experiment with various leaves after pruning or clipping shrubs and hedges, as many will impart various shades of yellow and green.

CLASSIC DYE CROPS

Traditional dye plants worth growing include the ancient woad (*Isatis tinctoria*), a leafy spinach-like plant whose use dwindled rapidly after the introduction of the more permanent blue dye from the indigo plant, *Indigofera tinctoria*, a subtropical species which needs to be grown in a warm greenhouse in temperate regions.

Dyer's madder (*Rubia tinctorum*) is a self-seeding perennial still cultivated

Above: *Woollen yarn dyed using homegrown* Polygonum tinctorum. *Shades are varied by the number of immersions in the vat.*

Right: *Indigo plants,* Strobilanthes flaccidifolius, *growing in a field in Guizhou Province, south-west China. Plants are cultivated annually from cuttings – the precursor of the dye is contained in the leaves.*

on a field scale in France and the Netherlands, and an important European source of strong red, while in North America bloodroot (*Sanguinaria canadensis*) was the main plant used by Indians for red body paint. Weld (*Reseda luteola*) (or dyer's greenweed, *Genista tinctoria*), a relative of broom, another dye source, is a traditional yellow dye plant with handsome flower spikes, and a tendency to colonize unless seedlings are kept in check.

The elder is guardian of all herbs according to folklore, and planting one of these will provide you with a green dye from the leaves and, from the berries, lilac (using alum mordant) or purple (using chrome).

SELECTED PLANTS FOR A DYE GARDEN

Part of the creative adventure of dyeing with plants is that the shades obtained can be varied considerably by using different mordants, so that madder, for example, can produce anything from light pink to dark brown.

- reds, pinks: bloodroot, chenopodium, madder, pokeberry, rose hips, sorrel
- yellows and orange: beetroot, coreopsis, dahlias, golden rod, heather, marigolds, Osage orange, pear leaves, rudbeckia, saffron, turmeric, weld, zinnias
- black: meadowsweet, walnut
- blues: blackberries, blueberries, dandelion root, elderberries, indigo, juniper berries, woad, yellow flag

- greens: bracken, dock, lily of the valley, nettles, weld
- browns: gipsywort, madder, sassafras, sumac, various barks (apple, birch, walnut), willow

Choosing Sites for Herbs

Thymus vulgaris

Choosing a suitable site for a herb needs preliminary assessment of factors such as the type of plant, the soil, the aspect, the exposure and the local temperature range. There are also practical considerations of space and appearance in relation to the rest of the garden. All this needs careful thought before starting to plant up sites.

Every form of gardening is artificial and depends for its success on matching as far as possible the natural environment of the plants. Herbs that you intend cultivating will be assembled in one place, and yet they come originally from all parts of the world and every kind of soil and climate.

Always find out where your herbs normally grow in the wild – it might be a sun-baked rocky hillside near the Mediterranean Sea or a well-watered rainforest where frost is unknown, a cool temperate woodland, or cold exposed cliff where wind keeps growth short and compact. Try to identify the warmest sheltered parts of the garden, the areas with the best drainage or dappled shade, corners where frost lingers or the sun arrives first in the morning, and allocate herbs according to their preferences. If you are planning a separate herb garden, assess its position at all times of the year and from all cultural aspects, and then choose the plants

Below: *A general mixed bed of herbs, combining, for example, borage, comfrey, lovage and lavender: this looks very effective against a backdrop of traditional wattle fencing.*

PLANNING A SMALL BORDER

Herbs for the back – 1 m/3 ft upwards
• *perennials: angelica, artemisia, bergamot, elecampane, fennel, liquorice, lovage, meadowsweet, rosemary, sea holly, shrub roses, European or American sweet cicely*
• *annuals and biennials: alexanders, foxglove, mullein*

Herbs for the middle – 45-100 cm/ 1 ft 6 in-3 ft
• *perennials: agrimony, balm, chicory, comfrey, costmary, curry plant, lavender, rampion, rue, sage, santolina, southernwood, St John's wort, tansy, tarragon, valerian, white horehound*
• *annuals and biennials: borage, bugloss, caraway, dill*

Herbs for the front – up to 45 cm/ 1 ft 6 in
• *perennials: bistort, calamint, catmint, chamomile, chives, herb bennet, hyssop, lady's smock, marjoram, mint, sedum, sorrel, thyme, winter savory, wormwood, yarrow*
• *annuals and biennials: anise, basil, chervil, clary, coriander, cumin, marigold, parsley, summer savory*

that are most likely to succeed in its various beds.

Remember that the term 'herbs' is used as a broad and imprecise classification, and includes plants with very different life cycles. Annuals and biennials are short-term plants, the former completing their growth from germination to shedding seed within a single season (some such as chervil can manage more than one generation per year). This partly determines where they are grown, for they will change rapidly in appearance and leave gaps in a planting scheme when they have died down. Biennials germinate and make leafy growth during their first season, survive the winter on the stored nutrients in their roots, and then flower and set seed the following year; if they are grown for their foliage, you can treat them as annuals, but for flower and seed crops they will need space for two years.

Perennials, which may be hardy or tender according to their origin, provide the framework of any herb garden design, for they are permanent and maintain continuity from one year to the next.

Size varies widely, with some herbs low-growing but liable to expand sideways into broad ground-hugging mats of foliage, while others are tall and dominating. Ultimate height and spread should always be taken into account when planning beds and herb gardens, together with a plant's tolerance of pruning and clipping, for many bulky subjects such as evergreen shrubs can be cut back to manageable size. Site plants of various heights according to their probable impact on an overall design: the tallest species work best in the centre of island beds viewed from all sides or at the back of borders, with the shortest plants at the

PLANTING A HEDGE

1 Mark out and excavate a shallow trench running the length of the proposed hedge, and thoroughly fork over the soil in the bottom to ensure good drainage.

2 Hedging plants need plenty of nourishment in their early years, so add a generous amount of garden compost to the trench and lightly fork in.

3 Mark the centre line of the hedge with string and pegs, and space out the plants, using a length of cane or wooden batten to measure equal distances between them.

4 Planted, firmed and watered in the refilled trench, the hedge will soon begin to fill out, ready for its first trim to shape.

front, although positioning a large, attractive specimen where it is least expected (within a sea of contrasting short plants, perhaps, or on a bend in a path to conceal an alcove) can produce a satisfying impact.

Growing herbs in containers is the ideal solution where considerations of space, soil or climate suggest a plant might be difficult to grow. This is not a poor substitute for open-ground cultivation, but an attractive branch of gardening in its own right. Most herbs

adapt to pots and other containers, and when well tended can create satisfying collections to enhance otherwise barren areas of the garden – courtyards, flights of steps, entrances and exits, for example – and make herb growing a practical choice for window boxes, balconies and roof gardens. It is easy to supply container-grown plants with the kind of soil they prefer, and to move them under cover or to sunny spots if they are sensitive to cold or exposure.

Above: *Raised beds built within stone walls are convenient sites for herbs such as rosemary. They offer good drainage and ease of picking.*

Above: *Shady woodland spots suit many herbs which do not tolerate direct sun and dry soil. Herbs such as peppermint may provide useful ground cover for barer patches beneath trees in cultivated gardens.*

Planning the Herb Garden

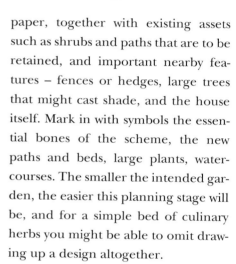

Formal or relaxed, utilitarian or decorative, a herb garden must be satisfying to look at and work in, and manageable in terms of your time, needs, energy and commitment. A complex parterre, for example, must be kept clipped, weed-free and carefully aligned for success, whereas the cottage garden approach of profusion without confusion may be more appropriate if you want plentiful supplies of useful herbs combined with cheerful diversity and low maintenance.

Levisticum officiuale

O nce you have explored the potential site and the chances of your chosen herbs liking the position, there is style to consider. This is an intangible but important matter, taking into account not only your personal tastes but the nature of the site, for any garden or border is intimately bonded to the house, and to the immediate and distant surroundings.

With a fairly clear vision of the garden you would like, you can draw together all the various elements in a final design. Measure the garden or plot, and mark its outline on graph

Above: *Design herb beds and borders to take advantage of contrasts between colours and shapes, but remember to match for height and impact.*

paper, together with existing assets such as shrubs and paths that are to be retained, and important nearby features – fences or hedges, large trees that might cast shade, and the house itself. Mark in with symbols the essential bones of the scheme, the new paths and beds, large plants, watercourses. The smaller the intended garden, the easier this planning stage will be, and for a simple bed of culinary herbs you might be able to omit drawing up a design altogether.

For larger plans always beware the illusion that you have more room in the garden than actually exists: it is easy on paper to draw a path or pack a large number of herbs into a given space, and then find that the result is hopelessly cramped or out of scale, or has unexpected visual effects on the rest of the garden. Look up the likely spread of trees and shrubs, mark this precisely on the plan, and then check frequently with the site itself; if necessary position stakes where significant plants and features are to go, or lay a garden hose on the ground to assess

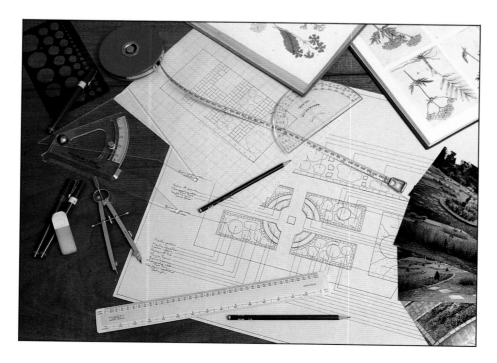

Left: *Avoid mistakes and disappointment by making careful preliminary plans, drawing out the proposed design to scale to check its impact and feasibility.*

LAYING A PATH

1 Mark out and excavate the path, arranging stout boards along the sides with their upper edges at the finished surface level. Spread and compact a foundation of hardcore such as stones or broken brick.

2 Cover the base with a bed of sand, lightly tamped with the head of a rake to fill any gaps in the hardcore, and then rake a loose level surface in which to bed the bricks.

3 Arrange the bricks on the widest side in an attractive bond or pattern, firming them into place with the handle of a hammer and checking the surface in all directions with a spirit level as you go.

4 With all the bricks set out, spread more sand over the surface and brush repeatedly to fill all the joints; clear away any surplus sand.

5 Ease sand from the joints with a knife to create pockets for prostrate herbs which may be sown directly or, as here, planted as divisions from established specimens.

6 Tuck a little compost around the plants, firm into place and water if necessary; they will soon spread into mats and cushions of fragrant foliage.

the shape and course of a path or bed.

Work out planting schemes for individual beds and borders on separate sheets of paper only when you are satisfied with all this preliminary work make any necessary basic adjustments after trying out possible variations on the ground.

In addition to pictorial plans, you should also draw up a schedule of the work involved, because the various tasks are often best done in a particular order, perhaps at certain times of the year to ensure the least amount of disorder, mess and delay. Planting itself is almost the final operation and best timed for autumn in mild areas, or spring where winters are severe.

Before then you will need to repair or renovate existing hard structures such as paths, fences and walls, prune or move plants at the appropriate season, and remove turf or weeds to leave a clear site for marking out. Separate smaller beds can be prepared and planted piecemeal, but when planning a complete herb garden it is best to complete all these preliminary stages before transferring your design to the ground, using pegs driven in securely and joined with strings to mark the basic outlines. You can then dig over beds and borders to a suitable depth and condition, and set about constructing paths and hard edges.

Plant Requirements

Consideration should be given to the requirements of individual herbs for successful growth and yield; different surroundings are suitable for different herbs and a little time spent researching the ideal environment will help to produce a wonderful crop of pungent and decorative plants.

Lavandula spica

Although most of the well-known herbs are of Mediterranean origin and therefore prefer a sunny, free-draining position, re-creating the ecology they evolved in does not mean aiming deliberately for impoverished conditions. Only the nasturtium is recommended for hungry sites, because these encourage the production of flowers that might otherwise be usurped by lush leaf growth; but the result of improved flowering in the case of the nasturtium is often early death. It is worth remembering that most plants grown in gardens are often superior in form, size and performance to their relatives in the wild: the fact that they have adapted naturally to spartan surroundings is no reason to deny them care and nourishment.

It is fair to say, though, that aromatic herbs grown for flavouring or medicinal use are best grown in full sun, whereas those grown as pot herbs and leaf crops prefer moister conditions and some shelter from hot sunshine if they are to make plenty of growth. Arrange beds or the distribution of plants within a herb garden according to these needs, assembling leafy plants, for example, at the shady end of a border, in the shadow of shrubs, near hedges or beneath the canopy of open-pruned trees to provide them with a little dappled shade. Remember that variegated plants yield their best colours when exposed to morning and evening sunlight with a little shade at midday.

Similarly, free drainage is important for plants that are intolerant of damp conditions. These include plants with silver and grey foliage, which is usually produced by dense fine leaf hairs intended to trap moisture, developed as an adaptation to very dry conditions. Other plants of dubious hardiness may also succumb to prolonged damp around the stems. Raised beds or gravel mulches around stem bases can sometimes improve their chances of survival. Most woody-stemmed perennials need plenty of warm sunlight to ripen their growth and ensure

DIVIDING A BED

1 Segregate herbs with underground runners from other, more vulnerable plants with wide slates or pieces of durable panelling inserted vertically.

2 Replace the soil on both sides of the division, and firm into place with your heel or the handle of a trowel.

3 An invasive herb such as mint can then be planted a little distance from the inconspicuous division.

that they are well prepared to withstand winter temperatures.

Herbs that like damp, partially shaded sites, on the other hand, only thrive where their needs are met, both hot dry soil and gloomy waterlogged positions proving intolerable to them. Herbaceous perennial herbs, in particular, need to make maximum growth during the growing season to stock their roots with enough nutrients for survival and re-emergence the following spring.

Most herbs need shelter of some kind from the extremes of wind and frost. Though they might survive in the wild, their growth is often stunted by wind-pruning and frost injury, and you will do them a favour by enclosing beds and borders with windbreak hedges or fences that reduce their exposure. You will reap the benefits in summer, when the still sheltered air is heavy with the concentrated fragrance of volatile oils. Make sure, however, that the garden is not so enclosed that it becomes a frost pocket, without gateways or openings for cold air to drain away from susceptible plants.

SLOPING GROUND

Level ground is not essential unless you are planning an impressive parterre or knot garden, which really needs construction on a prepared platform in the same way as a bowling green or formal lawn. For most other herb schemes sloping ground, especially a dry bank, is ideal as a means of guaranteeing good drainage and, if it faces the sun for a large part of the day, plenty of warmth and light. There are enough prostrate and trailing herb varieties to ensure adequate ground cover and protection against soil erosion on a bank, but for larger specimens or where the incline is very steep,

making simple terraces or small level planting pockets will help with rapid establishment and any watering needed until plants are self-reliant. Paths can be cut as a series of steps, their outline perhaps softened by cascading thymes, ground-hugging Corsican mint, or tufts of chamomile and the creeping savory *Satureja spicigera*.

Above: *Herbs that need warm conditions do well when planted along the base of a brick wall facing the sun, which remains warm even after nightfall.*

Right: *A simple pit surrounded with firm walls of bricks or old wooden beams provides a useful bed for larger herbs, or (as here) a propagation and nursery frame that can be covered in cold weather.*

Above: *Stepping stones made from sawn log sections or paving slabs are a simple means of providing access for planting and maintenance in larger beds, and soon merge with the herbs as these grow and spread.*

HERBS FOR HEAVY SOILS

Although wet clays and other intractable soils will always benefit from some improvement to open their texture and speed drainage, the following herbs can usually cope well, especially if the surface is mulched in summer to prevent drought and cracking. Sunny or shaded sites are suitable, except where stated otherwise.

• alexanders	• angelica
• borage (sun)	• calendula
• chives (sun)	• comfrey
• fennel (sun)	• lemon balm (sun)
• lovage	• mint
• nasturtium (sun)	• sage
• sorrel	• sweet cicely

Structuring the Herb Garden

The design of a formal herb garden, whether it is a complex of knots or a simple wheel with radiating spokes dividing beds of culinary plants, allows plenty of scope for imagination. As William Lawson wrote in the seventeenth century, 'For special forms in squares, there are as many as there are devices in Gardeners' brains.' Simplicity is essential, for an elaborate layout will merely look confused once plants start to grow, and will only be comprehensible if viewed from above.

Gratiola officinalis

Graph paper is essential, as are accurate measurements. Sketch in the outlines of beds and borders as a rough guide, by all means, but decide first on the layout and dimensions of paths. Ornament is one thing, access at all seasons for harvesting and tending plants another, and all paths should be wide enough for comfortable passage (especially between shrubs after heavy rain) and must reach all parts of the garden. Main paths should be at least 60 cm/2 ft wide, more if you use a wheelbarrow or need wheelchair access. You can make subsidiary paths narrower – 30 cm/12 in might be enough – or you could use stepping stones instead of a continuous surface. Position the odd slab in large beds to stand on, or limit their width to about 1.2 m/4 ft so that all herbs are within arm's reach.

While balance and good proportion are important in planning the layout of beds, there is no reason why an irregular herb garden cannot be as successful as a classically symmetrical one. Draw out several geometrical patterns of beds on tracing paper laid over the garden outline drawn to scale on squared paper, and check their measurements for practicality. Leave room for seats, statuary and other features, and remember that hedges occupy real space – allow a 30 cm/12 in width for dwarf hedges, more for taller ones.

A series of small beds, each planted with a single type of herb, provides simple bold blocks of colour and texture, but more comprehensive plant collections need larger beds, perhaps organized according to colour, height or use. With elaborate designs, always measure the diagonals to make sure they are truly symmetrical, and take all measurements accurately, starting where possible from a base line – that is, the longest straight line that can be measured on the site – which can be used as a reference for all other

Left: *Herbs adapt to a number of styles and designs, not least to a relaxed cottage garden arrangement where the plants can grow and flower with their natural informality.*

HERB SPIRAL

1 Arrange bricks in a gradually increasing number of courses to create the outline of a spiral bed.

2 Spread a drainage layer of pea-sized gravel on the surface of lower levels, omitting areas where moisture-loving herbs are to grow.

3 Add garden compost to part of the lower level for hungry herbs such as parsley, basil and leaf coriander.

4 Partly fill the upper levels with broken bricks and rubble to ensure good drainage for herbs that like dry soil.

5 Fill between the parallel walls with good topsoil, and tamp into place or leave to settle.

6 Arrange the herbs for dry soil near the top and moisture- and nutrient-loving species at the base.

7 Finally, plant out the herbs and water thoroughly.

distances. Leave a string marking this line in position if possible to allow easy transfer of the design from paper to ground.

RAISED BEDS

Early herb gardens comprised a series of beds, laid out as functional squares and rectangles or in decorative shapes; these were raised slightly above the level of intervening paths with the soil held in place by edging boards. Raised beds have several advantages over ground-level cultivation: their layout establishes a strong design pattern, and it is easier to improve individual beds than to change the nature of the soil on a large scale, and less bending is involved in cultivating the plants. A single layer of thick wooden planks or edging boards, or two or three courses of bricks, will considerably increase the rooting depth where soils are shallow, while the sides of beds can be raised as high as necessary for the comfort of disabled and elderly gardeners. Higher sides, though, may need foundations and footings for stability, together with a series of holes for drainage.

Preparing the Site

Many plants are site-specific, only growing well where conditions are perfect. Fortunately the commonest herbs tolerate a wide range of soils, although their performance may be less than ideal – silver and grey herbs, for example, thrive in light, sandy ground, but in the same place sage and winter savory soon develop bare stems and need frequent propagation, and leafy annual herbs quickly bolt to seed in a dry season.

Teucrium chamaedrys

R e-creating a plant's preferred habitat is the ideal way to ensure success. Most of us, however, have to compromise by making the most of our garden soil. For positive health plants need enough moisture to maintain growth but not so much that their roots decay in airless surroundings; a balanced supply of nutrients and minerals in a soil that is not too acid or alkaline; sufficient warmth to sustain active growth, and freedom from weed competition. Any soil improvement must take all these factors into account.

Sandy soil is easy to work and warms up quickly, but soluble nutrients are easily leached out by rain, and drought may seriously check the growth of all but the toughest Mediterranean species. Adding plenty of garden compost before planting, together with annual mulches and occasional supplementary feeding to restore depleted fertility, helps to fortify the soil without destroying its naturally free drainage.

The tiny particles of clay readily stick together, producing wet, airless soil that sets hard and cracks in dry weather. Heavy ground with a large proportion of clay is potentially very fertile if you can improve its texture by digging in grit, coarse sand, leaf litter and bulky manure or compost to help aeration. A permanent mulch will protect the surface from being compacted by heavy rainfall and from drying out in hot sunshine.

Pools of water lingering on the surface of heavy waterlogged soils usually indicate poor drainage. Digging can relieve the problem if this is due to surface compaction, while deeper cultivation will break up a hard 'pan' – an impervious layer some distance below the surface. If saturation recurs, you may have to install a system of drainage pipes for permanent improvement unless you confine your herb collection to marshy species.

BEDS FOR WET GROUND

An alternative treatment for wet ground is to increase the depth of free-draining topsoil available for plants by creating raised beds. These are equally effective for coping with

HERBS FOR LIGHT, SANDY SOIL

Many herbs tolerate light, dry soils, but these are particularly suitable. Winter rain may remove large amounts of lime and nutrients each year, so be prepared to feed or compost the soil annually.

- alkanet
- arnica
- broom
- chervil
- coriander
- dianthus
- fennel
- hound's tongue
- lavender
- lemon verbena
- marjoram
- artemisia
- savory
- tarragon
- wormwood

- anise
- borage
- centaury
- chives
- cumin
- evening primrose
- foxglove
- hyssop
- lemon balm
- alfalfa
- sweet clover
- rosemary
- southernwood
- thyme

soils that are shallow, or too acid or alkaline to suit most species. Raised beds are not a modern innovation, but date back to medieval gardens. They may be enclosed by low walls of bricks, stone or timber boarding and their width is best limited to about 1.2 m/4 ft so that you can reach the centre without walking on the soil.

Dig over the enclosed area thoroughly, work in as much organic material as you can to improve texture and drainage, and add 15 cm/6 in of topsoil, perhaps saved from the making of paths, or bought. Finally cover the surface with an organic mulch that can be stirred in annually with a fork to maintain fertility.

CLEARING GROUND

The site for a herb garden is best prepared in autumn. Start by eliminating weeds, especially invasive perennial kinds that will be difficult to remove after planting; these can be forked out carefully or cleared with one or two applications of systemic weedkiller. If the area is under grass, skim this off

HERBS FOR CHALKY SOIL

- calamint
- chickweed
- cowslip
- elder
- juniper
- lemon balm
- lungwort
- mignonette
- Pasque flower
- rosemary
- sage
- Solomon's seal
- wormwood
- centaury
- chicory
- dianthus
- hound's tongue
- lavender
- lily of the valley
- marjoram
- mullein
- periwinkle
- roses
- salad burnet
- thyme
- yarrow

with a spade, stack neatly and cover with black plastic sheet until it decays into fibrous loam for potting.

Correct any drainage problems and dig the bed thoroughly. Dress with lime if the soil is too acid, and leave the surface rough over winter to be broken down by frost. In early spring treat any weeds that have appeared, and then fork in a good dressing of compost or decayed manure. Rake the surface level, and leave the ground for a few weeks to settle before marking out the design.

Above: *A hand cultivator with prongs can be useful for clearing the site of weeds.*

COMFREY COMPOST

1 Recycling vigorous perennials such as comfrey returns precious minerals and nutrients to the soil. Cut the larger foliage, leaving the youngest leaves to provide further crops later.

2 Soak the leaves in water to make a liquid feed, or add them to the compost heap as this is built; there they will decompose and release their goodness.

Healthy Herbs

A good collection of herbs is an enduring asset and healthy herbs are essential for a functioning garden of plants. Sensible planting arrangements, soil types and the availability of light are all important considerations when beginning a new herb bed or renovating an existing one.

Mentha piperita

A herb garden is an enduring asset, so do not be over-hasty in getting started. With the site prepared, construct any edgings and paths, except for gravel which is best laid after planting to avoid depositing soil on it.

Although container-grown herbs can be planted at almost any time of the year, autumn is the perfect season (especially for bare-root plants) unless winters are very cold or the soil heavy, in which case wait until mid-spring. If you have to wait several months before planting, use the bed for a display of annual flowers or grow a 'green manure' crop of mustard, clover or vetch to dig in later as a soil improver.

Try to fill a whole bed at once, even if this means assembling a collection of herbs over a period of time. They can be kept in their containers, or transferred temporarily to a nursery bed where you might be able to take cuttings or divisions to supplement your stock. Bare-root plants must be heeled in to a piece of spare ground if they are not to be planted immediately.

Be generous with quantities; trees, shrubs and invasive herbs can be planted singly, but others, particularly small edging plants, are best ordered in quantity for an instant impression of lush establishment. Always choose young, short-jointed bushy plants with

PEST AND DISEASE CONTROL

Treating your herbs well by watering, feeding or propagating whenever necessary helps to maintain their vigour and so avoid disorders that normally affect ailing plants.

Any problems that do occur should be treated promptly. Aphids are perhaps the commonest pests, and may be controlled by spraying with derris, or rotenone, which is harmless to their natural predators. Quassia is effective against caterpillars if there are too many to pick off by hand. Slugs and snails are also best controlled by picking off.

Diseases are occasionally more serious, especially fungal disorders such as rust, which commonly affects mint, as well as violets and other subjects. Cut down rusted growth to ground level for burning, and scorch the crown and surrounding soil with a flame gun; if all else fails use a commercial fungicide or alternatively transfer clean-rooted divisions to fresh soil.

Left: *Some herbs are attractive enough to mass on their own. The many forms of thyme are favourites for planting as hedges, edgings and flowering borders.*

Right: *A healthy purple sage plant. For their strongest colour such plants need fuii sunlight, though even in light shade the young tips will display their characteristic leaf colours.*

PLASTIC MULCHES

If you suspect the ground is still full of weed seeds or root fragments, or if the soil is very light and liable to dry out quickly, you can use a plastic mulch to suppress weed growth and retain moisture. Prepare the soil in the usual way when it is moist and rake the surface level, removing as many stones as possible. Spread a sheet of heavy-duty black plastic sheet or woven matting across the bed, and secure the edges by wedging them in the soil. Cut holes or crosses in the sheet through which to plant the herbs, and then cover the whole surface with a layer of gravel, or shredded bark or cocoa shells.

a good, healthy colour, and make sure they are fully hardened off if bought in spring.

PLANTING

Choose a pleasant day for planting, and one on which you have the time to finish an area completely. Water plants well, whether they are in pots or the open ground, and then arrange them on the surface according to your ground plan – but mark the positions for bare-root plants with stakes or labels, rather than expose them to drying out. Check the overall effect and make sure everything has room to develop, although to avoid unsightly gaps you might prefer to space certain plants more densely and then sacrifice some later as others demand room.

INVASIVE HERBS

Herbs such as mint, tarragon and woodruff are irrepressible colonizers, their creeping roots eventually taking over large areas of ground and infiltrating neighbouring plants. Restrain their invasiveness by planting them in containers, either above ground or buried in the soil. Large pots, bottomless buckets or thick plastic bags perforated with drainage holes are ideal. They can be filled with good garden soil, or a soil and compost mixture, which will sustain them for two or three years before the contents need division and replanting in fresh soil.

Plant edgings first, together with strategic plants such as trees, shrubs or anything with a large rootball – stake these where necessary, and tread the soil firm around larger plants. Spread out the roots of bare-root specimens, working soil between them as you refill the hole, and make sure the

finished surface matches the soil mark on their stems. Re-level the intervening soil before planting the other herbs. Prune growing tips and side shoots of shrubby plants to encourage bushy growth. Label everything clearly, and then water the whole bed to settle the soil around the roots.

Looking after the Herb Garden

Herbs are relatively free from serious disorders, especially if you start with healthy plants in the first place. However, every plant depends for its welfare on the condition of the soil in which it grows, and the annual management routine in a herb garden should concentrate on building up and maintaining the soil's nutrients and vitality.

Origanum
marjoranum

WATERING AND FEEDING

Soils lose water through drainage or evaporation at different rates according to their type and condition: clay, for example, retains moisture for much longer than sandy soil, which in a hot dry season may need thorough watering at least every week. Plants can only absorb food in solution, so maintaining adequate moisture at the roots is essential for uninterrupted growth. The best way to ensure this is to add manure or compost to the soil to increase its content of humus, partly decomposed organic material that soaks up water like a sponge and releases it slowly, together with essential nutrients.

If the soil has been enriched with compost or decayed manure during initial preparations, it should be sufficient to spread a layer of compost annually over the surface of the moist soil in spring to maintain humus levels. Most aromatic herbs will then flourish without supplementary watering. Indeed, try not to be too generous when watering: too much water can dilute the essential oils, and may injure herbs that prefer relatively dry conditions.

Leafy herbs will need watering in a dry season to keep the soil constantly moist, while plants grown for their fruits or pods benefit most if watered when in flower and again while their crops are swelling. If you do water, soak plants thoroughly, and spread a further mulch afterwards to prevent evaporation. Plants in containers need regular watering, as will recently introduced herbs, especially if planted in summer. Be prepared to water new trees in dry weather for at least a season after planting.

As long as the soil is mulched annually with a light dressing of compost, most herbs will thrive without supplementary feeding. Too rich a soil, in fact, encourages soft rank growth with less flavour and perfume. Plants grown as bulky leaf crops sometimes benefit from an application of dried blood to supply extra nitrogen after a wet winter on light soils, and fruit quality is improved by a spring dressing of general fertilizer such as seaweed meal or blood, fish and bone. Avoid using artificial fertilizers, which may unbalance soil conditions and reduce the herbs' concentration of essential soils and active substances.

MULCHING

An essential part of soil care and plant health, mulching involves covering the

DIVIDING COMFREY

1 Vigorous clump-forming herbs such as bergamot, lovage and comfrey need dividing every few years to keep plants young and robust. Dig whole clumps for splitting, or use a spade to slice off outer portions from growing plants.

2 With a very sharp knife, cut these cleanly into small segments, each with a tuft of leaves or a dormant bud, and plenty of healthy roots. Replant immediately in good soil.

MAKING COMPOST

Apart from being a useful soil improver in the early stages of making a herb garden, animal manure is too rich for feeding all but the greediest plants. It can be used, however, as just one of the ingredients in a compost heap, where it will blend with plant waste to produce the ideal material for mulching and soil improvement. Site the compost heap on bare soil in a wire enclosure or commercial container, starting with a layer of plant stems and coarse material to let air penetrate the heap. Build the heap in layers, mixing organic household waste, manure, lawn mowings, weeds and discarded plants; avoid seeding and diseased plants, and pass any woody stems through a shredder first. Parts of herbs are particularly suitable ingredients, especially nettles, comfrey and yarrow, which all help the compost to ferment. Between the layers spread a thin dressing of garden lime, or gypsum if you do not want to increase the alkalinity of your soil. Cover the completed heap with plastic sheeting or old carpets. Leave it for a few months, then turn the contents to ensure even decomposition.

ground to protect it from erosion, rapid drying and structural deterioration after heavy rain or hot sun, and also to smother weeds.

An organic mulch of compost, pulverized bark or cocoa shells can be used for plants that like moist conditions, but herbs from hot dry habitats are better mulched with an inorganic material such as gravel or grit to prevent their stems from rotting – this is especially important on heavy soils that may remain wet for a large part of the year. Always spread a mulch when the soil is moist, and keep the material away from woody plant stems to ensure free drainage.

WEEDING

Although plants normally prefer to live in communities rather than alone, common weeds compete too energetically to allow them to grow

Above: *Herbs in constant use, as in this collection of culinary plants, need routine care if they are to prosper and stay in good condition: pruning or cutting back, watering, feeding and regular propagation all help maintain continuity.*

unchecked. A permanent mulch will suppress most annual weeds, which should otherwise be hoed or pulled by hand while still small. Perennial weeds such as buttercup, thistle and ground elder or goutweed are more tenacious and may be a problem even where the soil is mulched. Fork or pull them up with as much root as possible, or paint them individually with systemic weedkiller. Check when weeding, though, that you are not pulling up a potentially useful plant. Many herbs seed themselves and their seedlings can be transplanted to a nursery bed for growing on, while many weeds have

medicinal or culinary uses and so may be worth leaving or growing elsewhere.

The appearance and qualities of herbs change as the season progresses, but light pruning checks this by redirecting energy into new growth, keeping plants in good condition for longer. Dead-heading borage, pot marigolds and other annuals will prevent their setting seed and so prolong flowering for a few more weeks. This is also a useful precaution with prolific seed producers such as fennel and angelica, whose deep-rooted seedlings can take over a herb border – but leave a few heads to mature if you do need more seeds. Self-seeding may be a virtue, of course: you can have continuous supplies of chervil if this short-lived annual is left to seed itself in a permanent bed, while in its second year a parsley plant will sow a patch of seedlings for transplanting elsewhere.

Perennials grown for the soft tips of their shoots are best cut back once or twice as their stems start to age: mint and lemon balm, for example, will produce further flushes of young growth if pruned to ground level before their shoots reach full height. Shrubby perennials are best clipped lightly after flowering to keep the plants tidy and stimulate new side shoots, but if grown formally they will need more frequent trimming. Hedges of santolina, hyssop, rosemary and germander should be clipped in early summer and again two or three months later, and may be pruned hard in spring if they have grown too large.

AUTUMN CARE

As frost threatens, tender herbs such as basil, lemon verbena and scented pelargoniums should be dug up for potting and growing on indoors. Take cuttings from any of doubtful hardiness, or transplant a specimen to the cold frame as insurance against loss. Either leave dead stems on herbaceous perennials over winter to provide a little insulation against frost and wind, or cut them down for composting and insulate the crowns of cold-sensitive plants with a covering of bracken, leaves or straw held in place with wire netting. Remember that different varieties of the same herb may vary in hardiness, so check their individual needs. Always clear away fallen

FRESH CULINARY HERBS AVAILABLE IN WINTER

- burnet – outdoors or under cloches
- chives – under cloches or indoors in pots
- mint – in a cold frame or in large pots and boxes indoors
- rosemary – outdoors or in pots

- winter savory – outdoors or in pots indoors
- chervil – outdoors, in a cold frame or indoors in pots
- marjoram – outdoors or in pots indoors
- pelargoniums – indoors in pots
- sage – outdoors

leaves from prostrate herbs that might otherwise rot beneath them.

THE HERB GARDEN IN WINTER

With herbaceous plants now dormant, interest will focus on evergreen species. Not all these can withstand a bleak winter, so check their hardiness and if necessary arrange windbreaks of sacking or plastic mesh to filter cold winds. Shake off settled snow before its weight damages branches.

EXTENDING THE SEASON

To ensure a supply of basic herbs during winter, use some form of protection to keep them in active growth. Cloches and small covers set over parsley, chives and mint in autumn will prolong their usefulness for several extra weeks, or you can transfer a few plants to a cold frame where they will be available all winter if the frame is covered with matting in hard frost. Lettuce, coriander and chervil can be sown in cold frames to crop in winter. Many other herbs such as thyme, tarragon and sage may be dug up and potted for use indoors, with a few pots kept in reserve in a frame or greenhouse to take their place when they are exhausted. Some herbs respond to forcing, especially mint, whose roots can be dug up in late winter and buried in boxes of potting compost to make early growth in the greenhouse. Out of doors, cloches placed over dormant plants will revive them a little earlier than normal, while crops such as rhubarb, seakale and Good King Henry are usually forced into growth by covering them with boxes or blanching pots.

Right: *A sheltered area or potting shed is ideal for transplanting herbs and storing equipment.*

USING A COLD FRAME

1 A cold frame is a valuable accessory, both for growing plants out of season and for housing cuttings and young plants, such as these thyme seedlings, in their early stages.

2 Adequate humidity and protection from low temperatures or bright sunlight are essential, so cover the frame when necessary, but remember to admit ventilation whenever possible.

Propagating Herbs

Seasoned professionals and amateur gardeners alike get immense satisfaction from raising new plants. Your collection may start with a few bought herbs in pots, but sooner or later you will probably want to grow your own from seed or by rooting live parts of a plant. Some herbs can be started in more than one way while others need a particular technique; whichever method is used, remember always to start with healthy material or seeds from a reputable source to avoid disappointment.

Anagallis arvensis

GROWING FROM SEED

Most herb species can be raised from seed, although this method takes the longest to produce a mature plant and is not recommended for named cultivars, especially variegated kinds, as seedlings do not always resemble the parent plant. Seed sowing is the quickest way to grow a particular plant in large quantities, and the usual method of raising annual and biennial herbs, wild flowers, salad and vegetable herbs, species from other countries and easily germinated perennials such as chives, fennel, feverfew, lovage, rue, salad burnet, European and American sweet cicely and winter savory.

Although a seed is a potential plant just waiting to grow, it will only germinate when conditions are right. For most, a combination of adequate warmth, moisture and air is enough to trigger them into life, but others have special requirements which depend on the kind of surroundings they normally meet in the wild.

The seeds of juniper, woodruff, European sweet cicely and violets, for example, are protected by a hard, resistant coat against early germination when temperatures are too cold, and they depend on frost to break this down – a process called stratification.

SOWING

1 *Fill a sterilized tray with a moist seed growing medium. Level and firm lightly if this is soil-based; simply tap the tray to settle soil-less composts.*

2 *Scatter small seeds evenly and thinly over the whole surface of the compost; larger seeds can be spaced at regular intervals.*

3 *Some seeds need light for germination, but others prefer darkness and must be covered with compost that has been sifted to remove any lumps or debris.*

4 *Sprinkle this fine compost evenly over the seeds to the recommended depth, label the tray and cover with plastic or glass to conserve moisture.*

Sown in autumn, they may be left outdoors exposed to winter weather, or you can artificially break their dormancy by mixing the seeds with damp sand in a plastic bag, and leaving this in a refrigerator for about two months before sowing in warm conditions.

Hard-coated leguminous seeds need penetration by moisture before they will grow. This can be speeded up by scarification, a method that involves carefully nicking the coat with a sharp knife or gently thinning part of it with sandpaper; soaking overnight in warm water is an alternative way. Some ordinary seeds need light, others darkness, to trigger germination, so always follow the sowing instructions on seed packets carefully to make sure you have provided the right conditions.

SOWING OUTDOORS

The normal sowing time for the majority of plants is early to mid-spring, just as soon as the soil is warm enough to support active growth. Wait until new weed seedlings appear or the first hedgerow buds break as an indication of the best time.

Vegetables and herbs needed in quantity are sown in drills in the kitchen garden, others in shorter rows in a nursery bed; flowering herbs may be sown where they are to grow, either in short rows or in circular furrows made by pressing the rim of a pot into the soil surface. Wherever you are sowing, always fork, weed and rake the soil into a crumbly level seedbed first, and in cold weather warm the ground for a week or two beforehand by covering it with cloches.

Use a rake handle or garden stake to mark out a shallow depression in the soil for short drills, or draw the corner of the rake along a tight garden line for longer rows. Sow the

GROWING BASIL

1 Basil seeds may be sown individually in soil blocks to save pricking out later, or seedlings can be transferred from seed trays.

2 The richer compost mixture of the soil blocks combined with heat and regular watering encourage rapid early growth.

3 With two pairs of true leaves, these seedlings are well established and ready for potting up.

4 After hardening off, these young basil plants will soon be ready for transfer to the open garden.

seeds in the bottom of the drill, and then cover with a thin layer of soil and gently tamp with the back of the rake head to ensure good contact between soil and seeds. In very dry weather flood the open drill with water, allow to drain before sowing, and then cover with dry soil.

Keep the sown area moist until seedlings appear. When large enough to handle these should be thinned to leave plants 5-10 cm/2-4 in apart. Most annual herbs can be left to grow at this spacing, but biennials and perennials may need thinning again or transplanting to another patch of

ground until large enough to be moved to their permanent positions.

SOWING UNDER GLASS

This is the best method of raising half-hardy annuals and early crops, together with those herbs that need extra warmth or pot cultivation, and any that are particularly precious or expensive.

Use seed trays, pots or shallow pans according to the quantity of seeds, first cleaning and sterilizing the containers with soapy water and a little ammonia or disinfectant. Cover the drainage holes of earthenware pots with a few broken shards before filling with a moist seed compost; plastic containers can be filled without a drainage layer. Tap the pot sharply to settle the contents or gently firm with a flat board, and then scatter the seeds thinly and evenly over the surface.

Dust a thin layer of compost over them, as deep as the diameter of the seeds – but any that need light for germination should be simply pressed gently into the surface. Label and seal the pot and cover it with a clear plastic bag, or with a piece of glass and a sheet of opaque paper where darkness is required.

Stand the containers in a warm place, and keep the soil moist during germination, either misting it when dry or standing the container in shallow water until moist patches appear on the surface. Check frequently to see if seedlings are emerging - germination may take only a few days, or several weeks or more for slow growers such as parsley and bay. Once the first shoots appear, remove the covering and move them into the light, but avoid bright sunlight until they are stronger.

Mounding

Evergreen perennials such as sage can quickly develop into impressive mounds of shrubby growth.

1 When old woody herbs develop bare lower stems, they can be propagated by mounding.

2 Clear out any dead stems and leaves, and then heap soil in the centre of the bush.

3 Leave for a few months. Each of the branches will have rooted and can be detached as a new plant.

Layering Rosemary

1 Choose a low, flexible branch, remove some of the leaves where it touches the soil, and cut a shallow notch to induce rooting.

2 Scoop out a shallow depression for the prepared section of branch, and hold it in place with a wire loop or clothes pin.

3 Cover the wounded section and peg with good topsoil, and firm gently. In dry weather water the layer (but not the parent plant) to hasten rooting.

STRIKING CUTTINGS

1 Prepare a gritty, free-draining rooting mixture by blending sharp sand with an equal volume of peat, peat substitute or seed compost.

2 Trim the cuttings to size, using a very sharp knife to cut through the stem just below a node. Remove the lowest pair of leaves.

3 Fill a pot with the mixture and insert a cutting in each. Water in the cuttings and enclose in a plastic bag supported on short canes.

When seedlings are large enough (usually when they have made true leaves in addition to their seed leaves), they will need pricking out (transplanting singly) except in the case of large seeds sown individually in small pots and those to be planted out or potted on intact. Replant the seedlings up to the base of their seed leaves in separate pots of moist potting compost or about 5 cm/2 in apart in seed trays.

DIVISION

Division is used to multiply herbs that form clumps of rooted stems, and also to rejuvenate older specimens where the centre of the clump has died out, leaving a ring of young material. The whole crown of the plant is eased from the soil with a fork, during winter dormancy or in early spring as growth revives. Divide it into segments by plunging two forks back to back into the mass of growth and forcing them apart; smaller crowns can be split with a sharp knife or by tearing off rooted portions. Replant divisions firmly in fresh soil at the same depth as the original crown.

LAYERING

Layering is a slow but foolproof method of inducing the stem of a woody perennial such as sage, lavender or honeysuckle to make roots of its own while it is still nourished by the parent plant.

MOUNDING

When whole plants are layered to root large numbers of cuttings, or to restore a neglected herb that has become bare at the base, the technique is known as mounding or stooling. It is very useful for salvaging unpruned lavender bushes, but can be used on any woody herb; it is also the standard way to multiply rootstocks for fruit trees.

CUTTINGS

Cuttings are small portions of stem or root, trimmed off and induced to grow roots of their own. There are three main kinds of stem cutting: hardwood, taken in autumn from woody stems of trees and shrubs and rooted outdoors or in a cold frame over winter; semi-hardwood, taken in mid- to late summer from side shoots

with a ripe base and often a 'heel' of old wood; and softwood cuttings taken in spring or summer, using the soft tips of the current year's growth. The differences are largely technical and most plants can be propagated by more than one method; clipping shrubby herbs and hedges to shape often yields plenty of cutting material.

Always use sturdy, healthy non-flowering shoots about 8-10 cm/3-4 in long; hardwood cuttings rooted in the ground should be two or three times this length. Trim carefully just below a leaf joint with a razor blade or sharp knife. Strip the leaves from the lower half of the cutting using a knife or by pulling them away to leave a clean wound. The base of the cuttings can be dipped in a hormone rooting preparation as an insurance before inserting them firmly in a well-drained cuttings compost. Strike soft cuttings in pots in sealed plastic bags or a propagator, others in a cold frame or outdoors in a sheltered place. Shade from bright sunlight, and pot on or transplant to a nursery bed as soon as the cuttings are growing well.

Potted Herb Gardens

Lack of available ground need not stop you from making a collection of herbs, for most adapt readily to cultivation in pots and other containers. Even if most of your herbs grow in the open garden, growing some of your favourite kinds in pots adds a further dimension to herb gardening.

Origanum vulgare

Pots can be arranged near the house in decorative groups for easy access, their mobility allowing you to move them around to follow the sun as the season progresses or to shelter them from cold winds. You can bring them indoors in winter to maintain supplies or even for guests to help themselves to herbs at the table. Larger tubs or troughs provide room for several kinds to grow together as permanent miniature herb gardens, positioned where they get all the sun or shade they might need. In gardens on poor ground, container growing is the best way of providing perfect soil.

Almost any kind of container is suitable and the range is infinite, from wooden boxes, clay pots and stone urns, to used growing bags and large paint tins, cattle troughs and coal scuttles. Any you choose must be large enough to house plants comfortably – aim for a minimum 20 cm/8 in diameter and depth - and should have adequate free drainage at the base to shift surplus water and so avoid sour, stagnant conditions at the roots. Provide several drainage holes in the base, together with a few in the sides just above the base if the containers are not supported off the ground by small blocks or pieces of tile to let water drain away.

Try to match containers to their intended plants. Terracotta is an attractive material sympathetic to more decorative herbs such as a collection of coloured sages (golden 'Icterina', cream and pink 'Tricolor' and red 'Purpurescens', for example) or the many kinds of scented-leaved geraniums. A larger tub would suit an informal arrangement of rosemary, hyssop, thyme and golden marjoram, and if mounted on castors could be moved to a greenhouse or conservatory for winter use. Utilitarian containers such as bottomless buckets or 10 litre/2 gallon paint tins may be hidden behind more ornamental pots to house taller invasive herbs such as tarragon, sorrel, horseradish, comfrey and mint. Used growing bags are ideal for annual and biennial herbs such as basil, chervil and parsley, or for growing out-of-season supplies of mint in the greenhouse. Wooden 'Versailles' pots and similar large formal containers are best reserved for specimen bay trees, herb topiary, or perhaps a trained quince planted with annual nasturtiums, lettuce and trailing New Zealand spinach at the base.

POTTING ON

1 As plants develop they need to be moved on to increasingly large containers. Free drainage is essential and depends on a preliminary layer of small stones or gravel.

2 The pot is then part-filled with the appropriate growing medium, the plant is tapped from its old pot and centred in the new one, and the remaining space is filled with soil.

POTTING BAY

1 Leafy bushes of bay are reliable in containers, but be sure to plant in pots of adequate size; one such as this will sustain growth for several years before it is too small.

2 While there is still room in the container, smaller herbs such as parsley, thyme and marjoram planted around the base will transform the pot into a miniature garden.

Above: *Evergreen bay (*Laurus nobilis) *is a popular container shrub for formal situations, as here where a pyramid-trained specimen stands sentinel in a painted 'Versailles' box.*

PLANTING

The easiest way to start any potted collection is to buy pots of young herbs from a specialist nurseryman, and plant these straight into new containers. Cutting the tips of shoots for use will keep them compact for several months before they need potting on or exchanging for smaller plants. A stouter herb such as rosemary, lavender or sage can be started by rooting several cuttings together in a small pot and then transferring them as a single plant to the container until they become too large and need replacement.

At planting time check that drainage holes are clear and then cover them with a layer of gravel, stones or a few shards from broken clay pots. Over this spread a thin layer of peat or a moisture-retentive peat substitute before filling the pot with a soil-based potting mixture. Soil-less growing media can be difficult to moisten once completely dry, and as most contain fertilizers that are soon exhausted, supplementary feeding is often necessary after only a few weeks. They are easier to handle and lighter than soil-based mixes, but this may be a disadvantage outdoors where weight confers stability. John Innes No 2 or Cornell mix is a good commercial mixture, or you can blend your own from 7 parts good garden soil, 3 parts peat or leafmould, 2 parts horticultural sand, and a little seaweed fertilizer – but watch out for possible weed seedlings.

POT CARE

Herbs in pots need special attention, as they are totally dependent on the gardener for their welfare. Their greatest need is water: the toughest drought-loving herb cannot survive for long in bone-dry soil and you must therefore check regularly (daily or even twice daily in a hot summer) that the soil stays consistently moist. Leafy herbs will appreciate an occasional feed of houseplant fertilizer, but for others annual re-potting or top-dressing is enough to replenish their diet.

Young herbs in small pots need to be transferred to larger ones when their roots show through at the bottom of the pot. Once they are in their final containers, you need to replenish the nutrients annually in spring by gently knocking out the plants, and teasing away the soil from around the rootball before repotting them in fresh soil in the original container or one similar. Plants too large to repot in this way should have the top 5-7 cm/2-3 in of soil replaced annually with a fresh supply.

Container Herb Gardens

Herbs are ideal subjects not only for conventional pots, but also containers of all kinds – wall pots, troughs, window boxes, and anything you have handy, from a tatty old sink covered with 'hypertufa' to give it a new lease of life, to a beautiful terracotta chimney pot which can make a centrepiece in an informal cottage garden, especially if you put a few trailing plants around the edge. Containers have advantages of their own: they can be used to confine invasive herbs such as mint, or filled with ericaceous compost for lime-hating plants.

Ocimum basilicum

WINDOW BOXES

A window box makes an ideal herb garden, accessible at all times and changing with the seasons if a supply of potted plants is kept in reserve. Make sure brackets are strong enough to support the weight of moist soil, and use a box about 25-30 cm/10-12 in deep to allow a good root run for the plants.

Provide ample drainage in the same way as for other containers, and then fill with a moist soil-based potting mixture. Either plant young herbs directly into this or grow them in 10-12 cm/4-5 in pots, burying these just below surface level in the box and replacing them as they are exhausted. Small herbs, especially ornamental varieties,

HERBS FOR A SUNNY WINDOW BOX

- calendula
- dill
- lemon verbena – summer only
- nasturtium – in summer
- sage
- self-heal
- winter savory

- chives
- lemon thyme
- marjoram
- rosemary
- scented-leaved geraniums – summer only
- tarragon

Above: *A strawberry pot may be used not only for strawberries, but also for parsley or any other suitable herb. Always plant as you add the soil, firming each layer into place before filling the next hole.*

Left: *With regular watering and feeding, an ornamental pot on a wall can support alpine strawberries or an ever-bearing large variety that will fruit on trailing runners.*

are best but space can be made for taller kinds such as bay and rosemary, started as cuttings and grown in the box until they are too large, when they may be transferred to the garden.

HANGING BASKETS

A hanging basket holds only a small volume of soil and is often exposed to wind and sun from various directions. It needs dedicated attention to watering in hot, dry weather. Nevertheless, many herbs will grow well in a deep basket – seasonal kinds such as basil, nasturtiums and parsley, or permanent decorative crops of pennyroyal, lady's mantle or golden lemon balm. Try growing small-leaved ivies to cascade and cover the sides of the basket, and add a little trailing lobelia or a basket tomato variety for extra flair.

PLANTING IN A STONE TROUGH

1 Protect drainage holes with large stones or curved shards of broken pot and then spread a layer of pebbles or gravel.

2 Fill the trough with a moist, nutritious soil mixture almost to the rim, and help this settle by repeatedly plunging in the trowel.

3 Arrange and plant a few chosen herbs in the trough, but not too many as they will soon fill the available space as they grow.

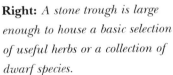

4 Complete the planting by covering the surface with a decorative mulch of fine gravel or chippings to conserve moisture.

Above: *Tall, emphatic containers such as chimney pots are perfect for displaying nasturtiums and other climbing or trailing herbs; fill the lower part of the pot with rubble for stability before topping up with soil or compost.*

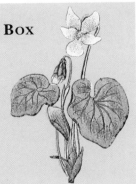

To plant a hanging basket, mix a soil-based medium 50-50 with a soil-less type to reduce weight, and either add a slow-release fertilizer or make sure you feed twice weekly from mid-summer onwards. Suspend the basket out of the wind in a position where you can reach the herbs comfortably for picking and watering. In the autumn transfer the complete basket to a cool greenhouse to prolong the season of use and help plants to survive the winter; the following spring you can take cuttings and remake the basket with fresh soil.

Right: *A stone trough is large enough to house a basic selection of useful herbs or a collection of dwarf species.*

HERBS FOR A LIGHTLY SHADED BOX

- bay
- catmint
- chervil
- corn salad
- mint
- lungwort
- violets
- French sorrel
- chamomile
- chives
- mignonette
- parsley
- salad burnet
- wild strawberry

Herbs Indoors

Herbs are not house plants, and all except the tenderest species need to spend most of their time out of doors if they are to thrive. But many kinds will stand some time indoors without permanent harm, and will add fragrance to your rooms. A pot of basil on an indoor window sill will, when the window is open, release its spicy odour every time the wind stirs the leaves. If you have a conservatory, of course, you can use it for a permanent collection of warmth-loving herbs of all shapes and sizes.

Origanum majorana

HERBS ON THE WINDOW SILL

Apart from shade-loving kinds and a few fleshy-leaved plants such as scented-leaved geraniums, most herbs remain in good condition only for a short time on domestic window sills, and soon suffer from lack of light. The best way to keep a supply of herbs near at hand is to grow several pots of each kind outdoors or in a cold frame or greenhouse, bringing them in one at a time to replace others as these are used up or become drawn and sickly. The superseded herbs are cut back and returned to the frame to revive, or may be planted outdoors after hardening off. All herbs thrive best in the open air, and even long-term pot plants are best moved outdoors in summer. With care, though, it is possible to keep a changing sequence of basic herbs on the window sill throughout the winter, supplemented by lettuce, coriander, and mustard and cress sown direct in pots to give two or three cuts of loose leaves for winter salads.

GROWING UNDER GLASS

In temperate climates a greenhouse or conservatory is essential for growing herbs from warmer parts of the world, and there is a wide enough variety of these to turn a fair-sized greenhouse into an indoor herb garden. Depending on their native habitat, some will be content with minimal frost protection, but tropical species

Above: *A greenhouse or conservatory admits plenty of light to keep plants healthy and compact; except for any in current use, keep potted herbs there where they will remain in good condition until needed.*

Left: *Although many herbs need preserving for out-of-season use, drying subtly alters their flavour and concentration. Parsley, basil, sage, mint and other fresh herbs grown in pots will supply an authentic and stimulating taste of summer.*

will need varying amounts of heat and humidity for good health all the year round. Check cultural needs and build your collection with compatible neighbours – the steamy conditions preferred by a vanilla orchid, for example, would prove lethal to a westringia or grapevine.

Use the walls and roof of the house for training climbers, especially fruiting kinds that will benefit from the good light and a long growing season: in a warm conservatory a fig tree can bear two or three crops of figs a year, compared with only one outdoors. These are best grown in deep containers or in a small soil border. Near the back of the bench arrange large pots of citrus fruit, tea and other greenhouse shrubs, filling the foreground with smaller herbs and trailing varieties to tumble down the front.

Like all pot plants these need regular watering and feeding while in active growth. During the summer paint the glass with shading to prevent sun-scorch and excessively high temperatures. Wetting down the staging and paths with a watering can helps

ESSENTIAL HERBS FOR WINDOW SILLS

• basil – sow a pinch in each pot, and prevent flowering for long life; sow again in midsummer for late supplies
• chives – pot up divisions from garden clumps, and keep well fed and watered
• parsley – choose a compact variety, sow in spring and again in late summer for winter cutting; use several pots in rotation
• thyme – start from seed or cuttings rooted direct in the pots; keep in full light and water sparingly

• chervil – sow in spring and again in late summer in quantity in a wide pan, and leave to seed itself when past its best
• marjoram – grow like thyme; choose sweet marjoram for warm rooms, or the hardier pot marjoram where it is cooler
• sage – strike cuttings and keep trimmed frequently; select a variegated kind for indoor colour

maintain a healthy atmosphere, and occasionally misting the leaves with water deters red spider mite. If pests and diseases do appear, treat them promptly, as they multiply rapidly in a closed environment. Insect predators are available to control most common pests, while attention to greenhouse hygiene – removing dead flowers and leaves, ventilating freely whenever possible, and maintaining steady growth – will discourage most diseases.

Above: *Bunches of herbs can remain where they were dried, adding their pervasive scent to the room.*

DIVIDING CHIVES

1 To propagate fibrous-rooted herbs or multiplier onions such as chives, lift a healthy clump and shake off the surplus soil.

2 Gently pull the clump into several pieces; heavy clay soil might need washing off before roots can be disentangled safely.

3 Pot up the divisions in good growing medium, and keep on a warm sunny windowsill for a regular indoor supply.

Pruning and Training

*Lavandula
spica*

Annual and biennial herbs need little interference with their growth, apart from dead-heading to prolong their lives and seasonal tidying as top growth dies. Herbaceous perennials, too, are largely self-sufficient, although thinning congested growth and cutting their dead flowers to prevent unwanted seeding are often an essential part of their care.

Perennial woody herbs, usually need some kind of restraint if they are not to grow too large. In thoroughly prepared ground a contented perennial herb may grow vigorously, a reassuring sign that all is well – although this should not be an excuse for avoiding pruning. Left to their own devices, perennials will continue growing until they reach maximum size, often with unfortunate results such as limited flowering or fruiting and the development of bare stems at the base, while increased competition and overcrowding encourage disease.

Timely pruning will avoid all these complications and banish disorder from the herb garden.

UNDERSTANDING PRUNING

Plants grow upwards and outwards because growth hormones concentrate at the ends of shoots, suppressing the development of buds elsewhere. Cutting off a growing tip redirects the plant's energies to lower buds and stimulates them into growth as replacements for the lost leading shoot. Pinching out the tips of a citrus bush, clipping a lavender hedge and

mowing a thyme lawn to remove some of the top foliage are all forms of pruning to limit upward growth and encourage bushy side shoots.

Picking the tips of herb bushes in the course of normal use is a valuable form of basic pruning, but most perennial kinds need one or more overall trims each season to maintain a well-balanced plant. As a general rule, clipping with shears immediately after flowering will restore shapeliness, but this may be done earlier to prevent flowering and allow a longer period of regrowth before the end of the season. A mid-season trim of variegated herbs will provoke a flush of brightly coloured new growth; at the same time cut out completely any shoots that revert to plain green. Herb hedges and topiary may need several trims a year, depending on the species used and the degree of strict formality intended.

RENOVATION

Plants such as rosemary, lavender and broom resent being pruned hard, but an annual trim after flowering is essential to maintain size and quality; confine cuts to young green growth, which regenerates freely, unlike older brown stems which may die after

CUTTING BACK

1 Once some herbs are past their best, often after flowering, it is a good idea to cut back their straggly stems almost to ground level.

2 With their long stems removed, young shoots at the base will be exposed to more light and will soon provide a fresh crop of usable leaves.

being pruned. Many other hedge and shrub species, on the other hand, can be cut back hard at the start of the growing season to restore their size. Always check first in a good handbook. Remember, the first rule of pruning is 'Think twice, cut once.'

The most conscientious pruning will not confer immortality on a plant, however, and once a woody perennial such as lavender or sage develops patches of bare stems, it is usually time to start again. Pruning should always be combined with taking cuttings to maintain a stock of available young plants; while these are growing, the older plants can be temporarily restored by hard pruning, layering side shoots of hedge plants to fill gaps, or tying adjacent branches together to disguise dead areas in an important specimen. Always cut out dead and diseased stems when starting pruning or before renovating a plant.

TRAINING

Training accompanies pruning to direct growth in a new direction. Knowing that the topmost bud of a pruned stem is usually the first to break and resume growth allows you to prune back to a bud facing a particular way in the knowledge that the plant will then grow in this direction. Pruning a lax species to upward-facing buds helps prevent it from sprawling too far sideways, while cutting vertical stems to outward-facing buds encourages bushiness.

This technique is particularly useful when training wall shrubs into decorative shapes, since rerouting growth in this way is often safer than attempt-

Right: *The sinuous curves of spiral topiary add a touch of whimsical artistry to a formally designed herb garden.*

ing to bend stubborn branches in a new direction. Some fruits and roses in trained forms need summer pruning to restrain growth and encourage the formation of productive buds, combined with winter pruning to maintain size and shape.

Climbing plants need careful training to prevent them from straggling. They need firm supports on which to climb, or trellis or horizontal wires so that the stems can be tied in evenly as they grow. The annual pruning of many climbers depends on the age of the wood on which flowers are borne – if they bloom on the current year's stems, prune hard in late winter to encourage plenty of young growth; thin this to retain the strongest stems for tying in. Climbers that flower on stems produced the previous year should be pruned immediately after flowering, cutting exhausted stems back to strong new shoots.

Right: *A young mop-head bay, its straight stem trained originally on a firm cane. The dense head of foliage is produced by repeatedly pruning or pinching off the tips of stems to encourage further side shoots.*

Above: *While many hedging and topiary evergreens can be clipped with shears, large-leaved species such as bay need pruning with secateurs or pruners to avoid leaving ugly wounds. Use the prunings as cuttings or for drying.*

Harvesting Herbs

Artemisia abrotanum

For all their ornamental value, herbs are intended for use, and the dedication that you have put into growing them will be jeopardized by careless harvesting and storage. First establish which parts of the plant are normally used – in most cases it is the leaves and stems, but sometimes the flavour or medicinal value is most concentrated in the seeds, flowers, roots or even bark. Often the concentration is highest at a particular time of year, or even time of day.

For routine culinary purposes leaves and sprigs can be picked fresh as needed and whenever available. However, many herbs are not evergreen or accessible all the year round, and it will be necessary at some point to gather larger quantities for preserving and subsequent storage for winter use. Top growth should be harvested when plants are in prime condition and active growth, normally during spring and summer. There is some evidence that oils and active principles are more concentrated in the morning before strong sunlight has affected them, so try to gather material early in the day – but after any dew has dispersed, because damp herbs soon turn mouldy. Only gather as much as you can handle immediately from clean, healthy plants, keeping different species separate and clearly labelled.

DRYING LEAVES AND FLOWERS

Living parts of plants contain large amounts of water, as much as seven-eighths of their weight in many cases, and this must be removed before they can be safely stored. In a warm, dry climate, leaves and flowers may be tied loosely together in small bundles and hung in an airy, dust-free place out of the sun until brittle enough to break easily between your fingers (in dusty places enclose bundles in perforated bags). You can also spread them on a table or shelf between sheets of newspaper or muslin, and turn daily, or lay them on a mesh screen raised to allow air circulation beneath. The aim is to retain most of the colour, flavour and aroma of the original, so avoid bright

Below: *Freshly gathered herbs in convenient bundles ready for tying and drying.*

sunlight which will bleach the colour, and cool conditions that increase drying time with a resulting loss of quality – in most cases a week should be long enough.

In a cool or wet season when natural air drying is not practicable, an airing cupboard, shaded greenhouse, warm attic or dry ventilated shed is an acceptable place. Herbs may be dried in a domestic oven or dehydrator, provided that care is taken to keep the temperature no more than 32°C/90°F for the first day or two, after which it can be reduced to 25°C/75°F until the process is complete, usually after a further three to five days. Turn the material occasionally and complete one batch at a time – adding fresh material during drying will reduce the temperature and raise humidity. Bunching several herbs together for bouquets garnis will be easier before drying than afterwards.

DRYING SEEDS

Ripe seeds need careful handling because of their natural tendency to shed at the slightest touch. Gather them when they are dry, shaking them from open capsules into paper bags or snipping off complete seedheads, holding them steady as you do so to

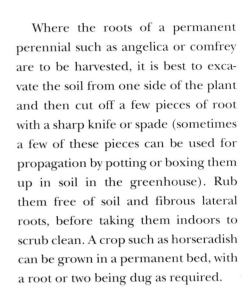

Right: *Bundles of drying herbs need a good circulation of air, for which a suspended drying rack is ideal – but make sure they are kept out of steamy surroundings. The bundles are decorative as well as highly practical.*

GATHERING WILD HERBS – A WARNING

There are several reasons for taking extra care when harvesting wild herbs, a practice once part of everyday life but no longer easy or even advisable in some districts. Check first that there are no laws or local byelaws against removing plants from the wild (British laws would prevent the digging of wild flower roots, for example), and as a matter of courtesy always obtain permission from the owner of the land. Pollution is an ever-present hazard, and plants should never be gathered from roadsides and near industrial sites, nor from agricultural land where chemical crop treatments are normally used.

There should be no doubt whatsoever as to the identification of the plants you intend using. Many well-known herbs are unmistakable in appearance or fragrance, but there are also a number of valuable wild herbs which are almost identical to useless or toxic near-relatives. Tasting is a risky identification test and not to be recommended. If you cannot distinguish a plant for certain by its appearance, leave it alone in case it is dangerous. Gather only from plants that are locally plentiful, taking just small amounts of material from any one plant so that its chances of survival are not diminished.

Hang up the open bags in an airy place under cover, or spread out seed-heads on paper, leaving them for two or three weeks to finish drying. When seed cases are quite crisp and papery, rub or shake the seeds from their capsules. Some kinds will inevitably be mixed with other plant remains such as broken pods or the aerial 'parachutes' typical of Compositae species, but these can be removed by shaking the seeds in a fine sieve, or simply by gently blowing away the debris.

HARVESTING ROOTS

In most cases roots are dried for storing with their skins intact, but a few such as liquorice, turmeric and marshmallow are best peeled. They are then cut into 1 cm/^{1}/$_2$ in slices, thicker roots being cut in two lengthwise. They take longer to dry than other parts of herbs, often several weeks with frequent turning, but the process can be accelerated in a warm oven set at 50°C/120°F/lowest gas setting. When the fragments are light and brittle, pack them in airtight tins or dark glass jars.

Where the roots of a permanent perennial such as angelica or comfrey are to be harvested, it is best to excavate the soil from one side of the plant and then cut off a few pieces of root with a sharp knife or spade (sometimes a few of these pieces can be used for propagation by potting or boxing them up in soil in the greenhouse). Rub them free of soil and fibrous lateral roots, before taking them indoors to scrub clean. A crop such as horseradish can be grown in a permanent bed, with a root or two being dug as required.

Below left: *Culinary herbs cut up small and packed in measured amounts with water in ice-cube trays lose little of their flavour when frozen, and are ready for almost immediate use.*

Below: *Herbs dried outdoors can be spread in layers if turned regularly, but in still conditions indoors it is better to arrange leaves separately on racks.*

avoid loss. Keep each variety separate and label the bags clearly. If you are saving seeds for sowing, always choose the best plants with typical growth and appearance; inferior plants yield seeds suitable for other uses as long as they are free from diseases. When dry, label and store in packets in airtight jars.

A-Z of Herbs

Achillea millefolium (Compositae)

🐌 **Yarrow**

milfoil, nosebleed, herb militaris, soldier's woundwort, thousand leaf, thousand seal, field hop

Description: hardy herbaceous pungent perennial, 15-60 cm/6-24 in. Finely feathered, bright grey-green leaves and flat heads of small white, pink or red flowers midsummer to autumn. Grows in grassy places, including lawns.

Use: folk remedy for rheumatism, toothache, haemorrhage and fever; fresh young leaves used sparingly in salads; herbal tobacco and substitute for hops in brewing.

Cultivation: prefers full sun and well-drained ground; good for chalky and seaside gardens. Spreads readily, so segregate from other plants. Divide roots in spring or autumn, or sow seeds from spring until autumn; plant 15 cm/6 in apart for lawns.

Parts used: top growth cut just before flowering. Dry outdoors in the shade or in gentle heat indoors.

Related species: *A. decolorans* (English mace): half-hardy perennial, 45-60 cm/18-24 in, native to southern Europe. Feathery leaves; yellow flowers, summer. Light soil in full sun.

A. moschata (musk yarrow): rhizomatous perennial, 20 cm/8 in, from European Alps. Ferny leaves; white flowers, summer. Needs good drainage and full sun.

Agrimonia eupatoria (Rosaceae)

🐌 **Common Agrimony**

church steeples, liverwort, sticklewort, cockleburr

Description: wayside perennial often found on chalk, 15-60 cm/6 in-2 ft. Attractive grey-green cinquefoil leaves, arranged in alternate large and small pairs, with pale yellow star-shaped flowers in summer on tapering spikes like a mullein; apricot scent, popular with bees. Seedheads are burrs which stick to clothes and fur.

Use: once regarded as a magic herb for healing jaundice; used as a spring tonic, as an astringent externally for treating wounds, and in oriental medicine to stop bleeding; a valuable yellow dye plant.

Cultivation: likes well-drained soil in full sun, but will also thrive in short grass. Sow in a seedbed outdoors in spring or autumn, or divide established roots in autumn.

Parts used: whole plant for dyeing; fresh leaves steeped in water to make an infusion; aerial parts except thick stems may be gathered just before flowering for drying gently in the dark; roots may be dried and grated to add to pot-pourri.

Related species: *A. odorata* (fragrant agrimony): highly aromatic plant with sticky, hairy leaves, larger in all parts than *A. eupatoria*. Often planted in wild and woodland gardens.

Ajuga reptans (Labiatae)

🐌 **Common Bugle**

creeping bugle, carpet bugle, carpenter's herb (note that North American bugle, bugleweed or gipsy wort refers to *Lycopus* spp.)

Description: short prostrate perennial, 15 cm/6 in. Rosettes of coarse shining green leaves, and spires of blue, white or rose flowers in midsummer. Spreads freely by runners. Several cultivated forms including 'Atropurpurea', with metallic purple leaves, and 'Variegata', cream and green, best in shade.

Use: medicinally to treat bleeding from cuts and other wounds; popular ground cover among other herbs and for edging containers.

Cultivation: grows in moist, rich soils in shade or full sun; flourishes beneath hedges if compost is added. Sow in spring or autumn in trays and barely cover seed – germination is slow and erratic. Separate established roots and transplant divisions in spring or autumn.

Parts used: leaves picked as required and simmered to make an infusion; whole herb cut down to ground level in summer and dried in shade.

Related species: *A. chamaepitys* (ground-pine, arthritic ivy): short bushy annual with pine scent, 10-15 cm/4-6 in. Red-spotted yellow flowers in summer. Whole herb used to treat bleeding and high pulse rate, and in Arab veterinary treatments.

Alchemilla vulgaris (Rosaceae)
🐚 Common Lady's Mantle

lion's foot, bear's foot, common alchemil

Description: an aggregate of closely related species, typically herbaceous perennials, 15-45 cm/6-18 in. Leaves cloak-shaped and pleated. Small yellowish-green flowers in summer.

Use: used by alchemists in attempts to make gold; folk remedy for eye disorders and to stop bleeding; traditional treatment for menstrual disorders and in childbirth.

Cultivation: grows in sun or shade, in walls, as edging and as ground cover under trees and shrubs, where it self-seeds freely. Sow in trays in summer, and plant out in autumn; or divide clumps in early spring or autumn.

Parts used: leaves and flower shoots picked as required; aerial parts gathered in summer and dried outdoors.

Related species: *A. alpina* (alpine lady's mantle): evergreen dwarf perennial, 20 cm/8 in, for sinks, rock gardens and short grass in sun; soft furry, silvery leaves, tiny yellow flowers.

A. arvensis (parsley piert, field lady's mantle): similar to *A. vulgaris*, popular Romany tonic and remedy for bladder stone.

Allium (Liliaceae)

The various species all possess the familiar sulphurous smell, but individually they are valued as vegetables, herbs, medicines and decorative garden bulbs. Only the most important in herbal terms are described here.
Caution: some people are slightly allergic to all forms of onions.

Allium sativum
🐚 Garlic

Description: subterranean white-skinned bulb, subdivided into numerous 'cloves'. Short, flat upright leaves, 15-30 cm/6-12 in, tall single flower stem bearing spherical head of pale pink or greenish-white blooms often mixed with tiny bulbils.

Uses: flavouring, vegetable and medicinal herb that has accumulated superstitions over the centuries. Used as an antibiotic, expectorant and digestive, and for treating high blood pressure.

Cultivation: cloves planted in autumn 5-10 cm/2-4 in deep in rich soil, or in pots in a frame for planting out in spring in cold regions. Harvested in summer when foliage dies down, and dried in sunlight or warmth.

Parts used: bulbs, separated into cloves.

Related species: *A. oleraceum* (field garlic, wild garlic), *A. triquetrum* (three-cornered garlic), *A. scorodoprasum* (sand leek) and *A. rosea* (rosy garlic) used in various parts of the world as wild substitutes for garlic.

A. ursinum (wild garlic, ramsons): white-flowered wild onion, widespread in damp woodland; pungent garlic smell, but mild when cooked.

A. vineale (wild garlic, crow garlic): wiry version of cultivated garlic, widespread in temperate regions. Used by North American Indians.

Allium schoenoprasum
🐚 Chives

Description: small perennial bulb growing in clumps, with fine hollow dark green leaves, 20-30 cm/8-12 in, and slightly taller flower stems bearing small clusters of mauve or purple blooms. Can be found wild in moist soils, but usually cultivated.

chives

Uses: mainly culinary for flavouring and garnishing where a mild onion flavour is required. Also a stimulant and digestive; high in vitamin C. Popular decorative herb for edging and for attracting bees. Chive tea is sometimes sprayed to prevent gooseberry mildew and apple scab. Chive flowers can be used in decorative dried flower arrangements.

Cultivation: sow seeds outdoors in spring, or divide clumps into small groups and plant in spring or autumn in moist rich soil. Lift and divide every 3-5 years according to growth. May be potted up in autumn for forcing winter supplies indoors.

(Continued)

Parts used: fresh leaves cut as needed. Chop and freeze in bags or ice-cube trays for use out of season.

garlic chive

Related species: Larger-leaved forms available; also Chinese or garlic chives (*A. tuberosum*) and Siberian chives (*A. schoenoprasum sibiricum*).

Aloe vera, syn. *A. barbadensis* (Liliaceae)

🐌 Aloes

Cape aloes, socotrine, medicine plant, burn plant

Description: succulent drought-resistant tropical plant forming clumps of short-stemmed rosettes of fleshy evergreen leaves, up to 60 cm/2 ft long, pointed and edged with teeth. Tall flower stem with spikes of yellow, orange or red tubular blooms. Often grown as a house plant in cool regions.

Uses: according to legend the sole survivor from the Garden of Eden. Gel-like sap from leaves used externally to heal wounds, burns and mastitis. **Caution:** traditional internal use as purgative bitters ill advised and may cause haemorrhage.

Cultivation: plants need sunny, arid conditions. May be started from seed in spring, or propagated from small offsets at base of parent plant. As house plants, best grown in gritty cactus mixtures in good light; minimum winter temperature of 5°C/41°F to ensure flowering, in summer may be stood outdoors. In frost-free gardens, ideal plants for sunny beds with fast drainage.

Parts used: broken leaves rubbed on affected part. Sap extracted from leaves and often dried to form a resin.

Related species: *A. aristata*: small relative with leaves 10-15 cm/4-6 in long, white spines and orange flowers. Popular house plant and hardiest of the tropical aloes; may survive mild temperate winters out of doors.

Althaea officinalis (Malvaceae)

🐌 **Marsh Mallow**

guimauve, mortification plant, schloss tea, sweet weed, wymote

Description: tough-rooted herbaceous perennial, 1.2 m/4 ft. Velvety stems and leaves; white or pink flowers in leaf axils in late summer. Found in damp, often saline places.

Uses: valuable and handsome herb with a long tradition of use in medicine and cosmetics, and as a vegetable and confection. Cultivated by the Romans and promoted by Charlemagne. Soothing and mucilaginous; tops of young shoots added to salads (popular with Bedu); flowers and leaves infused to treat lung and bowel disorders; roots sliced and boiled to poultice external inflammation and relieve gastric ailments; root was made into traditional 'marshmallows' (now just sugar and gelatin).

Cultivation: sow seeds in spring indoors in warmth, or outdoors in summer, and transplant to permanent positions in autumn. Roots may be divided in spring or autumn. On light soils mulch freely in summer.

Parts used: flowers, leaves and young tips of shoots gathered fresh; roots at least 2 years old, dug up during winter dormancy when the active constituents are most concentrated, and used fresh or dried.

Althaea Rosea
৯**Hollyhock**

Description: biennial or perennial of waste places, and traditional cottage garden flower; grows up to 3 m/10 ft. Wide hairy leaves, up to 30 cm/12 in across. Large flowers, often double, in summer; wild forms are white or pink; cultivated forms purple, red or yellow.

Uses: petals of purple-flowered variety once used to dye wine. Leaves used medicinally as a diuretic and to help some chest complaints. Provides relief for mouth ulcers; soothing to the face.

Cultivation: can be grown in any soil. Propagate from seed and prick out.

Parts used: flowers and leaves, fresh.

Anethum graveolens
(Umbelliferae)
৯**Dill**
dillseed, dillweed

Description: annual herb, 45-75 cm/18-30 in, with finely feathered blue-green leaves and hollow stems. Small open umbels of creamy-yellow flowers in summer, followed by dark brown seeds. Grows wild in waste places, but is also cultivated.

Uses: used as a condiment and flavouring and as a pickling spice. Often taken as 'dill water' to relieve digestive problems and flatulence. Occasionally used to perfume cosmetics; medicinal oil distilled from leaves, stems and seeds.

Cultivation: sow in rows or small patches in spring, and again in early summer for continuity, in a sunny, well-drained position. Grow well away from fennel, with which dill cross-pollinates readily. Choose right variety for seed or leaf production.

Parts used: young leaves gathered at any time for use fresh, also flowers for adding to soups; seeds harvested when dry for use whole or crushed. Leaves may be dried, but lose much of their flavour.

Related species: *A. sowa* (Indian dill, Japanese dill): similar in appearance and uses, popular in Asian cuisines.

Angelica archangelica
(Umbelliferae)
৯**Angelica**
garden angelica, Holy Ghost

Description: a robust biennial or short-lived perennial plant, 1.8 m/6 ft, of damp woodlands. Produces a few large, deeply indented leaves at ground level, followed by tall hollow stems bearing from their leaf sheaths heads of greenish-white flowers in midsummer.

Uses: all parts promote perspiration, stimulate appetite, and are used to treat ailments of the chest and digestion. Young leaves and shoots used to flavour wines and liqueurs, while the stout stems are candied as a cake decoration or cooked like rhubarb. Fresh or preserved roots have been added to snuff and used by Laplanders and North American Indians as tobacco.

Cultivation: sow fresh seeds outdoors in autumn for exposure to frost, or pre-chill in a refrigerator for a few weeks before sowing in spring. Transplant to a moist shady position as young as possible, before the roots become immovable.

Parts used: young leaves can be gathered any time during the growing season, the stems in the summer of the second year. Cut seedheads and ripen until seeds are dry enough to store. Roots are dug up just before flowering and dried slowly.

Related species: *A. atropurpurea*: a wild North American species used by Shakers as flavouring and medicine.

Anthriscus cerefolium (Umbelliferae)

Chervil

salad chervil, garden beaked parsley

Description: decorative annual, sometimes grown as a biennial, 60 cm/2 ft, with a tapering rootstock. A well-branched plant with sweet-scented and delicately cut pale foliage rather like parsley, and umbels of small white flowers in spring and summer, followed by large seedpods. Sometimes found wild as a garden escape, when it closely resembles young cow parsley (*A. sylvestris*). **Caution:** do not gather from the wild, as chervil may be confused with poisonous hemlock, fool's parsley and water dropwort.

Uses: leaves used in soups, salads and vinegars, and for garnishes. Medicinally the bruised plant is applied fresh or as poultices to wounds; an infusion aids digestion and encourages perspiration.

Cultivation: sow spring, summer or autumn *in situ* in rows or patches, in moisture-retentive soil in full sun or light shade. As plants often run to seed rapidly, sow little and often, or leave plants to self-seed. Sow in warmth for out-of-season supplies indoors.

Parts used: leaves gathered fresh as needed, and frozen or gently dried for storing. Roots sometimes dug and used in salad preparations.

Related species: *Chaerophyllum bulbosum* (bulbous chervil): a wild plant with tuberous roots; a close relative of *C. tenuilentum* (rough chervil).

Aquilegia vulgaris (Ranunculaceae)

Columbine

granny's bonnets, European crowfoot

Description: tough-rooted herbaceous perennial with prettily cut leaves on wiry stems, 60 cm/2 ft. Stout flowering stems in summer bear nodding spurred blooms in white, blue or pink. Found wild in meadows and waste places on chalky soils. Many garden forms with brilliant-coloured flowers, often double or with extra-long spurs.

Uses: all parts have been used medicinally, but now usually grown only as a decorative plant for herb gardens. Roots, flowers and leaves have antiseptic properties, and roots were once used to treat ulcers. **Caution:** internal use is not recommended as aquilegias contain prussic acid, and all parts are poisonous, especially the seeds.

Cultivation: sow in rows in a nursery bed in late spring for transplanting in autumn; or sow early under glass, and plant out in summer after hardening off. Plant in moist soil in partially shady sites; dead-head garden forms promptly, as self-set seedlings tend to revert to wild form.

Arctium lappa (Compositae)

Greater Burdock

beggar's buttons, lappa, cuckoo button, flapper-bags, bardana, clotburr, gipsy's rhizome

Description: short biennial with strong vertical roots up to 1 m/3 ft long, and a rosette of large coarse white-backed leaves like rhubarb. In summer thick hairy stems, 1.8 m/6 ft, bear reddish-purple tubular flowers, followed by seedheads (burrs) with hooked spines, lasting all winter. A handsome wild plant of waste places and roadsides.

Uses: a plant of widespread and varied virtues, burdock is cultivated in Japan as a vegetable (*gobo*); used everywhere as a folk remedy for skin problems, especially psoriasis and eczema; grown in China for its seeds, used for throat and chest ailments. A wild vegetable used by North American Indians. The chopped root may be cooked, and the stalks treated like angelica (these contain inulin, a mildly sweet substance useful for diabetics). Roots used as flavouring.

Cultivation: usually gathered from the wild, but seeds may be sown *in situ* in rich, loamy soil in the wild garden.

Parts used: roots of 1-year-old plants, split and dried slowly; young shoots and peeled stalks (before flowering) for salads or as a cooked vegetable; dried seeds for medicinal use.

Related species: *A. minus* (common, lesser or small burdock): a similar plant, but with more pointed leaves and smaller seedheads.

Armeria maritima
(Plumbaginaceae)

૪૦ **Thrift**

sea pink

Description: evergreen perennial form-ing mounds of narrow grassy leaves, 10-20 cm/4-8 in, on woody rootstock. In early summer produces short-stemmed white or rose flowers with a strong scent of honey. Grows wild in sandy soil beside the sea, but often planted in gardens, sometimes in improved forms.

Uses: an infusion of fresh or dried flowers was formerly used as an anti-septic and to treat nervous disorders, but now thought to cause allergic reactions such as dermatitis. A valu-able formal edging plant for herb gar-dens and for planting in paths; very popular with butterflies.

Cultivation: sow autumn or spring indoors in trays and plant out when hardened off. Tufts may be rooted as cuttings in a shaded frame in summer. Plant in full sun or light shade.

Related species: A. arenaria (Jersey thrift): plant of similar habit but altogether larger, with stout stems bearing deep pink flowers.

Armoracia rusticana, syn.
Cochlearia armoracia (Cruciferae)

૪૦ **Horseradish**

Description: coarse herbaceous peren-nial. Long-stalked oval leaves, up to 1 m/3 ft long; umbels of off-white flow-ers in mid- to late summer. Pungent roots, up to 60 cm/2 ft long.

Uses: used medicinally as a digestive, antiseptic and stimulant, and to make poultices for rheumatism, chest com-plaints and circulation problems. Young leaves may be used for flavour-ing in salads, or cooked; roots are often made into a sauce. **Caution:** use medicinally with care, as the roots may cause internal inflammation, affect the thyroid gland or, used externally, produce blisters.

Cultivation: although often grown as a perennial for occasional use, plants are invasive and virtually ineradicable, every fragment of bought-in root reviving to grow again. Better cultivat-ed as an annual crop by burying 15 cm/6 in long upper portions of bought-in roots about 30 cm/12 in apart in ridges of rich soil in early

spring. Water well in dry weather, and in late autumn dig out all the roots for storing in boxes of moist sand.

Parts used: young leaves gathered in spring; roots dug in autumn.

Arnica montana (Compositae)

૪૦ **Arnica**

mountain arnica, mountain daisy, mountain tobacco, fall dandelion, leopard's bane

Description: pungent ornamental perennial with creeping rhizomes and prostrate rosettes of downy leaves. Hairy flower stems, 30-60 cm/1-2 ft, bear bright yellow daisies in summer and autumn. Grows wild in hilly and highland districts, but often grown as garden ornamental.

Uses: homeopathic treatment for epilepsy and blood pressure. A for-merly popular Shaker salve; used in many countries to treat bruises and sprains, and also for throat infections, wounds and paralysis. Included in some French herbal smoking mix-tures. **Caution:** poisonous and not for self-medication, as the plant may be toxic and cause skin irritations.

Cultivation: sow seeds in a cold frame in spring (germination may be slow) and plant out in autumn in sandy acid soils in full sun; divide mature roots in autumn or spring.

Parts used: whole top growth, especial-ly flowers, either fresh or after drying slowly in shade; roots dug up in late spring or autumn and dried in artifi-cial heat.

Artemisia (Compositae)

A large genus of aromatic shrubs and herbaceous perennials, some with finely cut ornamental foliage ranging in colour from grey-green to bright silver. Most shrubby kinds are adapted to hot dry places in full sun, and, apart from their medicinal uses, provide valuable colour and form in the herb garden. Only the commonest types are described here.

Artemisia abrotanum
❧ Southernwood

lad's love, old man, Crusader herb

Description: graceful woody perennial shrub, up to 1 m/3 ft, with pungent feathery leaves, grey-green and downy. Inconspicuous yellow-green daisy-shaped flowers in late summer.

Uses: like all the artemisias, named after the Greek goddess Artemis, who had special care of women. Used medicinally as an infusion or tincture to regulate menstruation, but also as an antiseptic, insect repellent (in mothballs) and air freshener; used by medieval Crusaders to ward off plague. Has a reputation as a hair-wash and bitter stimulant, and even as an aphrodisiac. Stems yield a yellow dye.

Cultivation: prefers to be grown in sun, in well-drained soil. Propagate from soft cuttings in summer, or semi-ripe cuttings with a 'heel' in autumn. Cut back new growth of shrubs by half every spring, and disbud to prevent flowering. An ideal low hedge if trimmed in spring and again in summer.

Parts used: shoots and leaves, which may be dried slowly in the sun.

Artemisia dracunculus
❧ French tarragon

estragon, serpentarian

Description: herbaceous perennial of shrubby growth, with slim woody branching stems 1 m/3 ft. Smooth, dark green pointed leaves, and woolly white or grey flowers in late summer. Spreads by creeping rootstocks, which may be invasive.

Uses: popular culinary herb for stimulating the appetite and flavouring sauces, preserves and cooked dishes. Historically used for toothache, and by the Romans to treat snakebite. Useful for catarrhal and digestive problems, while tarragon tea is used to cure insomnia. An ingredient of perfumes and liqueurs.

Cultivation: may only be propagated by dividing the roots in spring or autumn, or from soft cuttings taken in early summer. Grow in rich, well-drained soil and confine roots in the same way as for mint. Renew every three years or so, and mulch in winter to protect roots. Young roots may be potted up for winter supplies but benefit from a dormant period.

Parts used: growing tips gathered for fresh use; all top growth may be harvested at flowering time for drying slowly in gentle heat.

Related species: A. dracunculoides (Russian tarragon): a more robust, coarser plant that may be raised from seed, as well as by division and from cuttings. Tolerates a wider range of soil types, but markedly inferior in flavour. Similar uses, but does not dry successfully.

Artemisia vulgaris
❧ Mugwort

felon herb, St John's herb, moxa

Description: herbaceous perennial with red-purple stems up to 1.8 m/6 ft. Long green ferny leaves with white undersides, and numerous reddish-brown flowers in late summer. Common in built-up areas and roadsides.

Uses: one of the nine Saxon magic herbs, used to make a tea for gastritis and digestive ailments, and to treat menstrual disorders. Insect repellent, and ingredient for herbal tobaccos and Chinese treatments for rheumatism. Used in stuffings for fatty meats. Leaves have been used to make fumigant candle wicks, flowers to flavour beer before the advent of hops.
Caution: may be harmful when taken internally in excessive doses.

Cultivation: may be grown from seeds sown *in situ* in spring and thinned to about 30 cm/12 in apart, in sun and light shade. Allow plenty of room, as plants grow quickly to full height. Take cuttings in autumn, or divide roots in autumn or spring. Take care that plants do not become invasive.

Parts used: all parts of the plant, either fresh or dried slowly in the shade.

Related species: A. verlotiorum: an Asian wild species, used in Chinese medicine.

Asparagus officinalis (Liliaceae)
ᴁ **Asparagus**
sparrow grass, sperage

Description: herbaceous perennial, up to 1.8 m/6 ft. Young, scaly edible 'spears' in spring grow into tall branched stems bearing fine ferny green needles. Greenish-white flowers appear in summer, followed on female plants by red berries in autumn. Fern or 'bower' turns bright yellow as it dies. Found wild on coasts, and widespread in the Middle East; stems may be prostrate.

Uses: an ornamental plant and early summer vegetable. Medicinally used as a laxative, while a tea brewed from the mature fern has been used for rheumatic and urinary disorders, and by Shakers to treat dropsy.

Cultivation: seeds may be sown in rows in spring, the strongest seedlings thinned to 15 cm/6 in apart; transplant 60 cm/2 ft apart the following spring in beds or single rows in light rich well-drained soil (on heavy ground create raised beds of suitable soil). Alternatively plant bought 1- or 2-year-old crowns. Start cropping when plants are 3 years old, cutting the 15-20 cm/6-8 in high spears just below ground level from spring until midsummer (in parts of Europe the spears are first blanched by earthing up plants). Use largest spears for eating, thinner ones ('sprue') medicinally. Cut down fern and top-dress beds every autumn with compost.

Parts used: young stems ('spears' or 'tips') and fern; roots sometimes dug up for medicinal purposes.

Atriplex hortensis
(Chenopodiaceae)
ᴁ **Orach(e)**
(red) mountain spinach

Description: an erect leafy annual, up to 60-90 cm/2-3 ft or sometimes taller still. Triangular fleshy leaves are dark green, or red in the attractive form *A. hortensis rubra* (red mountain spinach). Thread-like spikes of green or red flowers appear in summer. Common wild on sandy waste land, shingle beaches and salty sites.

Uses: traditional wild herb, often cultivated as a vegetable and garden ornamental; used as a spring tonic and stimulant, and in infusions to treat tiredness or exhaustion.

Cultivation: sow *in situ* in spring in sunny positions, either in rows or broadcast in small patches. Pinch out growing tips once and harvest shoots before plants flower, as they self-seed prolifically.

Parts used: larger leaves and whole young shoots.

Related species: *A. patula* (common orach, ironroot): mealy grey leaves and often trailing stems; common wild on warm beaches, used as a green vegetable.

A. prostrata (hastate orach): similar wild species with much larger leaves.

Borago officinalis (Boraginaceae)
ᴁ **Borage**
burage, bugloss, bee bread, bee plant

Description: stout herb, with hollow, bristly stems 60-90 cm/2-3 ft. Broad oval leaves, also stiffly hairy, and heavy bent clusters of blue star-shaped flowers (white form occasionally found), popular with bees, followed by oval seed capsules. A cultivated herb, sometimes occurring on waste ground.

Uses: a popular reviver included in some drinks. Young leaves add the flavour of cucumber to salads, older ones can be used as a vegetable, while in France and Italy the flowers are often cooked in batter as fritters. An infusion of leaves and seeds was a folk method of increasing the milk supply of nursing mothers, and to treat coughs, cold and depression. The roots are used to flavour wine, and the seeds are a source of gamma-linoleic acid, an essential fatty acid thought to reduce the risk of arteriosclerosis.

Cultivation: sow in early spring (outdoors or in pots) for flowers the same year, or in late summer outdoors to produce larger biennial plants that flower early the following summer. Grow in well drained soil in full sun. Plants self-seed freely to produce seedlings that usually overwinter safely.

Parts used: leaves and stems (latter said to have greater stimulating properties); flowers used fresh, candied, or dried in moderate heat and kept well sealed; seeds dried for medicinal use; roots dug after flowering.

Buxus sempervirens (Buxaceae)
❧ **Common Box**
boxwood, box tree

Description: a slow-growing evergreen shrub, occasionally small tree, up to 5 m/16 ft. Crowded oval leathery leaves, shiny and dark green above, paler beneath. Small greenish-white flowers in mid-spring, male and female blooms in separate groups. Grows wild on chalky commons, but widely cultivated as a garden ornamental, especially as formal hedges since the dense growth tolerates frequent clipping.

Uses: leaves yield a red dye, and are used homeopathically to treat fevers and rheumatism and to promote sweating. One of the best shrubs for topiary and hedges, the compact 'Suffruticosa' being the form grown as dwarf hedging around formal flower and herb beds. **Caution:** the foliage is too toxic for amateur medicinal use.

Cultivation: plant autumn or spring in rich, light soil, preferably in full sun although light shade is tolerated. Keep well watered and feed annually in spring. For hedging choose young plants and space about 10 cm/4 in apart, as older ones have very large rootballs and need more space when planted; trim in spring and again at midsummer for formal appearance. Propagate from cuttings outdoors in early autumn, or by layering lower branches.

Parts used: leaves at any time; bark and timber from larger pruned branches.

Related species: *B. macowanii* (Cape box): very similar species used for the same purposes in South Africa.

Calendula officinalis (Compositae)
❧ **(Pot) Marigold**
common marigold, marybud, marygold, English marigold

Description: perennial herb, usually grown as an annual or biennial, with sticky angular stems up to 60 cm/2 ft. Long oval leaves, hairy and fleshy, larger at the base; solitary yellow-orange flowers from early summer. Many cultivated forms in a range of yellow, orange and brown, often double.

Uses: apart from being popular old-fashioned cottage garden plants, pot marigolds have a long history of medicinal use. A tea made from the flowers is used for internal spasms and gastric disorders, but the main reputation is as an antiseptic and anti-inflammatory healer of wounds; a common ingredient of many proprietary salves and ointments. Used by Shakers to treat gangrene. Petals can be used as a hair rinse, a colouring agent for butter and cheese, and a substitute for the colour of saffron. Also used in cooking and as a garnish.

Cultivation: sow *in situ* in full sun or light shade, in spring for late flowering, or (better) in autumn to overwinter and make bushy plants that flower over a long season the following year. Dead-head regularly to prolong flowering. Although plants thrive best on heavier ground, they tend to self-seed most on light soils.

Parts used: petals fresh or dried in the shade; young fresh leaves in salads; whole flowers boiled as a dye.

Campanula rapunculus (Campanulaceae)
❧ **Rampion**
rampion bellflower

Description: herbaceous biennial with thick fleshy turnip-like taproot, and slim straight angular stems to 1 m/3 ft with milky sap. Slim, toothed leaves, oval near plant base; overwinters as a low rosette, producing in the second year pale blue or white star-shaped flowers in midsummer. A wild plant of meadows, fields and hedgerows.

Uses: an ornamental wild flower, whose leaves are used in winter salads. Popular enough in the sixteenth and seventeenth centuries to be cultivated as a root vegetable (but note that 'German rampion' is the root of evening primrose).

Cultivation: for leaves, sow in spring for autumn use, and in early summer for winter crops. For roots, sow in rich soil in a shady position in the kitchen garden, in rows 20 cm/8 in apart and thin seedlings to the same distance; sow in spring, but if plants flower early in a hot season, sow again in summer.

Parts used: leaves gathered any time before flowering; roots dug from autumn onwards – may be stored in sand in a cool place.

Centaurium erythraea, syn.
Erythraea centaurium
(Gentianaceae)
(Common) Centaury
bitterherb, centaury gentian, feverwort

Description: a delicate annual growing to 30 cm/12 in, often less. From a rosette of elliptical grey-green pointed leaves, several stems produce branching umbels of tubular flowers in late summer, pink with yellow centres, arranged in clusters and closing when rain is imminent. Found wild in damp meadows and grassy woodlands.

Uses: an ancient Greek and Celtic medicinal herb, used to make a poultice for skin disorders; taken as a bitter tonic by North American Indians. A tea made from the whole plant treats digestive disorders including heartburn, while homeopathic preparation is prescribed for the liver and gall bladder. One of the aromatic ingredients of vermouth.

Cultivation: although growing wild in damp places, it will adapt to most garden soils, thriving and self-seeding in sun or semi-shade in rock gardens and near the sea. Sow in autumn or spring where plants are to grow, and barely cover the seeds.

Parts used: whole plant gathered at flowering time and dried quickly in shade outdoors or in a warm room.

Related species: *C. littorale* (seaside centaury): smaller, with narrower leaves, flower paler but larger. A plant found on sand dunes, with similar uses.

Sabatia stellaris (American centaury): a biennial of marshes and wet localities, with similar uses.

Centaurea nigra
Knapweed
lesser knapweed, black knapweed

Description: tough perennial with sturdy ridged stems and dark green hairy leaves. Grows up to 90 cm/3 ft. Tubular purple flowers in summer. Grows wild on wasteland, roadsides and as a cliff plant.

Uses: a medieval wound salve; used to soothe sore throats and bleeding gums. Also acts as a diuretic.

Cultivation: grows easily in any soil; needs no particular attention. Self-seeds freely. May need containment.

Chamaemelum nobile, syn.
Anthemis nobilis (Compositae)
Lawn Chamomile
Roman chamomile, double chamomile, common chamomile, perennial chamomile

Description: a vigorous hairy creeping perennial, up to 45 cm/18 in, with ferny leaves and apple-scented white and yellow flowers in summer; non-flowering forms available for creating lawns. Grows wild in stony ground.

Uses: popular since early Egyptian times, a traditional strewing herb, and often used by Arabs in the form of the essential oil. Ingredient of a famous herb tea for settling nervous disorders, stimulating the appetite and cleansing the blood. Made into herb beers and tisanes, hair rinses and eye lotions, as well as being used in the preparation of cosmetics and perfumes. Essential oil is said to revive cut flowers. Plants often grown as herbal lawns and on ornamental seats.

lawn chamomile

(Continued)

(*Lawn Chamomile* continued)

Cultivation: sow seeds in spring out-doors or under cover, but do not cover as the seeds need light for ger-mination. Established plants may be divided in spring, the only way to propagate named forms. Plant in fer-tile, well-drained light soil, 45 cm/18 in apart for specimen plants and 15 cm/6 in for lawns, and be sure to water well in dry weather.

Parts used: whole plant for distillation; flowers for essential oil and teas, col-lected as petals begin to reflex in the sun; dried rapidly in shade.

**double
chamomile**

Related species: A. *arvensis* (corn chamomile), A. *cotula* (stinking chamomile), *Tripleurospermum inodo-rum* (scentless mayweed): all simi-lar-looking wild flowers with wholly or partly downy leaves, but without the characteristic pleasant subtle apple fragrance.

True wild chamomile is *Matricaria recutita*, q.v.

Chelidonium majus
(Papaveraceae)
❧ **Greater Celandine**
swallow-wort, tetterwort

Description: herbaceous perennial with brittle fleshy branching stems up to 1 m/3 ft, with soft, finely hairy leaves, yellowish above and blue-green beneath, divided into toothed leaflets. Numerous small yellow flowers appear in summer (double form also avail-able), followed by erect green seed capsules. All parts contain an acrid bright orange sap that may be irritat-ing to the skin.

Uses: once widely grown as a decora-tive cottage garden herb, but now regarded as a weed of waste and culti-vated ground, and walls. Antispas-modic and mildly sedative, traditional-ly valued for its sap as a treatment for warts and source of an orange dye. Flowers are beneficial for thyroid con-ditions, while the roots have been used to treat liver and gall bladder dis-orders. **Caution:** in large doses may be poisonous, and an internal and exter-nal irritant.

Cultivation: sow seeds in autumn or divide roots in spring, and plant in dry chalky soils in sun or light shade. Plants normally seed freely but are rarely a nuisance.

Parts used: top growth at flowering time, fresh or dried slowly in darkness; sap at any time from top growth or dormant roots; roots dug in autumn.

Chenopodium bonus-henricus
(Chenopodiaceae)
❧ **Good King Henry**
all-good, mercury, poor man's asparagus

Description: herbaceous perennial with smooth, slightly fluted stems up to 75 cm/2 ft 6 in, and thick fleshy tri-angular leaves, grey and mealy at first. Small yellow-green flowers in clusters appear at midsummer. Found wild on light, rich soils, but often cultivated.

Uses: cultivated as an early green spinach-like crop, the first shoots sometimes blanched by earthing up for use like asparagus.

Cultivation: sow in spring *in situ* or in a seedbed, and thin or plant at 45 cm/18 in distances in light, fertile soil. Plants seed freely, so dead-head to prevent invasiveness.

Parts used: young leaves and shoots.

Related species: C. *album* (fat hen, common pigweed, common lambs-quarter, white goosefoot): red-stemmed salad ingredient, tonic herb for livestock and source of a red dye; seeds once used for flour.

C. *ambrosioides anthelmiticum* (Ameri-can wormseed), Mexican tea): annu-al wild plant, source of chenopodi-um oil widely used for the treatment of internal worms. **Caution:** large doses may be poisonous.

C. *quinoa* (quinoa): Peruvian annual, widely cultivated in South America .

C. *botrys* (ambrosia), C. *leptophyllum*, C. *nuttaliae*: other sources of fatty and nutritious seeds.

Chrysanthemum balsamita
❧ Alecost
costmary, bible leaf

Description: sharp-tasting herbaceous perennial, growing up to 60 cm/2 ft. Finely haired creeping rootstock, pale green ridged stems and pointed oval leaves with a minty fragrance. Small yellow flowers often with outer white petals, late summer.

Uses: in medieval times used to ease childbirth; formerly used in brewing as a preservative. Medicinally, used in infusion to soothe colds and digestive disorders. Can be added in small quantities to salads, game, soups and cakes.

Cultivation: sow seed in warm climates, or divide roots and plant in rich, well-drained sunny position. Thin the roots each year. Can also be grown as a pot herb indoors.

Parts used: leaves and flowers; gather young leaves at any time, and flowers as they begin to open.

Cichorium intybus (Compositae)
❧ Chicory
succory, witloof, blue sailors

Description: tough herbaceous perennial, sometimes grown as an annual crop, with a large deep taproot that exudes a milky sap, and a basal rosette of long smooth leaves, green and jagged like a dandelion (wild species) or greyish and oval (cultivated forms). Hairy flower stems up to 1.5 m/5 ft bearing bright blue daisies (occasionally white or pink) all summer. A common weed in parts of the USA.

Uses: a vegetable and salad ingredient with a bitter flavour; often forced and blanched (witloof or Belgian chicory) to reduce bitterness. Leaves yield a blue dye. Roots and seeds often roasted as a coffee substitute and additive. Chicory tea used to stimulate bile secretion and to treat gout, rheumatism, anaemia and liver complaints. **Caution:** excessive use can lead to digestive upsets, and handling may cause dermatitis.

Cultivation: sow in rows in late spring in rich soil, and thin to 20 cm/8 in apart. Roots of witloof varieties are dug in autumn, trimmed to leave a stump of foliage and stored in sand until forced in heat and darkness to produce young buds ('chicons').

Parts used: roots and flowering stems, fresh or dried slowly in the sun; woody core of dried roots discarded before rest is shredded and roasted for coffee; seeds also roasted for drinks.

Related species: *C. endivia* (endive, escarole): a bitter salad vegetable, with numerous decorative forms, sometimes blanched to reduce bitterness.

Clinopodium calamintha, syn.
Calamintha ascendens (Labiatae)
❧ Common Calamint
mountain mint, mountain balm

Description: hairy herbaceous perennial, with creeping rootstock and bushy growth up to 60 cm/2 ft. Square stems bear greyish oval, toothed leaves with a mint-like fragrance, and dense branched whorls of lilac or purple flowers in late summer. Found wild in dry waste places, usually on chalk.

Uses: a medicinal plant of ancient Greek and medieval physicians, used in infusions as a tonic and expectorant, and in pleasant mint-flavoured tisanes. The whole crushed plant can be used to make poultices for bruises and sprains. Flowers attract butterflies and bees.

Cultivation: sow direct in early spring or autumn outdoors, or in seed trays in autumn to overwinter in a cold frame; germination may be slow and erratic. Alternatively divide mature roots in late spring, or take cuttings from side shoots in early summer. Plant in well drained soil in full sun; will tolerate poor soil.

common calamint

(Continued)

(*Common Calamint* continued)

Parts used: leaves gathered any time, and dried slowly in warmth.

lesser calamint

common calamint

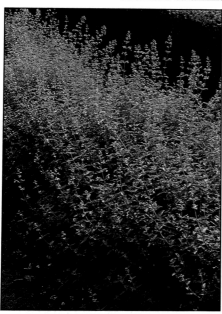

Related species: *C. vulgare*, syn. *Calamintha clinopodium* (wild basil): similar plant with clusters of purple flowers and bristly bracts in summer, and a scent between those of thyme and basil.

C. grandiflorum, syn. *Calamintha grandiflora*: smaller plant, grey-leaved and decorative, with bright lilac flowers in summer.

C. calamintha calamintha, syn. *Calamintha nepeta* (lesser calamint): similar in appearance and uses to common calamint, with greyer leaves and almost white flowers.

Cnicus benedictus, syn. *Carduus benedictus* (Compositae)

Holy Thistle

blessed thistle, spotted thistle, St Benedict thistle

Description: branching annual with a single taproot, hairy, reddish stems up to 60 cm/2 ft, and long white-veined green leaves, deeply cut and spiny. In late summer thistle heads of yellow flowers and brown bracts appear, almost enclosed in a tuft of small leaves and followed in autumn by fat achenes (single seedpods).

Uses: ancient remedial herb used as digestive tonic, to treat liver and gall-bladder complaints, and to induce sweating. A poultice of the leaves relieves chilblains, wounds and burns. Roots used in aperitifs and may be boiled as a vegetable, flowerheads sometimes eaten like globe artichokes.

Cultivation: usually found wild, but may be sown in spring or autumn in patches *in situ*, or for transplanting to loose fertile soil in full sun. For crops sow in rows 45 cm/18 in apart.

Parts used: roots dug just after flowering; leaves picked before flowering and dried slowly; flowers used whole; seeds gathered when dry.

Convolvulus arvensis (Convolvulaceae)

Field Bindweed

lesser or pink bindweed, cornbine, devil's guts

Description: climbing or scrambling herbaceous perennial, with twining stems up to 1 m/3 ft long and deep, often tightly coiled rhizomatous roots. Leaves neat and arrow-shaped with basal lobes, in summer and autumn white (or pink on soils rich in iron) funnel-shaped flowers. Difficult to eradicate.

Uses: a tonic and blood cleanser, sometimes used in infusion for fevers and constipation. The flowers may be added to salads.

Cultivation: rarely necessary, but may be propagated from stolons and planted in full sun.

Parts used: flowering top growth, fresh or dried.

Related species: *C. floridus*: North American species whose roots and stems are dried and ground into fragrant *bois de rose*.

Calystegia sepium, syn. *Convolvulus sepium* (hedge bindweed, bellbine): much stronger growing than field bindweed, up to 3 m/10 ft, with large white flowers.

Coriandrum sativum
(Umbelliferae)
Coriander
cilantro

Description: rigid, strong-smelling annual with pronounced taproot, and slender stems up to 60 cm/2 ft. Ferny pinnate leaves, rounded and parsley-like at base, and umbels of small white or pink flowers in midsummer, followed by round red-brown seed capsules, aromatic when ripe. Many named forms selected for leaf or seed production; small-seeded varieties are usually grown in temperate regions, large-seeded kinds in warmer climates. Grows wild in bare places, usually as an escape from cultivation.

Uses: one of the oldest recorded spices, mentioned in ancient Sanskrit texts and in Exodus (coriander is one of the bitter Passover herbs). The leaves and shoots are added to salads, soups and stews, especially in India, South America and China (the leaf is sometimes known as 'Chinese parsley'). The seeds are a stimulant and digestive, often ground and included in curries and regional meat dishes. They are used as a flavouring for bread, and yield an essential oil for soaps and perfumes. They are sometimes added to pot-pourri, and to other herbs to disguise their unpalatability. The root supplies a stronger flavouring, and is often cooked as a vegetable in South-East Asia.

Cultivation: sow *in situ* in autumn or spring, and thin to 15 cm/6 in apart. Grows fast in full sun, in well-drained soil with a little lime. Protect the brittle stems from wind. Plants usually self-seed freely. Several sowings are advisable for good leaf production.

Parts used: young leaves and shoots at any time; mature seeds dried, roasted and pulverized before use; roots dug after flowering.

Cymbopogon citratus (Gramineae)
Lemon Grass
oil grass, takrai, sereh

Description: coarse tufted tender perennial grass, lemon-scented, with strong roots and spear-shaped, brownish-green leaves up to 90 cm/3 ft, growing from a tough, fibrous bulbous base.

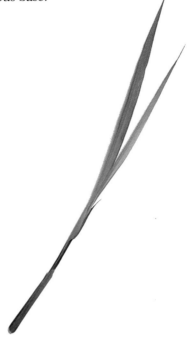

Uses: leaf buds and chopped stems are added to oriental dishes, and made into a tea for liver complaints. The plant yields lemon-grass oil, rich in vitamin A, which is used as a tonic and stimulant, antiseptic, and oily skin cleanser, as an ingredient of cosmetics, and as an aromatherapy oil.

Cultivation: divide clumps and plant offsets with their bottom 2.5 cm/1 in buried in rich soil in a warm, sunny site sheltered from cold winds.

Parts used: leaf buds; stems fresh and finely chopped, or dried and ground.

Related species: *C. flexuosus* (Indian lemon grass): an alternative source of lemon-grass oil and an antiseptic.

C. martinii (ginger grass): a source of ginger-grass oil and palma-rosa oil.

C. nardus (citronella grass): yields Ceylon citronella oil for perfumery.

Cynara cardunculus
Cardoon

Description: a close relative of the thistle and globe artichoke, this short-lived perennial grows up to 1.8 m/6 ft. Impressive silvery leaves, ridged stems, often grown as an ornamental garden plant. Grey-blue thistle-like flowers appear in late summer.

Uses: an ornamental garden favourite, also an edible vegetable crop with a delicate flavour. Especially popular in Mediterranean countries. Best eaten in winter and spring.

Cultivation: from seed in almost any soil. To increase yield, cut down to ground level in early summer, feed and water copiously. New growth will be produced until well into autumn.

Parts used: stems, blanched, braised or fried; also added to sauces.

Cynoglossum officinale
(Boraginaceae)
❧ Hound's Tongue
gipsy flower, rats-and-mice

Description: hairy grey-green herbaceous biennial, smelling of mice, with stems up to 90 cm/3 ft. Leaves roughly hairy, large and oval or tongue-shaped near base of plant, upper ones much narrower. Clusters of hooded flowers, dull maroon or occasionally white, appear in midsummer, followed by hard, flat fruits covered with short-hooked spines. A wild plant of dry, grassy areas, especially near woods.

Uses: infusion from shaved root or crushed leaves used to bathe cuts, bruises, burns and eczema, and to treat coughs and bronchitis; leaves produce a potent poultice for external relief. A nectar-rich plant for bees and butterflies. **Caution:** self-medication is not recommended, as internal use can be dangerous, and external applications may cause dermatitis.

Cultivation: usually gathered from the wild, but seeds may be sown in late summer *in situ:* these need frost to stimulate germination and will not appear before the following spring. Grow in light, well-drained soils in full sun. Plants succeed in seaside gardens, and self-seed freely.

Parts used: flowers and leaves, fresh or dried in shade or a warm room; root fresh or dried.

Related species: *C. germanicum* (green hound's tongue): a similar plant, with leaves shiny and hairless, and lacking the distinctive odour of *C. officinale.*

Dianthus caryophyllus
(Caryophyllaceae)
❧ (Clove) Pink
(clove) gillyflower, carnation, sops-in-wine, divine flower

Description: an evergreen perennial with grey-green branched stems 60-90 cm/2-3 ft divided into sections by hard knuckles or nodes, from which long, thick grey-green waxy leaves, stiff and smooth-edged, arise in pairs often joined at their base. Showy, very fragrant flowers, rose-pink or white, appear in summer and early autumn. Found wild on walls and in chalky places in warm climates; cultivated in numerous forms and colours, especially as perpetual-flowering and border carnations.

Uses: an outstanding ornamental plant, whose fresh flowers are used in tonics, and to flavour drinks and syrups; dried petals are often added to pot-pourri.

Cultivation: easily grown on light, well-drained chalky soil in full sun. May be raised from seed sown under glass in spring, the seedlings potted on or transplanted outdoors to a nursery bed for planting in autumn. Propagate named forms from pipings in summer, or cuttings with a heel in early autumn.

Parts used: flowers, fresh or dried. Before culinary use remove the bitter petal base.

Related species: *D. plumarius* (cottage pink, grass pink): smaller plant with slender rough-edged leaves, and fringed flowers in white, pink or purple; one of the parents of the garden pink.

Dryopteris filix-mas
❧ Male Fern

Description: a fern with large fronds which grow up to 1.2 m/4 ft. Veins on the underside of fronds are covered with sporangia. Grows in damp woodlands and in hilly and mountainous areas.

Uses: once used to expel tapeworms, and formerly believed to soothe wounds, cure rickets and ease rheumatism. **Caution:** recent research suggests many species of fern are carcinogenic; male fern should be avoided; it should never be taken internally, especially not by those suffering from cardiac problems or by pregnant women.

Cultivation: grows freely in damp areas and on hedge banks. Should be avoided in the herb garden because of possible health risks.

Echium vulgare (Boraginaceae)
🐦 Viper's Bugloss
blue weed, blue devil

Description: herbaceous biennial with an exceptionally long drought-resistant taproot and coarse, hairy stems up to 90 cm/3 ft. Greyish freckled leaves, long and narrow with rounded tips near the base of the plant, shorter on the flowering stem. Plants flower at midsummer, the dense panicles of pink buds opening into bright blue flowers with long, conspicuous stamens. A wild plant of dry, stony or grassy places, often near the sea; cultivated blue or white forms grown in gardens.

Uses: an outstanding ornamental plant, originally used to treat snakebite (both the seeds and stem markings resemble the features of snakes), the whole plant being crushed and applied to the bite. Flowers are mildly tonic and antiseptic, and may be added to drinks or candied. Leaves may be cooked like spinach.

Cultivation: sow in late summer in any soil where plants are to flower, and thin seedlings to 45 cm/18 in apart; transplant others to new sites while still young and their taproots undeveloped. Plants self-seed freely where happy.

Parts used: fresh young leaves and shoots before flowering; flowers when fully open.

Related species: *E. lycopsis* (purple viper's bugloss): more softly hairy, with larger red-purple flowers and fewer stamens. Similar uses.

Eruca vesicaria spp. *sativa* (Cruciferae)
🐦 (Garden or Sweet) Rocket
rocket-salad, rocket-gentle, rocquette

Description: fast-growing annual, with a rosette of smooth, dark green leaves, indented like a dandelion. Branched, leafy main stems, hairy and reddish, growing to 60 cm/2 ft, producing sparse simple flowers of loose, floppy creamy-yellow petals with purple veins, followed by fat, crisp seedpods.

Uses: salad herb with pungent flavour, especially popular in Mediterranean countries. A tonic, mild stimulant and cough remedy. Crisp seedpods are edible, seeds used to treat bruises and supply mustard oils.

Cultivation: for succulent leaves grow in rich, moist soil in full sun or light shade; on hot, dry soils plants run to seed quickly and produce tough, bitter leaves. Sow in spring and again at midsummer (all year round in warm districts), and keep well watered. Plants usually self-seed.

Parts used: leaves gathered in succession as soon as plants are large enough; seedpods while young and juicy; seeds from ripe seedpods.

Eupatorium perfoliatum (Compositae)
🐦 Boneset
thoroughwort, agueweed

Description: perennial herbaceous herb, with branching rough stem up to 1.5 m/5 ft. Long narrow pointed leaves, dark green and shiny above, and white and downy beneath. Dense heads of small white, occasionally blue, flowers, followed by feathery seedheads.

Uses: a popular tonic and stimulant, best known as a hot infusion for treating coughs and colds, or as' an ointment or syrup for muscular aches.

Cultivation: sow on the surface of seed trays in autumn or spring in a cold frame; divide mature plants in spring or autumn, and grow in damp or marshy soil in sun or light shade.

Parts used: whole plant as flowers open, fresh or dried quickly in warmth.

Related species: *E. ayapana*: Brazilian species, producing a stimulant and digestive tea.

E. cannabinum (hemp agrimony, water hemp): contains eupatorin, used to treat dropsy; flowering herb or root also used as a tonic and laxative.

E. purpureum (joe-pye weed, gravel-root, queen of the meadow): white- and purple-flowered plant up to 3 m/10 ft; North American Indian red dye plant; roots and seedheads used to treat rheumatism, backache and urinary disorders.

Filipendula ulmaria, syn. *Spiraea ulmaria* (Rosaceae)

🐚 **Meadowsweet**

queen of the meadows, meadsweet, meadwort

Description: herbaceous perennial with a pink aromatic creeping rootstock. Reddish stems, up to 1.2 m/4 ft, bear pinnate leaves. Dense panicles of fragrant, creamy-white flowers in late summer.

Uses: an early source of salicylic acid. Tea from the flowers reduces fever, and is used to treat stomach acidity, influenza and rheumatism. Flower buds produce oil for perfume, and the dried flowers are added to home-made wines. Leaves flavour drinks, especially beer and mead. Dyes made from the roots (black) and flowers (yellow).

Cultivation: sow in spring or autumn *in situ* or in trays of compost under glass, or divide roots in spring. Plant in moist, rich soil in sun or light shade.

Parts used: flowers fresh or dried gently in warmth; roots dried for homeopathic use; leaves for flavouring.

Related species: *F. vulgaris* (dropwort): smaller plant, up to 60 cm/2 ft, with less dense flowerheads. Roots sometimes used as a vegetable.

F. rubra, syn. *F. magnifica* (queen of the prairie): similar North American species with pink flowers.

Foeniculum vulgare (Umbelliferae)

🐚 **Fennel**

spigel

Description: greyish-green, strong-smelling herbaceous perennial, with slim stems up to 1.8 m/6 ft, bearing soft lacy, dark green leaves with thread-like lobes and swollen bases. Creeping rootstock gradually extends plant into a sparse clump. Small mustard-yellow flowers appear in summer, followed by small egg-shaped seed-

pods. Grows wild in waste places and damp sites; may become an invasive weed, as in Australia and New Zealand.

Uses: one of nine Anglo-Saxon sacred herbs; much used by ancient Greeks and throughout the Middle Ages. Roots once boiled as a vegetable, and used as an expectorant in cough mixtures. Dried stalks are an essential ingredient of Provençal cuisine. Soft growing tips are widely used to flavour and garnish fish dishes, soups and baked foods, and may be made into fennel tea to treat indigestion and colic. A popular flavouring for liqueurs and a scent for soaps and cosmetics. Oil produced from seeds is antibacterial. In warmer regions foliage attracts swallowtail butterflies. **Caution:** avoid large doses.

Cultivation: for lavish growth light, moist soils are best. Divide roots in spring and plant in a warm sunny place, or sow seeds in spring or summer, either in pots or *in situ* 50 cm/20 in apart. Roots become long and

tough, so transplant while still young. Water well in dry weather. Fennel self-seeds freely, so dead-head if seeds not needed. Plants become congested and exhausted after 3-4 years, and are then best replaced. Do not grow near dill, as these two species cross-fertilize readily to produce useless hybrids.

Parts used: growing tips, fresh or dried in early summer (leaves and stems may be cropped several times before flowering); seeds, from seedheads cut in autumn before fully mature and dried in warmth; roots dug in autumn and dried slowly.

Related species: *F. vulgare* 'Dulce' (Florence fennel, finocchio, sweet fennel): annual cropped from the wild for its essential oil, and cultivated as a vegetable for its juicy, swollen stem base.

F. vulgare 'Piperitum' (carosella, cartucci): local Italian vegetable with blanched young stems.

Ferula foetida (asafoetida): perennial herb used as an Indian condiment and in sauces; medicinal resin extracted from the root.

Ferula galbaniflua (galbanum): Middle Eastern species, the stem and roots of which yield an aromatic gum used for incense.

Fragaria vesca (Rosaceae)
﷽ **(Wild) Strawberry**
wood strawberry

Description: deciduous herbaceous perennial, spreading by runners or stolons. Single white flowers on stems in summer, followed by red or white berries with numerous yellow seeds on the outside. Grows wild in woods and grassy places on dry soil.

Uses: mildly laxative fruits are a nerve tonic, rich in iron. Leaves can be made into a popular tea that is a diuretic and astringent; fresh leaves sometimes added to salads. **Caution:** excessive consumption sometimes leads to allergic reactions.

Cultivation: plant young runners in spring or autumn, or sow seeds under glass in spring (sow on the surface and keep moist – germination may be slow and erratic). Plant in sun or light shade, in any soil except clay.

Parts used: fruit when fully coloured; leaves at any time; roots dug in winter.

Related species: F. moschata (hautbois strawberry, musk strawberry): wild species with larger flowers.

F. virginiana (wild strawberry): red-fruited wild species, an important North American Indian legendary and medicinal plant, and one parent of most large-fruited forms.

Galium odoratum, syn. *Asperula odorata* (Rubiaceae)
﷽ **(Sweet) Woodruff**
kiss-me-quick, master of the woods (Waldmeister)

Description: herbaceous perennial, often evergreen. Branched stems up to 30 cm/12 in bear neat whorls of dark green leaves. Clusters of star-shaped flowers on long stalks appear in early summer.

Uses: flavours wines and other drinks, and scents linen, pot-pourri and perfumes. Medicinally used to poultice wounds and scabies, and to stimulate milk flow of nursing mothers. **Caution:** excessive use may produce dizziness and respiratory allergies.

Cultivation: divide roots at any time, or sow ripe seeds in late summer *in situ.* Grow in rich, alkaline soil in shade, and harvest from second year onwards.

Parts used: green plant cut at or just before flowering time, and dried slowly.

Related species: G. verum (lady's bed-straw): taller and with thinner leaves; sweet-scented yellow flowers used to curdle milk and colour cheese; stems yield a red dye.

Asperula tinctoria (dyer's woodruff): white-flowered species, giving a yellow-orange dye.

Gaultheria procumbens (Ericaceae)
﷽ **Wintergreen**
partridge berry, tea berry, chequerberry

Description: evergreen perennial shrub with prostrate creeping stems from which erect branches grow to 15 cm/6 in high. Top of each branch bears a few leathery, serrated oval leaves, shiny and paler beneath. Drooping white or pink flowers appear in mid-summer, followed by pea-sized scarlet berries. A wild plant of woodlands on acid soils.

Uses: leaves made into aromatic infusion for use as a gargle. Leaves are pain-reducing, and when dried can be made into a tea. Oil distilled from the leaves rubbed in externally to treat muscular aches and pains, and also used to flavour dental preparations.

Cultivation: excellent ground-cover plant for moist, acid soils and rock gardens. Plant in autumn or spring in peaty soils in full sun or light shade. Propagate by seeds sown in a seedbed outdoors in autumn, or from rooted prostrate stems in spring.

Parts used: leaves fresh or dried in the sun, distilled for oil of wintergreen.

Related species: G. antipoda: New Zealand species, either prostrate or a medium-sized shrub, with edible red berries.

G. shallon (shallon, salal): vigorous, shrubby North American species, with purple berries.

Genista tinctoria (Leguminosae)
🌿 Dyer's Greenweed
dyer's broom

Description: dwarf deciduous broom-like shrub, sometimes prostrate or erect to 90 cm/3 ft. Bright green branches and narrow pointed glossy leaves; long, leafy racemes of bright yellow pea-type flowers in summer. A wild plant of dry grassy places and heaths; numerous cultivated forms, including one with double flowers.

Uses: a decorative ground-cover plant to grow with heathers. Infusion made from young flowering shoots is diuretic and laxative, and used to treat dropsy and skin disorders. Young flower buds may be pickled like capers. Flowers yield a yellow dye, rich green if mixed with woad.

Cultivation: poor soil in an open, sunny position with good drainage is ideal. Plant autumn or spring, or sow seeds outdoors in autumn after rubbing them between sheets of sandpaper; named varieties may be grafted on to laburnum rootstocks in spring. Prune soft growth after flowering.

Parts used: flower buds; flowers for dye; young flowering shoots fresh or dried in shade.

Geranium maculatum
(Geraniaceae)
🌿 American Cranesbill
spotted cranesbill, alum root, crowfoot

American cranesbill

Description: hairy herbaceous perennial with stout rhizomatous root and stems up to 60 cm/2 ft. Leaves elegant and downy, divided with scalloped edges and blotched with white as they age. Small pink-purple, occasionally white, flowers appear in late spring, followed by fruits with long barbs like the bill of a crane. A wild plant of hedgerows and woodlands.

Uses: a popular North American Indian herb; root is astringent, used in infusions or as a powder to treat diarrhoea, dysentery and bleeding, and ulcers, both internal and external.

Cultivation: divide mature plants in early spring, or sow in autumn or spring where plants are to grow after rubbing seeds between sheets of sandpaper. Grow in full sun or light shade in moist, leafy soil. Plants self-seed profusely and soon develop into thick clumps.

Parts used: roots gathered in autumn or winter, dried and powdered.

herb robert

Related species: *G. robertianum* (herb robert, stinking cranesbill): annual with pink or white flowers; whole plant (including roots) is a powerful wound herb, used to stop bleeding and heal oral inflammations.

Geum urbanum (Rosaceae)
🐦 **Herb Bennet**
wood avens, clove root

Description: downy herbaceous perennial with strong thick aromatic pink root and branched stems up to 60 cm/2 ft. Grows as a rosette of dark green oval leaflets of unequal size, the terminal one largest, toothed or deeply lobed. In summer and autumn bears loose open panicles of yellow flowers. A wild plant of woods and shady fertile places, and 'weed' of cultivated soil.

Uses: spicy root, a medieval pot herb and substitute for cloves, can be made into an infusion for stomach and liver disorders, to increase appetite and stop bleeding, or into a strengthening tea to reduce fever; also used as a mouthwash. Young leaves can be eaten in salads.

Cultivation: sow in spring or autumn where flowers are to grow, and thin to 15 cm/6 in apart. Grow in fertile soil in full or semi-shade.

Parts used: roots fresh or dried in shade or warmth; young leaves.

Related species: G. rivale (water avens, Indian chocolate): delicate perennial with trefoil leaves and nodding bell-shaped pink flowers, preferring damp shade or the margins of ponds. Similar uses, but milder in effect; also used to make chocolate-flavoured drinks.

Glycyrrhiza glabra (Leguminosae)
🐦 **Liquorice**
licorice, sweet root

Description: vetch-like herbaceous perennial, with long yellow fibrous taproot, numerous subroots and creeping stolons. Stems to 1.5 m/5 ft, bearing pale green pinnate leaves with small oval leaflets in pairs. From the leaf axils loose, conical lilac-blue pea-type flowers appear in midsummer, followed by long brown seedpods.

Uses: cultivated for its sweet aromatic roots since the Middle Ages; used by Arab physicians as a laxative, and for treating stomach problems such as ulcers, and bladder and kidney complaints. Infusion given for bronchial catarrh and sore throats, and to reduce fever. Popular sweetener and flavouring for confectionery, beers and tobacco. Waste fibres after processing used to make wallboard. **Caution:** long-term use can raise blood pressure, lower potassium levels and lead to sodium retention.

Cultivation: grow in deep, well-drained soils in full sun. Divide roots in spring and plant 10 cm/4 in deep and 45 cm/18 in apart. Cut down foliage annually in autumn and remove any creeping stolons.

Parts used: roots from 3-4-year-old plants, dug in autumn or spring, peeled and dried; juice may be extracted from fresh roots.

Hamamelis virginiana (Hamamelidaceae)
🐦 **(Common) Witch Hazel**
winterbloom, spotted alder

Description: deciduous perennial shrub or small spreading tree with smooth pale bark, up to 4 m/13 ft. Small elliptical hazel-like leaves, downy when young, and ragged spidery bright yellow flowers on bare stems from late autumn onwards. A wild shrub of damp woods and watersides, widely grown as an ornamental and rootstock for cultivated witch hazels.

Uses: traditional astringent and cooling wound herb, sacred to North American Indians. Made into an infusion for treating bruises, sprains, varicose veins and bleeding, and an ointment for relieving piles. Commercial witch hazel is made from young flowering twigs. **Caution:** tinctures made from the leaves and bark may cause allergic reactions.

Cultivation: prefers lime-free soils in full sun or light shade, may be grown as a decorative lawn specimen or among other shrubs, or trained against walls. Sow seeds in spring in trays under glass or a seedbed outdoors, or layer branches in autumn. Cut out suckers annually; if rooted these may be transplanted for new plants.

Parts used: bark and leaves for tinctures; flowering twigs for distillation.

Hedera helix (Araliaceae)

Ivy

English ivy

Description: long-lived evergreen climber, with woody stems clinging by aerial roots, up to 30 m/100 ft. Dark green glossy leaves, often with paler veins; juvenile foliage pointed and lobed, often palmate. When stems reach full light they branch freely and bear smaller simple pointed oval leaves and globular heads of greenish fragrant flowers in autumn, followed by black berries. A wild plant growing in trees and hedges or prostrate on shaded soil; numerous ornamental forms.

Uses: once regarded as a protective magical plant, with numerous internal medicinal uses: berries were taken as a purgative, and leaves used to treat fevers and glandular disorders. They may safely be turned into an effective poultice for bruises and stiff joints. Plants produce a resin sometimes included in varnishes; flowers attract bees, and birds depend on the berries in winter. **Caution:** whole plant is poisonous and should be restricted to external use.

Cultivation: plants prefer rich, well-drained soil in full or semi-shade. Sow in autumn, exposing seed trays to frost over winter, or use pieces of stem bearing aerial roots as cuttings. Peg shoots to soil surface at first to encourage more rapid growth and coverage of walls. Prune in spring, trimming off old leaves and shortening or removing any unwanted straggly stems.

Parts used: young leaves, fresh or dried in shade.

Helichrysum italicum, syn. *H. angustifolium* (Compositae)

Curry Plant

everlasting flower, helichrysum

Description: evergreen aromatic bush with branched woody stems up to 60 cm/2 ft. Fragrant narrow, silvery-white leaves; rich yellow daisies on long stalks in summer.

Uses: intensely aromatic herb for flavouring meat dishes, drinks and jellies, and effective as an insect repellent. Essential oil used in cosmetics, and for treating respiratory problems.

Cultivation: grow in poor soil in a sunny, well-drained position, protected from frost and cold winds in winter. Divide plants in spring, take cuttings from side shoots in summer, or sow under glass in spring. Plant in autumn or spring; in formal positions trim off flowering stems as these detract from the foliage, but never cut into old wood.

Parts used: leaves; flowers in bud dried for arrangements; flowerheads and shoots in summer for distillation.

Related species: *H. cochinchinense.* South-East Asian species, leaves used to flavour rice dishes.

H. serpyllifolium, syn. *Plecostachys serpyllifolia:* South African species, leaves made into tea.

H. stoechas (goldilocks): bright yellow-flowered dwarf shrub; leaves used as a vermifuge.

Humulus lupulus (Cannabinaceae)

Hop(s)

Description: hairy aggressive perennial climber, with long spreading stolons and twining stems ('bines'), often twisting around each other into ropes, up to 9 m/30 ft. Leaves heart-shaped or palmately lobed, with toothed edges. Clusters of greenish male and female flowers appear on separate plants in summer, female flowers ripening into large cones of overlapping bracts in autumn. Grows wild in hedges, cultivated commercially and grown as a garden ornamental.

Uses: common flavouring and antibacterial preservative in beer; female cones used to treat insomnia and nervous tension, and included for their hormonal content in skin creams and lotions. Hop poultices applied to boils and swellings. Young shoots and leaves cooked as vegetables; fibres from the stems are used in the textile industry.

Cultivation: grow from cuttings or divisions from the base of the plant in spring, or sow seeds in late summer and autumn in a cold frame. Plant in rich, moist soil in full sun or light shade, and grow up sturdy tall supports. Mulch in spring with rotted manure, thin young shoots to 5-6 per crown, and water freely in dry weather.

Parts used: female cones gathered in early autumn while still green, and dried until brown, sometimes powdered; young shoots 15-20 cm/6-8 in long in spring.

Hypericum perforatum (Guttiferae)
🌿 (Perforate, or Common) St John's Wort

Description: low evergreen perennial, with long, wiry runners or stolons and branched stems up to 90 cm/3 ft, woody at base and marked with two raised parallel lines. Small, pale green leaves arranged in opposite pairs and speckled with translucent dots, which are oil glands. Bright yellow flowers appear in late summer, petals edged with black dots. A wild plant of grassy and shady places, usually chalky.

Uses: leaves mildly sedative, and stimulate gastric and bile secretions. Sometimes used to treat poor blood circulation and irregular menstruation, but best known as an antibacterial remedy for slow-healing wounds and burns. Young leaves eaten in salads; flowers yield red and yellow dyes. **Caution:** avoid exposure to the sun during treatment, as the plant causes photosensitivity.

Cultivation: grow in sun or light shade in well-drained soil. Divide roots in spring, take cuttings in summer, or sow seeds in trays in spring. Plant in autumn or spring, and prune damaged stems after frosts.

Parts used: young leaves and flowers fresh or dried in shade.

Related species: *H. androsaemum* (all-heal, tutsan): larger, shade-loving plant with unspotted leaves and black berries in autumn; a noted wound herb.

Hyssopus officinalis (Labiatae)
🌿 Hyssop

Description: perennial evergreen shrub with branching stems up to 60 cm/2 ft. Long narrow green fragrant leaves, hairy and dotted with oil-bearing glands; whorls of blue, pink, purple or white flowers on long narrow spikes in autumn, popular with bees. A wild plant of dry stony soils on chalk, and an ornamental herb, sometimes used for dwarf hedging.

Uses: a valuable expectorant; flowering tips infused in water used to treat coughs and sore throats, also to heal bites, burns and stings. Often added for flavouring to soups, stews and salads. Distilled oil used in liqueurs and perfumes.

Cultivation: grow in full sun in well-drained, light soil. Sow in spring under glass, take cuttings in early summer, or divide in spring or autumn. Plant 20 cm/8 in apart for hedging and clip to shape in spring.

Parts used: leaves fresh at any time; flowering tips fresh or dried in sun.

Related species: *Agastache foeniculum* (anise hyssop): aromatic herbaceous perennial, dried leaves used for seasoning and teas.

A. urticifolia (nettle-leaved giant hyssop): herbaceous perennial, used by North American Indians medicinally and as flavouring.

Isatis tinctoria (Cruciferae)
🌿 Woad
dyer's weed

Description: biennial or short-lived perennial, with basal rosette of long-stalked, oval toothed leaves, blue-green and downy, with branched leafy stems up to 1.2 m/4 ft, stem leaves smaller, sessile and arrow-shaped. Graceful loose panicles of small yellow flowers in early summer, followed by pendulous black seeds. A wild plant of waste places on chalk, widely cultivated until this century.

Uses: an ancient dye and healing plant, fermented leaves producing a blue dye eventually superseded by indigo. Leaves were also traditionally used to stop bleeding and heal the wounds of battle. **Caution:** for external use only.

Cultivation: grow in full sun in well-drained, rich chalky soil. Sow *in situ* in late summer and thin seedlings to 30 cm/12 in apart. Removing stems before they can flower extends the life of plants, which will otherwise seed themselves freely as biennials.

Parts used: leaves repeatedly fermented and dried in a complicated sequence of operations.

Juniperus communis
(Cupressaceae)
Juniper

Description: evergreen coniferous shrub or tree, prostrate or upright to 6 m/20 ft. Needle-like leaves, prickly and emitting scent of apples if bruised. Yellow-green flowers in early summer, followed by fleshy berries, green at first, turning blue-black with a white bloom in the second year.

Uses: Oil from unripe berries used in massaging rheumatic or gouty parts of the body. Ripe berries are added as a flavouring to drinks such as gin, and meat dishes, especially game. Wood of stem and roots is burned to smoke preserved meats. **Caution:** use internally only under medical supervision; may also be an external irritant.

Cultivation: plant in autumn or spring in good, well drained soil in an open position. Propagate from seeds sown in a cold frame in spring, or from cuttings in autumn.

Parts used: leafy shoots at any time; fruit gathered in late summer and dried in sun; woody stems and roots when available.

Related species: *J. sabina* (savin): poisonous shrubby species used under supervision as a veterinary herb.

J. oxycedrus (prickly juniper): oil of cade (juniper tar) distilled from the roots as a veterinary vermifuge.

J. virginiana (eastern red cedar): source of cedar oil for perfume and medications.

Laurus nobilis (Lauraceae)
(Sweet) Bay (Tree)
sweet laurel, bay laurel

Description: large dense evergreen shrub or ornamental tree up to 15 m/50 ft, with glossy dark green, oval pointed leaves. Small creamy-yellow flowers appear in early summer, followed in warm climates and on mature plants by black berries.

Uses: an ancient aromatic and antiseptic plant, used to weave a victorious Roman general's crown or 'laurels'. Leaves are a popular culinary flavouring, and stimulate the appetite; when pulped they can be applied as an astringent to burns and bruises. Berries are pressed to make oil for liqueurs, perfume and veterinary uses.

Cultivation: grow in rich, well-drained soil in full sun, sheltered from cold winds; sometimes scorched or cut back by severe frost especially while young. Plant in early autumn or spring, and trim to shape in summer; may be clipped into formal topiary. Propagate by layering shoots in autumn, or from cuttings of side shoots in a shaded cold frame in early autumn. Best grown in containers and moved to a cool greenhouse in areas with severe winters.

Parts used: leaves at any time, dried in darkness and lightly pressed flat; ripe berries pressed for oil.

Related species: *Umbellularia californica* (Californian laurel): similar shrub or tree, with more aromatic foliage.

Lavandula angustifolia, syn. *L. officinalis*, *L. spica* (Labiatae)
(English) Lavender
true lavender

Description: evergreen perennial woody shrub, dense and branching up to 90 cm/3 ft. Long narrow, aromatic leaves, grey-green and downy, and intensely fragrant blue-mauve flowers in long spikes in midsummer. A wild plant of Mediterranean hillsides; numerous varieties widely cultivated as garden ornamentals and hedging.

Uses: an early strewing herb, often burnt on low fires to perfume rooms. As an essential oil and in infusion used as a cough suppressant, and to treat headaches and nervous disorders. As an embrocation an external stimulant and antiseptic. Flowers attract bees, and are gathered for perfume, potpourri and to scent clothing.

Lavandula 'Hidcote'

Cultivation: grow in light, dryish soils in full sun for maximum fragrance and colour. Sow seeds in trays in late spring; take soft cuttings in spring or hardwood cuttings in late summer; or layer old plants by mounding soil
(Continued)

Lavandula 'Nana Alba'

French lavender

English lavender

Levisticum officinale, syn.
Ligusticum levisticum
(Umbelliferae)

❧ Lovage

love parsley, lovage angelica, smallage

Description: pungent, clump-forming herbaceous perennial with rhizomatous roots and stout hollow ridged stems up to 2.4 m/8 ft. Broad glossy leaves, with large, dense umbels of greenish-yellow flowers in summer, followed by ridged golden-brown seedpods.

Uses: leaves can flavour soups and casseroles; stems are blanched like celery or candied like angelica; roots may be peeled and cooked as a vegetable; savoury seeds are added to bread and other baked foods. Powdered root sometimes used as a condiment. Medicinally digestive and carminative. Essence of lovage used in perfumes. **Caution:** avoid taking large quantities.

Cultivation: mature plants are large and bulky, and so need plenty of room in deep rich moist soil, preferably in shade. Sow in spring outdoors in a seedbed or under glass, or divide roots in autumn or spring. Cut back once or twice during summer if a continuous supply of young leaves is needed.

Parts used: young leaves, avoiding the central flower stem; hollow main stems before flowering; roots of 2- or 3-year-old plants dug in autumn, sliced and dried; ripe seeds.

around the stems. Prune annually to shape in spring to prevent straggly growth and bare stems, especially on hedges, but do avoid cutting back into old wood.

Parts used: flowers gathered just before fully opened and dried slowly; flowering shoots and leaves distilled for essential oil.

Related species: L. a 'Hidcote': slow-growing species, with low stems and deep purple flowers.

L. a. 'Nana Alba': pale flowers; a low-growing species.

L. stoechas (French lavender): slightly tender species, with a stronger scent than most.

Related species: Ligusticum scoticum (Scots lovage): smaller wild plant of cliffs and seashores with milder flavour.

Levisticum chinensis: used in Chinese medicine for menstrual disorders.

Ligustrum vulgare (Oleaceae)

(Common) Privet

wild privet

Description: densely branched deciduous shrub up to 3.6 m/12 ft, with smooth leathery oval pointed leaves and short spikes of white strong-smelling flowers in early summer, followed by small black or yellow shiny berries. Grows wild in scrubland and open woods, especially on chalk, and often cultivated as a hedging plant; numerous attractive garden forms.

Uses: valuable hardwood timber for tools and charcoal; leaves once used by Shakers to make a mouthwash. Yellow dye made from the leaves. **Caution:** all parts are poisonous if ingested.

Cultivation: tolerant of most soils and positions. Sow seeds in autumn outdoors; put cuttings of young shoots in a cold frame in summer, or hardwood cuttings in a shady position outdoors in autumn. Plant and prune to shape in autumn.

Parts used: leaves at any time during the growing season; wood of larger pruned stems.

oval-leaved golden privet

common privet

Related species: *L. ibota* (ibota privet): small elegant shrub, grown in China where insect damage to the stems produces a wax with industrial uses.

L. japonicum (Japanese privet, wax-leaved privet): dense, large-flowered species, with seeds sometimes roasted as a coffee substitute.

L. lucidum (wax tree): handsome small Chinese tree, seeds made into an infusion for strengthening general metabolism.

L. ovalifolium (oval-leaved privet): best species for hedging, dense and semi-evergreen, with popular golden variety.

Linaria vulgaris
(Scrophulariaceae)

(Common) Toadflax

yellow toadflax, butter and eggs

Description: herbaceous perennial with vigorous underground creeping rhizomes and numerous long slender greyish flax-like leaves. Stems up to 60 cm/2 ft bear in summer and autumn dense spikes of long-spurred brilliant yellow flowers like those of antirrhinums, each with a bright orange spot on the lower lip, followed by capsules of numerous flat round black seeds. A wild plant of bare waste ground.

Uses: a highly ornamental plant, used in the Middle Ages for laundry starch. Used homeopathically to treat diarrhoea and cystitis, and by herbalists to treat jaundice. Has a folk reputation as a fly poison when boiled in milk. Flowers yield dyes: yellow, orange, green or brown depending on the mordant used.

Cultivation: best grown in the wild herb garden, in a confined space, or in mown grass to restrain the invasive stolons. Sow in spring or early autumn, either where plants are to flower or in trays of compost for transplanting; established roots may be divided in autumn or spring. Plant 60 cm/2 ft apart in full sun. Plants self-seed liberally, so dead-head after flowering to restrain seeding.

Parts used: whole flowering herb, fresh or dried in shade.

Linum usitatissimum (Linaceae)
⁊ Flax
flaxseed, linseed

Description: slender annual with wiry stems to 90 cm/3 ft. Linear pointed leaves; pale to bright blue flowers (best for fibre production) or white in summer, followed by pods of flat oval brown seeds, rich in oil. Grows wild in dry grasslands, usually as an escape from cultivation. A taller variety is grown for flax production in cool, moist regions, and a more compact type in warm climates for seed.

Uses: stem varieties are soaked ('retted') in water to release fibres for making linen cloth. Linseed oil from seed varieties is one of the most important commercial drying oils, used in paints, varnishes and putty. Oil used medicinally as a laxative and vermifuge; the seeds soaked overnight and strained can be used to treat gastritis, constipation and indigestion, and in poultices for cuts, bruises and other abrasions. **Caution:** large doses may be poisonous.

Cultivation: sow in late spring or early summer in dry, well-drained soil in sun.

Parts used: whole fresh flowering plant for medicinal purposes; stems of green plant for fibre; seeds used fresh or dried and powdered.

Related species: *L. catharticum* (purging flax): white-flowered annual with oval leaves; used homeopathically to treat bronchitis and piles.

Lippia citriodora, syn. *Aloysia triphylla* (Verbenaceae)
⁊ Lemon Verbena
sweet-scented verbena, herb luisa, Spanish thyme

Description: perennial evergreen shrub, almost small tree up to 3 m/10 ft in warm climates, with sparse, slender branches and long narrow pointed leaves, grey-green and downy in groups of 3 or 4 with oil-bearing glands forming dots on the underside, giving off a penetrating lemon scent. Long terminal racemes of tiny white or lavender flowers in late summer.

Uses: tea (sold in France as 'verveine') made from leaves is tonic, calming and sedative, and can be used to treat nausea, palpitations and flatulence. Essential oil ('Spanish verbena') distilled from leaves used as flavouring in cakes, drinks, stuffings and desserts, in pot-pourri, and formerly in perfumes – largely replaced by lemon-grass oil. Hot leaf pulp is effective against toothache. **Caution:** large doses or prolonged use can cause internal irritation.

Cultivation: grow in fertile, well-drained soil in full sun, under glass in temperate regions as plants are frost-shy; in warm gardens may be trained as a climber against a sunny wall. Sow seed under glass in early spring, or take cuttings in summer. Propagate every few years, as older plants become threadbare and more sensitive to cold.

Parts used: leaves any time, fresh or dried in shade; shoots picked just before flowering and distilled for essential oil.

Lonicera periclymenum (Caprifoliaceae)
⁊ (Wild) Honeysuckle
woodbine

Description: deciduous woody twining shrub or climber to 6 m/20 ft, with oval glossy leaves. Clusters of fragrant pink-cream flowers appear in summer, followed by bright red berries.

Uses: as perfume, and a traditional remedy for a number of ailments. Bruised leaves used to treat skin disorders; flaked and infused bark for rheumatism and painful joints; flowers raw or infused in a tea for asthma and as a heart tonic; inside of the root as a veterinary vermifuge. Today only external uses are recommended. **Caution:** the berries of all honeysuckles may be poisonous.

Cultivation: grow in any good soil, in sun or shade, and train up walls or as standards on pillars. Sow seeds in autumn in pots (germination may be slow) or take cuttings in summer. Prune and mulch with compost in spring.

Parts used: leaves and flowers fresh or dried in shade; fresh bark from prunings; roots dug in autumn and dried.

Related species: *L. caprifolium* (perfoliate honeysuckle): yellow-flowered species with orange berries, used as an expectorant and antiseptic.

L. japonica: rampant semi-evergreen climber, an invasive weed in USA; widely used in Chinese medicine.

L. nigra (black honeysuckle): hard-wooded shrub with orange flowers, and black berries used homeopathically to treat neuroses.

Lythrum salicaria (Lythraceae)
❧ Purple Loosestrife

Description: herbaceous perennial with creeping rhizomes and square angled stems up to 1.5 m/5 ft. Narrow, pointed leaves without stalks, in opposite pairs or whorls of three, and long, dense spikes of bright mauve-pink flowers in midsummer, followed by ovoid seed capsules. A plant of river banks and damp places, with several cultivated garden forms.

Uses: high tannin content, so once often used in leather tanning, but now a mainly decorative and medicinal plant. Antibacterial, used as a gargle and eyewash.

Cultivation: sow on surface of pots of moist compost and stand in trays of water until seedlings emerge; divide mature plants in spring or take cuttings in summer in a moist cold frame. Plant in damp soil in light shade, or full sun where the plants will flower best. Be careful that it does not choke out native plants when naturalized.

Parts used: flowering herb, fresh or dried in shade.

Malva sylvestris (Malvaceae)
❧ Common Mallow

Description: coarse herbaceous biennial, sprawling or bushy to 90 cm/3 ft. Leaves hairy, crinkled and deeply veined, palmate but almost circular at base of plant and toothed with long stalks, sometimes marked with a distinct black spot. Flowers pink, white or mauve with purple veins, in pairs or groups, in summer and autumn, followed by flat green button-like seed capsules. A wild plant of banks and waste places, especially near the sea, but also cultivated as a flowering plant in gardens.

pink mallow

Uses: whole plant is mucilaginous and therefore soothing. Leaves used to reduce inflammations and ease bee stings, and in poultices to treat ulcers and haemorrhoids. Tea made from an infusion of the flowers given for colds and bronchitis. Leaves can be added to soups or cooked like spinach, seedpods eaten raw or boiled. **Caution:** large amounts may be purgative and cause indigestion.

Cultivation: grow in full sun in well-drained ordinary soil. Sow in spring or autumn where plants are to grow, and thin seedlings to 60 cm/2 ft. Older plants may develop severe rust, and will need to be sprayed with fungicide or replaced regularly with young stock.

Parts used: flowers repeatedly over the long season, picked when fully open and dried fast in warmth; young leaves

white mallow

used fresh, or the entire plant cut down at flowering time and dried; seedpods picked while still green.

Related species: *M. neglecta* (dwarf mallow): almost prostrate bushy annual with pink or white flowers; similarly used, especially by North American Indians.

M. parviflora (least mallow, little mallow): short annual with pale pink flowers and similar culinary uses.

Matricaria recutita, syn. *M. chamomilla, Chamomilla recutita* (Compositae)

🐝 **Wild Chamomile**

scented mayweed, German chamomile

Description: aromatic annual with branched stems up to 45 cm/18 in. Sweetly fragrant small white daisies with prominent yellow flowers with central hollow cones appear in early summer. A wild plant of fields and roadsides, and a cereal 'weed' on chalky soils.

Uses: popular herb with a wide range of applications. Chamomile tea is refreshing, digestive and mildly sedative. Flowers reduce inflammation; used to soothe teething pains and poultice wounds. Essential oil used to scent shampoos and soaps. **Caution:** may cause a severe reaction in those with ragweed allergies.

Cultivation: sow in autumn or spring where plants are to flower, and water seeds in gently (do not cover). Grow in dry, chalky soils in full sun. Plants self-seed freely and may spread weedily unless checked.

Parts used: flowers, fresh or dried in shade.

Melilotus officinalis (Leguminosae)

🐝 **(Common or Ribbed) Melilot**

yellow sweet clover

Description: trailing or upright biennial with sturdy taproot and branched stems up to 1.2 m/4 ft. Leaves trefoil with long, toothed leaflets; flowers creamy-yellow and sweet-scented in loose stalked spikes in summer, followed by brown oval, wrinkled seedpods. Grows wild in pastures and bare waste places, and widely cultivated as a fodder and green manure crop.

Uses: the tea is tonic and anti-colic, used to treat sleeplessness, nervous tension, thrombosis and digestive disorders. Externally, often added to relaxing baths and made into a compress for slow-healing wounds. Both flowers and seeds are used for flavouring. **Caution:** excessive consumption may cause vomiting and dizziness.

Cultivation: sow seeds in late spring where plants are to grow, in fertile well-drained soils in full sun.

Parts used: leaves and shoots of flowering plants, fresh or dried in shade.

Related species: M. alba (white melilot, white sweet clover): taller plant with fragrant white flowers; widely grown as a fodder crop ('Bokhara clover') and bee plant.

Melissa officinalis (Labiatae)

🐝 **(Lemon) Balm**

bee balm, melissa, sweet balm

Description: hairy clump-forming herbaceous perennial with creeping roots and erect square stems up to 90 cm/3 ft. Lemon-scented leaves, heart-shaped, toothed and deeply veined; flowers white or pale pink, sparsely arranged in a loose terminal spike in late summer. A wild plant of waste and derelict ground, widely grown in gardens, especially in golden and variegated forms.

Uses: vigorous and indestructible herb with a strong lemon fragrance. Young leaves used to flavour teas, soups, milk, custard, sauces, and added to liqueurs; pungent oil extracted from them is used in perfumery. Medicinally, balm lowers blood pressure, and is used in infusion to treat colds and influenza, nervous tension, insomnia, indigestion and other stomach ailments. A notable bee plant. Leaves and stems are sometimes used to polish and scent wooden furniture.

Cultivation: grow in rich, moist soil in full sun or light shade. Readily self-sows, or sow seeds in spring *in situ* or in trays under glass, or divide mature plants (advisable every 4-5 years to keep plants young and vigorous). Cut back in summer before flowering to encourage a further supply of young leaves.

Parts used: leaves and tips picked just before or after flowering, and used fresh or dried quickly in the shade (freezing retains more volatile oils than drying).

Mentha (Labiatae)

There are at least 18 species of mint and many more hybrids, most of them difficult to classify because of their variability and readiness to hybridize between each other. All are aromatic perennials, most containing menthol (essential mint oil) to some degree. **Caution:** handling mints may cause skin rashes and other allergic irritations; mint teas should not be drunk in large amounts over a long period.

Mentha x *piperita*
🌿 Peppermint

Description: hairy perennial with underground stolons and square pink or red stems up to 90 cm/3 ft. Red-tinted oval, pointed leaves, deeply toothed and long-stalked, with mauve or white flowers on long spikes in mid-summer. A hybrid between water mint and spearmint or corn mint (*M. arvensis*), found wild as an escape in hedgerows and rich moist soils; widely cultivated in gardens, and commercially for the essential oil.

Uses: the most medicinally valuable of all mints, with great cooling properties due to its high content of menthol. Used to treat gastric and digestive disorders, and nervous complaints such as tension and insomnia. Essential oil used to flavour confectionery, liqueurs and pharmaceutical products, and to scent cosmetics.

Cultivation: divide roots in autumn or spring, and plant in moist, fertile soil, cool in summer and with plenty of potash; cut back in summer to rejuvenate growth. Remake beds every 4-5 years, sooner if plants develop rust; or cultivate as an annual by containing the roots and replanting divisions every spring.

Parts used: leaves and stems, fresh or dried – gather before flowering for culinary use, in full flower for distillation of oil.

Mentha pulegium
🌿 Pennyroyal
pudding grass

Description: downy, bushy perennial with surface runners, and prostrate or erect stems up to 20 cm/8 in. Small oval dark green leaves, hairy and slightly serrated, and mauve flowers in dense whorls in late summer. Grows wild on moist, light soils.

Uses: a very pungent herb, once used to disguise the flavour of putrid meat and still included in a few local dishes. Valued since Roman times as a flea repellent; also popular today as an aromatic ground-cover plant. Used medicinally to treat gastric ailments, headaches, colds, bites and minor abrasions.

Cultivation: sow in spring under glass, or divide plants in autumn or spring, and plant in light free-draining soil as edging or ground cover, or in the joints of paving stones.

Parts used: whole green plant, used fresh or dried.

pennyroyal

peppermint

Mentha x *rotundifolia*
🌿 Round-leaved Mint
apple mint

Description: sweetly aromatic perennial with shallow runners and slender, branched stems up to 90 cm/3 ft. Oval, serrated leaves, soft green but paler and downy underneath, and slim spikes of white or pink flowers in late summer. Found wild as an escape on damp waste ground, and commonly grown in kitchen gardens, often in variegated or improved forms such as 'Bowles' Variety'.

Uses: the main culinary mint species in continental Europe, used to flavour both savoury and sweet dishes, sauces and drinks.

Cultivation: as for *M.* x *piperita.*

Parts used: fresh leaves as required; can also be frozen or dried.

round-leaved mint

spearmint

Mentha spicata
❧ **Spearmint**
garden mint

ginger mint

Description: branching perennial with underground runners and square stems up to 75 cm/30 in. Short-stalked leaves are oval and sharply pointed, deeply veined and serrated, either smooth and bright green or sometimes greyish, downy and wrinkled. Slim pointed spikes of mauve flowers appear in late summer. Found wild in moist shade on waste ground.

Uses: the least pungent species, subtly fragrant; one of the main culinary mints, yielding an essential oil used for flavouring confectionery, and dental and pharmaceutical preparations.

Cultivation: as for *M.* x *piperita*.

Parts used: fresh, frozen or dried leaves.

Related species: M. arvensis (corn mint): coarse wild species, sometimes gathered for culinary flavouring.

M. arvensis var. *piperascens* (Japanese mint): cultivated widely in the Far East as the main commercial source of menthol.

M. x *gentilis* 'Variegata' (ginger mint): popular compact ornamental variety with gold variegation.

M. x *piperata* var. *citrata* (eau de Cologne mint, bergamot mint): highly aromatic form with predominantly citrus fragrance, used to perfume cosmetics.

M. requienii (Corsican mint): prostrate tiny-leaved species; occurs wild, cultivated as ground cover; peppermint fragrance used in preparation of crème de menthe.

M. x *smithiana*, syn. *M. rubra raripila* (rust-free mint): purplish leaves and stems, spearmint flavour; least prone to mint rust.

M. suaveolens, 'Variegata' (pineapple mint): a variegated species with a distinct fragrance. Often grown as a decorative border herb.

pineapple mint

eau de Cologne mint

Monarda didyma (Labiatae)
❧ **Bergamot**
bee balm, Oswego tea, horsemint

Description: robust aromatic perennial with mat-like roots and runners that are sometimes invasive, and square stems up to 90 cm/3 ft. Rough oval, serrated leaves, dark green or red-tinted, and large whorled heads of tubular red flowers in late summer, attractive to bees. Found wild, occasionally as an escape, in moist shaded woodland and on the banks of streams; more colourful but less fragrant varieties grown for ornament in gardens.

Uses: traditionally used to make a relaxing anti-depressant tea which can also be used to treat nausea and flatulence. An infusion is inhaled for colds, or used as an antiseptic for ulcers, wounds and acne. Included in potpourri mixtures and as a perfume in cosmetics. **Caution:** bergamot may cause photosensitivity in some people.

Cultivation: prefers rich moist light soil in sun or partial shade, mulched in dry seasons. Sow in spring, or divide mature plants every 2-3 years in spring.

Parts used: leaves and flowers, fresh or dried.

Related species: M. fistulosa (wild bergamot, purple bergamot): North American Indian tea and medicinal plant with purple (occasionally white or pink) flowers and a preference for drier soils.

Myrica gale (Myricaceae)
Bog Myrtle
sweet gale, sweet willow

Description: deciduous shrub with shiny reddish, upright twiggy stems to 1.2 m/4 ft, and long narrow, grey-green leaves. Dense, yellow-brown catkins in spring are followed by orange, waxy berries. A rare wild plant of wet heaths, bogs and moorland.

Uses: tonic tea made from leaves, which are sometimes used with berries for flavouring cooked dishes and treating dysentery; dried leaves used as moth and flea repellent. Roots and bark give yellow dye.

Cultivation: grow in damp acid soils in shade, and prune in winter. Propagate in autumn from seeds sown outdoors, or from cuttings, layers or division.

Parts used: leaves, fresh or dried, or distilled for essential oil; berries fresh or dried; roots and bark.

Related species: *M. carolinensis* (bayberry): bushy shrub up to 2.4 m/8 ft, found on dry sandy soils; blue-grey waxy berries, used for candles.

M. cerifera (wax myrtle, candleberry): large shrub up to 9 m/30 ft; root bark used as circulatory stimulant and to treat diarrhoea; wax from berries made into candles.

M. rubra: oriental species, cultivated for edible seeds.

Myrrhis odorata (Umbelliferae)
(European) Sweet Cicely
myrrh

Description: bushy herbaceous perennial with a thick taproot and stout hollow grooved stems branching to 1.5 m/5 ft. Hairy, sweetly scented bright green leaves, soft, thin and ferny; loose umbels of small white flowers in early summer, followed by dark brown seeds, ridged and sharp-tipped. Grows wild in hedgerows and grassy shade on high ground, and cultivated locally.

Uses: leaves and unripe seeds are eaten raw in salads, roots and leaves boiled as vegetables. One or two leaves at a time are included in conserves and tart fruit dishes to add sweetness and aniseed flavour; also added to brandy and liqueurs. Whole plant is tonic and gently laxative, and used in healing ointments. Dried seeds ground as a spice in Germany; leaves used to polish and scent oak furniture; horses are sometimes lured with a piece of the root.

Cultivation: divide roots in spring or autumn, or sow seeds in autumn in trays outside or where plants are to grow (frost is needed for germination). Transplant while young to deep, rich, shady soil in a moist location; plants self-seed freely and may be invasive in heavy soils.

Parts used: leaves fresh or dried, seeds, green and immature, or dried; roots dug in autumn; whole green plant for medicinal infusions.

Myrtus communis (Myrtaceae)
Myrtle

Description: evergreen shrub, slow-growing in cool climates to 3 m/10 ft, stems with flaking red-brown bark. Long oval, leaves, dark green, shiny and dotted with oil glands. Scented flowers, white or rose-pink in late summer, followed by dark purple berries (some varieties white). Grows wild on Mediterranean scrubland and seashores.

Uses: The perfume *eau d'ange* is distilled from flowers and leaves to scent soaps and cosmetics; leaves added as flavouring to meat dishes; fruits fermented into alcoholic drinks. Medicinally, crushed leaves applied to external wounds, rashes and skin irritations; juice of berries good for stomach and digestive ailments. Dried buds and fruits used as a peppery condiment; roots and bark for tanning leather.

Cultivation: plants prefer fertile well-drained, acid soils, in full sun with good light; in cool regions the added warmth of a sunny wall is beneficial, or plants may be grown in large pots under glass. Prune to shape after flowering; dense foliage can be clipped into simple topiary. Propagate from cuttings under glass in summer, or seeds sown in greenhouse in spring.

Parts used: leaves fresh or dried; flower buds dried; flowers fully open; fruits fresh or dried; roots and bark.

Related species: *M. ugni*, syn. *Eugenia ugni*, *Ugni olinae* (Chilean guava, murtillo): small shrub with fragrant rose-pink flowers, and mahogany-red fruits used in jams and preserves.

Nasturtium officinale, syn.
Rorippa nasturtium-aquaticum
(Cruciferae)
Watercress

Description: lush aquatic or marginal perennial, almost evergreen, spreading by hollow brittle fleshy stems that root at each leaf joint. Leaves dark green and silky, oval or pinnate, older leaves burnished bronze. Racemes of small white flowers in summer followed by short, fat pods containing two rows of seeds (only one in some species). Grows wild in ditches and streams and widely cultivated in flooded beds as a salad herb in two main varieties: green or summer, and frost-hardy brown or winter cress.

Uses: leaves, rich in minerals and vitamins C and A, prized since Roman times for biting, rich flavour, raw or cooked as a vegetable and in soups. Also used as a cough remedy. Crushed leaves are applied as poultice for rheumatism and gout; raw seeds used as vermifuge. **Caution:** do not consume excessive quantities, and gather wild plants only from clean running water; plants in stagnant and polluted water may be host to the dangerous liver fluke.

Cultivation: sow in a moist, shady border in spring; divide plants, or root pieces of stem in pans immersed in water in spring. Plant in beds irrigated with flowing water, in tubs of soil and water, or in trenches of fertile moist soil. Water frequently.

Parts used: older leafy stems, fresh or dried; seeds when ripe.

Related species: *Rorippa palustris* (yellow cress): Australian wild herb with crinkled leaves and yellow flowers.

Nepeta cataria (Labiatae)
Catmint
catnip, catnep

Description: pungent, hairy perennial growing in a dense leafy mound. Long branching leafy stems up to 90 cm/3 ft bear light grey, heart-shaped leaves, coarsely serrated and almost white beneath; and from summer to autumn persistent flowers, white with mauve markings, in whorls. Grows wild in open spaces and roadsides on moist chalky soils, and commonly cultivated in gardens.

Uses: well known for its popularity with cats – volatile oil is a feline aphrodisiac and also distilled for perfumes. Leaves made into a mint-flavoured tea for colds, nervous tension, flatulence and gastric disorders, or poultices for cuts and bruises.

Cultivation: divide roots in spring or autumn, or take cuttings in summer, and grow in light, well-drained soil in full sun. Also easily grown from seed. Cut back after flowering.

Parts used: leaves and flowering stems, fresh or dried in shade.

Nicotiana alata, syn. *N. affinis*
(Solanaceae)
Flowering Tobacco
sweet-scented tobacco

Description: tropical perennial, usually grown as ornamental annual, with fleshy roots and strong, simple stems up to 1.8 m/6 ft. Long, tubular flowers, highly fragrant and white or pink, are followed by capsules of small seeds. Numerous cultivated strains, some dwarf, in various colours.

Uses: occasionally used as stimulant for nervous system, but normally grown as a handsome flowering plant in herb gardens.

Cultivation: sow under glass in spring, or outdoors in frost-free areas, and transplant to flowering positions in full sun. Water frequently in dry weather.

Related species: *N. bigelovii, N. attentuata, N. benthamiana* and numerous other wild species have been used by indigenous peoples in North America and Australia as snuff and ritual smoking tobacco.

N. rustica (nicotine tobacco) and *N. tabaccum* (common tobacco) are the main cultivated forms for commercial production of smoking tobacco, nicotine insecticide and citric acid.

Ocimum basilicum (Labiatae)
(Sweet) **Basil**
St Joseph wort

Description: bushy aromatic annual with brittle branched stems to 60 cm/2 ft. Leaves oval, shiny, fleshy and fragile, dark green or red tinted, such as dark opal basil; flowers creamy white or mauve in whorls, in midsummer. Grows wild in hot, humid regions, and cultivated extensively in numerous forms such as Greek, lemon, red or ruffled basils.

Uses: popular culinary flavouring, typical of Mediterranean cuisines and used since ancient times (remains have been found in Egyptian burial chambers). Oil of basil used in perfumery, soaps, cosmetics and liqueurs. Plant is claimed to be an insect repellant, and can be used medicinally to soothe pain and treat vomiting, nervous stress and headaches.

Cultivation: sow under glass in spring or outside after risks of frost are past. Grow in rich, moist soil, with full sun and shelter from cold winds; or treat as a pot plant, sowing in small pots to avoid root disturbance. Pinch out flowering shoots to extend useful life of plants, and root non-flowering side shoots in pots during summer for winter use.

Parts used: leaves fresh or frozen, or dried in shade (flavour will change considerably).

Related species: *O. kilimandsharicum* (camphor basil): African hairy perennial used to treat coughs and colds.

O. minimum (bush basil): hardier small-leaved dwarf plant, 15 cm/6 in, uses as for sweet basil; flavour bitter-resinous.

O. sanctum, syn. *O. tenuifolium* (holy basil): large, hairy plant with pink flowers; sacred in India, where it is known as *tulsi*.

O. viride (fever basil): West African species, used as a tea to treat fevers.

sweet basil

dark opal basil

purple ruffled basil

bush basil

Oenothera biennis (Onagraceae)
(Common) **Evening Primrose**
evening star, king's cure-all

Description: coarse biennial herb with thick fleshy taproot, and overwintering rosette of long, narrow willow-like leaves, bright green and wavy-edged with a reddish midrib. Robust flower stems to 1.8 m/6 ft bear large, sweet-scented pale yellow trumpets with red sepals in summer, individual blooms lasting only a single day, followed by elongated seed capsules. Grows wild in dry, sandy places; occasionally cultivated as a crop.

Uses: leaves are a winter pot herb, and may also be used to treat coughs and chest ailments. North American Indians have many uses for the plant, especially the roots, used in poultices for piles and boils; roots, sometimes known as German rampion, also eaten raw or cooked; ripe seeds used in bakery like poppy seeds. Medicinally the plant is an important source of gamma-linoleic acid, with other uses still under test.

Cultivation: sow in summer where plants are to grow, or in a seedbed for transplanting in autumn. Grow in full sun in light, well-drained soil.

Parts used: leaves, shoots and flowers for fresh culinary use; roots dug in autumn or early the following spring before growth resumes.

Related species: *O. erythrosepala* (large-flowered evening primrose): larger flowers with red stems, and edible shoots and roots.

Olea europaea (Oleaceae)
Olive

Description: slow-growing evergreen tree with gnarled trunk and slender grey, fissured branches, to 9 m/30 ft. Leaves dark green, scaly and grey beneath, narrow oblong or pointed. White, fragrant flowers in panicles in summer are followed by hard ovoid fruits, green at first but later purple-black, with a single hard stone. Thorny wild form grows on stony hillsides in Mediterranean regions, cultivated forms widely grown in groves.

Uses: since ancient times the principal source of edible oil in the eastern Mediterranean area; biblical symbol of peace. An olive wreath was given to victors in the Olympic Games. Not only the fruits but also the leaves are edible. Oil pressed from the fruits is a major culinary and medicinal product, sometimes used as a laxative and in enemas, and in treatments for minor wounds.

Cultivation: trees only grow well away from frost and tropical heat. Grow in dry, well-drained warm soils, with winter protection in cool regions, or in large pots under glass. Prune where necessary in spring. Propagate from seeds sown in warmth in autumn, or from cuttings taken in summer and rooted under glass.

Parts used: leaves; fruits picked when green, pink or red, or fully ripe, sometimes cracked, fermented and soaked in brine, or pressed for oil.

Origanum vulgare (Labiatae)
Oregano
wild marjoram, joy of the mountain, Mexican sage

Description: bushy, spicily aromatic perennial with horizontal woody rootstock and stems, often reddish, to 75 cm/30 in. Downy grey-green leaves, oval pointed and toothed, and small tubular flowers in clusters, pink or mauve with darker bracts, in late summer. Found wild on dry, fertile hillsides, usually on chalk, and widely grown both as a crop and a garden plant, often in variegated forms.

Uses: tonic, digestive and expectorant herb, used to treat coughs and sore throats, indigestion and gastric upsets. Antiseptic leaves are chewed for toothache, and added to baths and poultices. Important culinary flavouring for meat dishes and salads, the leaves are also made into tea and beer, or distilled into an oil for perfumes and cosmetics.

Cultivation: sow in spring outdoors and thin or transplant to 30 cm/12 in apart, or divide mature clumps in spring. Plant in light, well-drained soil in full sun (flavour more pungent in warmth), or grow in pots or a greenhouse border in cool regions.

Parts used: sprigs of leaves and flowers, or whole clump cut almost to ground

oregano

pot marjoram

level when in flower, for use fresh or dried in shade.

Related species: *O. dictamnus* (dittany of Crete): grey-leaved perennial with large, pink flowers; leaves have oregano flavour, used medicinally since Minoan times as painkiller and wound healer. *O. prismaticum* and *O. heracleoticum* (winter marjoram) have similar flavour, especially effective when dried.

O. majorana (sweet marjoram, knotted marjoram): sun-loving tender perennial often raised from seed each spring as an annual; mainly European culinary herb, with same medicinal uses as oregano.

O. onites (pot marjoram): tender perennial with white or pink flowers, for cooler gardens; ornamental plant also used like sweet marjoram.

Osmunda regalis (Osmundaceae)
❧ Royal Fern
buckthorn brake

Description: dense, clump-forming perennial terrestrial fern, with heavy rootstock of tangled, matted fibrous roots, and elegant buff-pink fronds up to 1.8 m/6 ft, streaked with creamy yellow in spring, later vivid green and turning golden brown in autumn. Leaflets at tips of fronds have spore-bearing sori in late summer. Grows wild in wet shady meadows.

Uses: handsome ornamental fern with mucilaginous roots, often boiled in water to produce royal fern jelly, once given to invalids as a nutritious, easily digested food, and also used to treat dysentery, coughs and pulmonary disorders. Dried roots (osmunda fibre) are a traditional ingredient of orchid potting composts.

Cultivation: grow in rich, moist soil, in damp shade or semi-shade. Mulch with compost every spring; water freely in dry weather. Divide in autumn or spring, or sow spores on surface of moist compost under glass in spring.

Parts used: main roots, fresh or dried, for medicinal use; thinner fibrous roots dried for compost.

Pelargonium graveolens (Geraniaceae)
❧ Rose Geranium

Description: tender perennial, green and succulent at first but later woody with light brown bark, up to 1.2 m/ 4 ft. Flowers small and pale pink in dense umbels in summer and autumn. Commercially grown for oil distillation; popular house plant in temperate regions.

Uses: rose-scented leaves used to scent desserts, cakes and teas, pot-pourri, drinks and fingerbowls. Oil distilled from the leaves is an insect repellent, used in perfumes.

Cultivation: sow seeds indoors in spring, or take cuttings in late summer and plant out the following summer in dry soils and full sun. Often grown as a house plant, best stood outdoors in summer to keep compact. May be grown permanently outdoors in warmer regions, cutting plants down in autumn and mulching with leaves or straw where light frost is possible.

Parts used: leaves, fresh or dried; all green parts, cut just before flowering for oil distillation.

Related species: *P. capitatum, P. radens*: alternative sources of rose-geranium fragrance. Other common species include *P. crispum* and *P. citriodorum* (lemon), *P. fragrans* (nutmeg), *P. nervosum* (lime), *P. odoratissimum* (apple), *P. parviflorum* (coconut), *P. tomentosum* (peppermint).

Petroselinum crispum (Umbelliferae)
❧ (Wild) Parsley

Description: biennial or short-lived perennial with rosette of rich green leaflets (tightly curled in many cultivated forms). In early summer a glossy, solid sharp-edged leafy flower stem, up to 75 cm/30 in, bears flat-topped umbels of yellow-green flowers, followed by capsules of brown seeds. Cultivated in gardens in numerous forms such as curly, plain 'Italian' and turnip-rooted Hamburg parsley.

Uses: tea made from leaves or roots used to treat jaundice, coughs and menstrual problems, rheumatism, kidney stones and urinary infections; juice expressed from them soothes conjunctivitis and eye inflammations. Both seeds and dried roots are used as spices; seeds, which contain poisonous apiol, are sometimes infused to produce an external vermifuge. **Caution:** avoid parsley during pregnancy or if suffering from kidney inflammation.

Cultivation: sow in spring in trays or outdoors in rich, moist soil – soak seeds for 24 hours in warm water or pour boiling water into seed drills immediately before sowing, as fluctuating temperatures hasten germination. Sow again in midsummer for winter use or for pots indoors.

Italian or continental parsley

curly-leaved parsley

Parts used: leaves, fresh, frozen or dried; roots dug in winter and dried; seeds when capsules are ripe.

Phlomis fruticosa (Labiatae)
🐦 **Jerusalem Sage**

Description: aromatic evergreen shrub with stout branching stems up to 3 m/10 ft. Silvery-green, wedge-shaped leaves are wrinkled and densely covered with yellow woolly hairs. Clear or rusty yellow tubular flowers appear in whorls in late summer. Grows wild in arid Mediterranean and Asian regions, and commonly grown as a shrub in herb and mixed borders.

Uses: mainly a handsome ornamental shrub; leaves sometimes made into an aromatic sage-flavoured tea, especially in Greece and neighbouring Mediterranean countries.

Cultivation: sow seeds in spring, take cuttings in summer or divide in spring or autumn. Grow in dryish, well-drained soil in full sun.

Parts used: leaves, fresh or dried in the sun.

Plantago major (Plantaginaceae)
🐦 **Greater Plantain**
broadleaf plantain, rat's tail plantain, waybread, white man's footprint

Description: tough-rooted perennial with coarse basal rosette of long-stalked, elliptical leaves, pointed and deeply veined. Tall, dense cylindrical spikes of tiny greenish-yellow flowers appear in summer, up to 45 cm/18 in, followed by a spike of seeds enclosed in sticky gelatinous pods. Found wild in cultivated land, waste ground, lawns and footpaths, where the spread of its sticky seeds is helped by passers-by. A local field crop in France, and also cultivated in gardens in improved forms.

Uses: an old herb, one of the nine sacred Saxon species and recovered from remains of Iron Age Tollund Man. The crushed leaves are cooling and pain-relieving, used in poultices and ointments for wounds and abrasions; an infusion of leaves or boiled roots is a useful gargle and eyewash; fresh leaves may be taken for both constipation and diarrhoea, according to the dosage. Very young leaves may be cooked like spinach; seeds are popular in Chinese and Malaysian drinks, and complete seedheads are fed to caged birds.

Cultivation: wild variety rarely grown deliberately, but seeds may be sown *in situ*, barely covered, in moist, fertile light soil or loam, in spring or autumn. Plants self-seed freely.

Parts used: leaves, fresh or dried quickly in sun or shade; roots, dug in winter and boiled; seed spikes, gathered in bags when they turn brown, and rubbed to free the seeds.

Related species: *P. coronopus* (crowfoot plantain, buckshorn plantain): biennial with dandelion-like leaves, used in salads while very young.

P. lanceolata (ribwort plantain): perennial with long, narrow leaves and short dense ribbed stem of yellow-brown flowers, used as cough remedy and wound healer.

P. media (hoary plantain): decorative perennial with scented, pink and white fluffy flowers, a great favourite with bees.

P. ovata (ispaghula): annual with medicinal seeds, producing a laxative and emollient oil.

P. psyllium (fleaseed), *P. indica* (branched plantain): annuals with branching globular heads of greenish flowers; known in Latin America as *llanten*, used in same way as ispaghula.

Portulaca oleracea (Portulacaceae)
(Wild) Purslane
pigweed

Description: warm-climate annual, with fleshy pinkish stems, prostrate and branching to 30 cm/12 in, bearing fleshy spatulate leaves, green or red-tinged. Small yellow flowers appear in the leaf axils in late summer, followed by seed capsules with opening lids and filled with numerous tiny black seeds. Grows wild in dry soils in vineyards and on hillsides in warm regions, a common weed in Australia, New Zealand and the United States; cultivated as an edible crop in the form var. *sativa* (kitchen-garden purslane), a larger erect plant with fleshy green or gold leaves.

Uses: ancient vegetable crop in India and Iran, still used as a salad herb and cooked vegetable. Infusion of the green plant is cooling and soothing, taken for fevers, headaches and chest complaints, and applied to skin rashes and abrasions. Seeds are an Australian Aboriginal wild condiment.

Cultivation: sow mid-spring in light, well-drained soil; water and feed regularly. Sow again for succession at monthly intervals until late summer.

Parts used: fresh leaves and stems, preferably before flowering, cut just above ground level.

Poterium sanguisorba, syn.
Sanguisorba minor (Rosaceae)
Salad Burnet

Description: clump-forming perennial with strong woody rootstock, and red, furrowed stems branching to 60 cm/ 2 ft. Grey-green pinnate leaves with rounded leaflets, each deeply indented, and small, bright red-brown petalless flowers in dense globular heads in early summer. Found wild in fields, woods and waste ground on dry chalk.

Uses: young leaves eaten as salad herb with cucumber-like flavour, and added to soups, sauces and cheeses. Leaves are digestive, and in infusions used to treat diarrhoea and haemorrhages. Decoction of root applied to cuts and burns; roots also produce a black dye and are used in tanning leather.

Cultivation: sow in spring in trays under glass, or divide roots in spring and plant in fertile soil in sun or light shade. Remove flowers to extend useful season for leaves. Plants self-seed very easily.

Parts used: young leaves before flowering; whole green plant, fresh or dried; roots dug in spring and dried.

Related species: *P. officinale,* syn. *Sanguisorba officinalis* (great burnet, bloodwort): taller herb with deep red, rectangular flowerheads; similar uses.

Prunella vulgaris (Labiatae)
Selfheal
heal-all, woundwort, carpenter's herb

Description: downy perennial with creeping rhizome and square stems to 30 cm/12 in. Long narrow oval leaves, bright green, pointed and toothed; flowers purple, pink or white in dense whorls in midsummer. Grows wild in moist meadows and pastures; many cultivated forms with larger flowers grown in gardens.

Uses: used in Middle Ages according to the 'Doctrine of Signatures' to treat throat conditions and internal bleeding, and regarded as a panacea by North American Indians and Chinese physicians, the latter using the seeds for nervous complaints. Flowering plant may be eaten in salads and cooked vegetable dishes, used to prepare a styptic for wounds, and made into gargles or mouthwashes for mouth ulcers and sore throats.

Cultivation: take cuttings or divide plants in spring, and plant out 20 cm/8 in apart as ground cover in moist shade or full sun. In fertile soils plants are much larger than normal and may be invasive; growing in turf helps restrain unnatural growth.

Parts used: green flowering plant, fresh or dried in shade.

Pulmonaria officinalis
(Boraginaceae)

❧ **Lungwort**

maple lungwort, spotted dog,
Jerusalem cowslip

Description: downy perennial with
creeping rootstock; stems hairy and
unbranched, up to 30 cm/12 in.
Rough leaves in a rosette over winter,
broadly oval and pointed, green with
grey spots, stem leaves narrower.
Flowers bell-shaped in small, leafy
sprays, pink at first and later becoming blue, or white or purple, in early
spring. Grows wild in woods and
hedgerows on chalk; often cultivated
as ground cover in shade.

Uses: ancient cure for lung disorders
according to 'Doctrine of Signatures'.
Young leaves used as spring pot herb
in soups, stews and salads; flowering
plant made into a tea for gastro-
intestinal and pulmonary ailments;
homeopathically used for bronchitis
and colds. Powdered roots and lower
leaves are wound-healing.

Cultivation: divide in autumn or after
flowering, and plant in light soils, not
too dry, in shade or semi-shade. Lift,
divide and replant every 4-5 years.

Parts used: young fresh leaves gathered; green flowering plant, fresh or
dried; roots dug in winter, cut, dried
and powdered.

Related species: *P. saccharata*
(Bethlehem sage): larger plant,
with leaves heavily marked with silver, flowers appear as lilac, white or
blue; grown as a foliage plant; similar uses to *P. officinalis*.

Reseda luteola (Resedaceae)

❧ **Weld**

dyer's rocket

Description: coarse unbranched biennial with an overwintering rosette of
long, narrow wavy-edged leaves. In
summer stout leafy stem, 1.5 m/5 ft,
terminates in long, slim spike of small
bright yellow or yellow-green flowers.
Found wild in dry disturbed soils in
chalky areas.

Uses: traditional dye plant, once widely cultivated or gathered from the wild
for brilliant yellow or reddish-yellow
colour extracted from leaves, flowers
and stems.

Cultivation: sow seeds where plants are
to flower, in late summer in well-
drained, fertile soil with a little lime.
Seedlings appear in spring and should
be thinned to 45 cm/18 in apart.

Parts used: whole green plant gathered
at flowering time.

Related species: *R. lutea* (wild
mignonette): similar to weld, but
shorter with divided, wrinkled
leaves; popular and decorative bee
and butterfly plant.

R. odorata (common mignonette):
perennial normally grown as an
annual, both outdoors and in pots,
for its intensely fragrant tiny yellow
and white flowers, from which oil is
extracted for perfume; a soothing
herb for calming nerves, healing
wounds, and treating asthma and
hayfever; once used to stuff pillows
as a remedy for insomnia.

Rosmarinus officinalis (Labiatae)

❧ **Rosemary**

Description: dense, woody evergreen
perennial, up to 3 m/10 ft. Bushy
stems with cracked grey bark and
downy young shoots are covered with
narrow aromatic, hard leaves, dark
and shiny above, greyish beneath.
Short racemes of small blue flowers
appear in early summer. Grows wild
on dry, rocky slopes and cliffs in warm
regions, and widely cultivated both
commercially and in gardens in
numerous forms.

Uses: ancient strewing herb and
Romany charm, hung up to ward off
evil; popular culinary flavouring
added to meat dishes, baked foods
and Mediterranean recipes. Leaves
medicinally valuable and for treating
depression, migraine, and disorders
of the liver and digestion. Leaves also
made into ointment for neuralgia,
rheumatism, eczema and minor
wounds, and used in hair rinses
and mouthwashes. **Caution:** excessive
quantities or frequent use may cause
poisoning.

Cultivation: sow seeds in trays in
spring, take cuttings in summer in a
cold frame, or layer plants in autumn.
Plant in well-drained, alkaline soil,
in a sunny position sheltered from
winds. Some forms are slightly tender
and may need protection in winter.

Parts used: leaves gathered at flowering time, used fresh or dried in shade.

Rubia tinctorum (Rubiaceae)
🌿 **Dyer's Madder**
dyer's cleavers

Description: herbaceous perennial with long fleshy complex yellow rootstock and red fibrous roots, and stiff square, prickly climbing stems up to 90 cm/3 ft, with whorls of pale green bristly leaves, long and pointed. Clusters of small greenish-yellow flowers appear in midsummer, followed by blue-black berries. Grows wild in hedges and thickets on chalk, often as an escape from former wide cultivation.

Uses: infusions of leaves and stems treat constipation, and liver and bladder disorders; powdered root is wound-healing, often used for skin ulcers. Homeopathically used to treat anaemia and ailments of the spleen. Most popular use of the roots is as a variable red to purple dye.

Cultivation: sow seeds or divide plants in spring or autumn, and plant in deep well-broken, alkaline soil in full sun or semi-shade.

Parts used: leaves and stems; roots peeled and dried quickly, and powdered or fermented.

Related species: R. *peregrina* (wild madder): similar plant, though coarser in appearance, producing a paler red dye.

Rumex rugosus, syn. *R. acetosa* (Polygonaceae)
🌿 **Common Sorrel**

French sorrel

common sorrel

Description: leafy perennial with thin vertical rootstock, and basal clumps of thick shiny, arrow-shaped leaves. Leafy slender flower stems in early summer, slightly branching to 1.2 m/4 ft, bear loose spikes of small red-brown flowers. Grows wild in damp fields and waste land.

Uses: popular, sharply flavoured pot herb since ancient Egyptian times, widely used by medieval apothecaries. Cooling and blood-cleansing, often taken as a spring tonic tea. Leaves made into poultices for acne and other skin complaints, and if picked very young can be eaten raw or cooked, notably in sorrel soup; juice of leaves will curdle milk and has also been used as a stain remover ('salts of sorrel'). Roots make a bitter tonic and a treatment for diarrhoea. **Caution:** leaves are high in oxalic acid and should be eaten sparingly; handling them may cause skin irritations.

Cultivation: sow in spring, thinning seedlings to 30 cm/12 in apart, or divide roots in autumn. Grow in rich, moist soil, and keep well watered.

Gather leaves frequently and remove flower stems to extend cropping.

Parts used: young leaves and buds, picked before flowering, and used fresh or frozen; roots fresh in summer.

Related species: R. *acetosella* (sheep sorrel, red sorrel): small smooth arrow-shaped leaves, piquant in salads or less sour cooked.

R. *alpinus* (monk's rhubarb): broad leaves, and thick creeping rhizome used in infusion as a treatment for constipation.

R. *crispus* (curled dock, yellow dock): tall with large, wavy leaves, used for skin complaints; root is laxative, powdered to make mouthwash and gargle; stems stewed like rhubarb; seeds ground and used in baking.

R. *patientia* (herb patience, sorrel-dock): tall and branched, leaves with low acidity, can be used as spinach substitute.

R. *scutatus* (French sorrel, round-leaved sorrel): short leafy plant, low in oxalic acid, used as a salad ingredient and pot herb.

R. *vesicarius* (ruby dock, wild hops): thick broad leaves and tall, bright red flowers; leaves popular vegetable with Bedu, young shoots can be added to salads.

Ruta graveolens (Rutaceae)

❧ **Rue**

herb of grace

Description: semi-evergreen perennial shrub with woody base and branching stems up to 90 cm/3 ft. Powerfully aromatic green or blue-green leaves divided into a number of spatulate leaflets, dotted with shiny oil glands. Loose racemes of small pungent yellow or yellowish-green flowers appear in summer. Found wild on dry, rocky limestone soils; cultivated in gardens as an ornamental shrub, often in blue, gold or variegated forms.

Uses: ancient medicinal herb, formerly used as an antidote to poisoning and a talisman against witchcraft. A favourite Arab herb, the only one to be blessed by Mohammed; leaves used homeopathically to treat phlebitis and varicose veins, and herbally for epilepsy, nervous complaints and uterine disorders. Essential oil used in perfumery and cosmetics; small amounts of the pungent foliage used for flavouring foods and alcoholic drinks. **Caution:** to be taken internally only under medical supervision, and used externally with care as allergic skin reactions are possible.

Cultivation: sow in a seedbed outdoors in spring, or take cuttings in late summer, and plant in full sun in well-drained soil with a little lime.

Parts used: leaves from flowering plant, fresh or dried in shade.

Salvia officinalis (Labiatae)

❧ **Sage**

Description: variable evergreen perennial shrub, with strong taproot, and square woody, branching stems up to 75 cm/2 ft 6 in, grey and woolly when young. Grey-green, pebbly-textured soft leaves are oblong or lanceolate, and finely toothed. Whorls of violet-blue flowers appear in spikes in summer. Found wild on hillsides and grassland on chalk in warm regions; widely cultivated as a pot herb in Mediterranean countries; popular herb garden shrub with numerous forms and decorative varieties, some gold or variegated. Best culinary sages are the plain narrow-leaved and non-flowering broad-leaved types.

Uses: an ancient herb, popular as a potent condiment for meat, fish, Mediterranean dishes, English Sage Derby cheese, and as a basis for sage tea, taken to counteract sweating. Infusion used to treat depression, nervous anxiety and liver disorders; homeopathic preparations given for circulation and menopausal problems. Leaves are also antiseptic, used in gargles for laryngitis and tonsillitis,

common sage

and as a mouth freshener and tooth cleanser. Essential oil used in perfumery.

Cultivation: grow in well-drained, rich soil, in full sun and with shelter from cold winds. Propagate from cuttings in spring and summer, or by layering (mounding for older bushes). Nip off points of shoots to induce bushy growth, and renew every 4-5 years as shrubs become leggy.

Parts used: leaves fresh, or dried in shade, picked before flowering for herbal use or when in flower for oil distillation.

variegated sage

clary sage

(Continued)

(*Sage* continued)

Related species: *S. azurea*: large blue-flowered perennial shrub, used in Mexico as a herbal panacea.

S. sclarea (clary sage): biennial with white, blue or pink flowers; leaves infused as a gargle and skin healer; source of muscatel oil for flavouring and perfumery.

S. viridis, syn. *S. horminum* (clary): annual, very similar to clary sage and similar uses; often grown as a flowering bedding plant.

S. horminoides (wild clary), *S. verbenaca*: purple-flowered species with jagged, toothed leaves and red stems; uses similar to clary sage.

S. fruticosa, syn. *S. triloba* (three-lobed sage): large perennial with lobed leaves, grown in Mediterranean countries for making the popular sage tea.

S. rutilans (pineapple sage): tender perennial with scarlet flowers in autumn and winter; fresh leaves add strong pineapple flavouring to desserts and drinks.

Sambucus nigra (Caprifoliaceae)

(Common) Elder (Berry)

Description: deciduous shrub or small tree with roughly fissured bark and numerous straight branches, up to 9 m/ 30 ft. Leaves pungent and dull green, with 5-7 elliptical leaflets; red flowering stems bear broad, flat-topped heads of small white, fragrant flowers in midsummer, followed by numerous edible purple-black berries. Found wild in hedgerows, woods and built-up areas; commercially cultivated on a local scale; ornamental varieties (white, gold, cut-leaf) frequently grown in gardens.

Uses: legendary tree, long held to be guardian over all other herbs, with numerous virtues according to the part used. Leaves are an effective insect repellent, and soothing in ointments for skin complaints. Flowers soothe the eyes, are added to cosmetics, make a calming tea, and are popular for their sweet fragrance in drinks and fruit dishes. Fruits are used in cordials, syrups and preserves; medicinally to induce sweating and to treat coughs, colds, catarrh and throat infections; and as a blue-purple dye. Bark is an old treatment for epilepsy, and (together with the leaves) is laxative; root used for kidney ailments.

Cultivation: usually harvested as a wild plant, but may be grown in almost any soil and position (variegated forms best positioned in full sun for maximum colour). Propagate by hardwood cuttings, easily rooted outdoors in autumn, or by suckers.

Parts used: leaves, flowers and fruits, fresh or dried; root and bark gathered as needed.

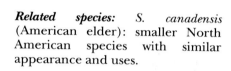

Related species: *S. canadensis* (American elder): smaller North American species with similar appearance and uses.

S. ebulus (dwarf elder, danewort): dwarf, strong-smelling perennial with creeping rhizomes, otherwise similar to common elder; used homeopathically for dropsy; berries give a blue dye; bark and flowers purgative (berries dangerously so).

S. racemosa (red-berries elder): small tree with more pointed leaves, flowers in early dense clusters, and scarlet berries in summer; purgative oil extracted from the seeds.

Santolina chamaecyparissus, syn.
S. incana (Compositae)
❧ Santolina
cotton lavender

Description: pungent evergreen perennial shrub with branched white stems up to 50 cm/20 in, silver-grey filamentous leaves, toothed along the edges. Fragrant small, bright yellow flowers like hard round buttons appear in midsummer. Grows wild in dry rocky places and warm soils; popular in gardens as an ornamental shrub and dwarf hedging plant.

Uses: grown and used since classical Greek times as a vermifuge and moth repellent. Infusion of leaves used as a rub for rheumatism and painful joints; flowers make a tonic tea. Perhaps most popular today as a decorative hedging plant for parterres and knot gardens.

Cultivation: grow in well-drained, light soil in full sun. Propagate by layering, or root cuttings with a heel in autumn or spring outdoors or in a cold frame. Clip hedges to shape in spring, and again at flowering time if only foliage is important.

Parts used: leaves before flowering, dried and stripped from stalks; flowers.

Related species: S. *neapolitana* (Italian lavender): taller plant with very feathery grey foliage and pale lemon-yellow flowers; similar uses.

Satureja hortensis (Labiatae)
❧ Summer Savory
bean herb

Description: hairy aromatic annual with tough straggly or erect stems, up to 45 cm/18 in. Long, dark green leaves, leathery and pointed, and lilac-pink or white flowers in small spikes from the leaf axils in late summer. Grows wild in dry, light soils and on rocky hillsides on chalk; locally cultivated for commercial use; popular garden herb.

summer savory

Uses: culinary herb whose use dates back to the early Romans; potent flavouring enhances all others in the same way as salt. Used sparingly in meat dishes and stuffings, with peas, beans and cabbage to improve their digestibility, and liqueurs. Infusion of leaves treats gastric upsets, indigestion and loss of appetite; tea is tonic. Spreading flowering shoots between clothing repels moths.

Cultivation: sow seeds in spring where plants are to grow, in well-drained soil in full sun. Species is sensitive to cold: delay sowing until the worst frosts are past, or grow the hardier winter savory. Plants self-seed freely.

Parts used: leaves gathered before flowering, fresh or dried in shade; flowering shoots fresh or dried.

winter savory

Related species: S. *montana* (winter savory): semi-evergreen bushy and woody perennial shrub, with smaller pink or white flowers and a stronger flavour; commercially cropped for essential oil; other uses similar.

Scabiosa arvensis, syn. *Knautia arvensis* (Dipsaceae)
❧ **Field Scabious**
blue buttons, pincushion flower

Description: evergreen perennial, with short rootstock and creeping stolons, long indented leaves. Bristly stem, up to 90 cm/3 ft, bears flat heads of mauve flowers in late summer, followed by densely hairy seedheads.

Uses: infusion of roots treats cuts, sores, abrasions and itching; whole herb used as a remedy for dandruff. Homeopathically used for eczema and skin disorders.

Cultivation: sow in trays in autumn or spring, divide roots in spring or take cuttings of short side shoots. Grow in full sun in fertile, well-drained soil.

Parts used: whole flowering herb including roots, fresh or dried; roots dug in autumn, fresh or dried.

Related species: *Succisa pratensis*, syn. *Scabiosa pratensis* (devil's bit, daisy fleabane): perennial with purple, blue or white flowers; root used for wounds and diarrhoea; leaves eaten raw or cooked like spinach.

Scutellaria galericulata (Labiatae)
❧ **(Common) Skullcap**
helmet flower

Description: downy perennial with creeping rhizome; short-stalked oval pointed leaves, bluntly toothed and dark green, with red veins on underside. Stems, up to 30 cm/12 in, in summer bear large slender tubular bright violet-blue flowers in pairs. Found wild in moist lowlands, especially wet meadows.

Uses: bitter tonic and digestive herb; powerful nerve tonic, used in infusion to treat depression, headaches, insomnia, irritability and similar disorders. (Out of flower, skullcap is easily confused with wood sage, *Teucrium scorodonia*.)

Cultivation: sow seeds outdoors in spring, or divide roots in spring, and grow in good moist soil in an open, sunny position.

Parts used: all green parts during flowering, fresh or dried.

Sedum acre (Crassulaceae)
❧ **Biting Stonecrop**
wall pepper, golden-carpet, gold moss

Description: succulent mat-forming perennial shrub with sprawling stems, and erect branches up to 20 cm/8 in crowded with overlapping cylindrical short green fleshy leaves, hot and peppery to the taste. Leafy stems extend in midsummer and produce bright yellow flowers, 5-petalled and star-shaped, in loose clusters. Grows wild on walls and roofs and in dry stony soils, often on lime; and in gardens as a wall, rock garden and edging plant.

Uses: plants were often grown deliberately on roofs as charms against lightning. Homeopathically used to treat piles; bruised leaves, fresh or in ointments, are soothing for wounds, abcesses, bruises and minor burns. ***Caution:*** slightly poisonous; internal use may cause dizziness and nausea.

Cultivation: grow in full sun in dryish, sandy soil with a little lime. Sow seeds outdoors or divide roots in spring, or scatter some of the cylindrical leaves which root freely where they fall.

Parts used: leaves, fresh or dried in warmth.

Related species: *S. reflexum* (reflexed stonecrop): long-stemmed robust perennial, with long cylindrical leaves and golden-yellow 7-petalled flowers. Fresh non-flowering shoots are often added to soups and salads, or cooked as a tangy vegetable.

Sempervivum tectorum
(Crassulaceae)
❧ **Houseleek**
hen-and-chickens

Description: fleshy perennial with short-stemmed rosette of tightly packed fleshy grey-green leaves, sometimes red-tipped, arranged in a spiral. Stem elongates in summer to form a thick leafy flower stem, 20 cm/8 in high, with clusters of small rose-pink star-like blooms. Grows wild on walls, roofs and rocky mountain sites; often cultivated in pots, sinks and rock gardens.

Uses: ancient magical herb, planted on roofs as an insurance against fire and lightning. Sliced or crushed leaves used to poultice stings, burns, rashes and itching skin, and to cure warts and corns. Sometimes used as a skin lotion. In some parts of Europe young leaves and shoots are eaten as a vegetable.

Cultivation: grow in full sun in crevices and mortar joints packed with a little ordinary soil, or in sinks and pots filled with gritty compost. Propagate from seeds or leaves in trays at any time.

Parts used: leaves, sliced or pulped, as needed.

Silybum marianum (Compositae)
❧ **Milk Thistle**
variegated thistle, Our Lady's milk thistle, spotted thistle

Description: prickly annual or biennial, with a thick taproot and downy white, furrowed stems up to 1.2 m/4 ft. Leaves oblong, wavy and spiny-edged, glossy dark green with clear white veins, and flowers red-purple and thistle-like above a collar of spiny bracts in midsummer.

Uses: the herb has had a reputation for treating liver disorders since classical Roman times, and is included in several proprietary medicines for this purpose. Used in herbal infusions and homeopathic preparations for liver and abdominal ailments. Young shoots and leaves are edible and an Arab delicacy; roots may be cooked like parsnips, and base of flowerheads in the same way as artichokes; stems can be peeled and boiled as a vegetable; seedlings eaten raw in salads.

Cultivation: sow in spring in a sunny bed where plants are to grow, and thin seedlings to 60 cm/2 ft apart.

Parts used: seedlings; young leaves and shoots; flower stems just before flowering; roots after flowering; flowerheads for medicinal use, fresh or dried in thin layers in warmth.

Smyrnium olusatrum
(Umbelliferae)
❧ **Alexanders**
black lovage, horse parsley

Description: pungent biennial with solid ridged stems up to 1.5 m/5 ft, and large shiny, dark green leaves divided into several trefoil toothed leaflets. Flowers yellow-green and glistening with nectar, in small round umbels in midsummer, followed by globular capsules of aromatic black seeds. Grows wild on rocky banks and sea cliffs.

Uses: bitter herb cultivated since early Greek times; root is diuretic, seeds a condiment, crushed leaves or their juice a soothing and healing treatment for cuts and minor abrasions. Grown as a salad and pot herb before celery became popular, with the leaves, stems, shoots and flower buds all used, sometimes after blanching, in soups and fish dishes.

Cultivation: grow in full sun in moist soil. Sow in spring and grow as an annual leaf crop, or in autumn to overwinter and produce larger stems the following year.

Parts used: young leaves; young stems, after blanching with soil or straw if preferred; roots fresh or dried; ripe seeds.

Solidago virgaurea (Compositae)
ఎ **Golden Rod**

Description: herbaceous perennial with a stout knotted rhizome, and downy slender leafy stems occasionally branched, up to 1.5 m/5 ft. Leaves narow oval or lanceolate, and toothed; flowers tiny, bright yellow and powdery, in panicles on branched spikes in late summer. Found wild in woods, hedges and the edges of fields; commonly grown as an ornamental plant in several cultivated forms.

Uses: a medieval Arab healing herb, also used by North American Indians; made into poultices for external wounds, and infusions for fevers and digestive upsets. Occurs in several proprietary medicines for kidney and bladder ailments, and used homeopathically to treat these, as well as arthritis and rheumatism.

Cultivation: sow in spring outdoors, or divide in autumn or spring, and grow in light soils in full sun or light shade. Lift, divide and replant every 3-4 years.

Parts used: green flowering plant before flowerheads fully opened, fresh or dried in shade.

Stellaria media
ఎ **Common Chickweed**

Description: variable fast-growing clump-forming or sprawling annual, with weak branching straggling stems, up to 45 cm/18 in long, each with a single line of longitudinal hairs. Small soft, oval fleshy leaves, long-stalked and yellowish-green, and tiny white flowers with separate thin petals, at any time. A common 'weed', forming dense mats on moist, cultivated and waste ground.

Uses: an ancient pot herb; seeds found in Neolithic burial sites. Traditionally fed to domesticated birds and fowls; a bitter salad and pot herb; homeopathic remedy for rheumatism. Poultice of stems and leaves used to ease arthritis and pains of the joints, cuts, skin irritations and inflammation.

Cultivation: seldom necessary. Plants self-seed themselves all too freely in all soils`and positions, especially in dry weather.

Parts used: young stems and leaves, fresh or dried.

Symphytum officinale (Boraginaceae)
ఎ **Comfrey**
knitbone

Description: stout rough perennial with thick brown, fleshy rootstock, and clumps of upright basal hairy leaves, long, oval and pointed. Branched stems up to 1.2 m/4 ft bear purple, pink or white bell-shaped flowers in forked, curled clusters in summer. Found wild in streams, ditches and other wet places; widely cultivated in selected forms for garden use.

Uses: root formerly a popular internal remedy for gastric disorders and a homeopathic treatment for ulcers. Leaves used in infusion for bronchitis, and in poultices for wounds, bruises and eczema. Young leaves and shoots were eaten as a vegetable, cooked with a change of water. Older leaves commonly used after wilting as an animal feed, for making compost and liquid fertilizer, and for mulching plants. **Caution:** absolutely not to be used internally under any circumstances – recent evidence suggests the plant is carcinogenic.

comfrey

Cultivation: divide roots in spring or autumn, or take root cuttings in spring. Plant in moist soil in sun or shade, and mulch annually with decayed manure for maximum leaf production. Lift, divide and replant every 3-4 years. May need containment.

Russian comfrey

variegated Russian comfrey

Parts used: leaves, fresh, wilted or dried; roots fresh or split lengthways and dried in sun.

Related species: *S.* x *uplandicum* (Russian comfrey): stiffly hairy, vigorous hybrid with larger leaves, cultivated for leaf production (up to 4-6 cuts per year); often found wild in dry places as an escape.

Tanacetum parthenium, syn. Chrysanthemum parthenium, Matricaria parthenium
(Compositae)
🐌 Feverfew

Description: robust downy perennial with branched stems up to 90 cm/3 ft. Leaves yellow-green and pungent, divided into several smaller rounded leaflets. Flowers small white daisies with prominent yellow centres, in dense clusters in midsummer.

Uses: a bitter-flavoured herb, long used as a tonic and to treat indigestion, but currently popular as a treatment for migraine. Leaves are made into pain-soothing poultices for limb and joint aches, and whole flowering stems are an insect repellant, keeping moths away from clothing. A popular bee plant. **Caution:** not to be taken during pregnancy; fresh leaves may cause mouth ulcers.

Cultivation: sow in spring outdoors on the surface and water in, or take cuttings in summer. Grow in dry, well-drained soil in full sun. Plants self-seed very easily.

Parts used: leaves or whole green flowering plant, fresh or dried in shade.

Related species: *T. vulgare,* syn. *Chrysanthemum vulgare* (tansy): pungent perennial, with feathery dark green leaves and flat heads of yellow button-like flowers; an old strewing herb, insect repellent (companion plant to ward off aphids) and vermifuge; crushed leaves used to treat bruises and varicose veins; leaves once added to lamb dishes and spring puddings.

Taraxacum officinale agg.
(Compositae)
🐌 Dandelion
blowball

Description: complex group of perennials with long, stout taproots, and milky sap. Flowers on hollow stems, often reddish and downy near the top, up to 45 cm/18 in; large, sweet-scented and yellow, in late spring to early autumn, followed by fluffy heads of numerous seeds, each with a parasol of white hairs to aid wind distribution.

Uses: leaves are a diuretic; dried to make tonic teas; added to herbal beer; blanched for salads. Flowers used in wines, schnapps, pancakes and in Arab baking; inside surface of flower stems soothes burns and stings (also stains skin). Roots roasted as a coffee substitute, cooked in Japanese cuisines, and give a magenta dye (with the leaves they produce brown dyes). Medicinally, given for gall-bladder and liver complaints.

Cultivation: often gathered from the wild, but may be grown as an annual by sowing in full sun in spring, barely covering seeds.

Parts used: leaves fresh or dried in warmth; flowers when fully opened in sun; roots dug in summer for medicinal use, or autumn for drying and grinding for coffee.

Related species: *T. kok-saghyz* (Russian dandelion): similar Russian wild plant, with rich milky sap, producing latex, used together with roots of *Scorzonera tau-saghyz* to make rubber.

Microseris scapigera (Australian dandelion): similar plant with larger flowers and stout yam-like root used as a vegetable by Aborigines.

Teucrium chamaedrys (Labiatae)
Wall Germander

Description: semi-evergreen perennial with purplish stems, sprawling or upright to 30 cm/12 in. Leaves oval with rounded teeth; flowers dark lilac-purple, pink or white, in summer.

Uses: leaves used in tonic teas, wines and liqueurs, and for treating digestive and gall-bladder disorders. Plants used for edging and hedges in herb and knot gardens.

Cultivation: sow seeds in spring outdoors, take cuttings in summer, or divide plants in autumn. Grow in well-drained soil with a little lime. Clip hedges in spring and again in midsummer.

Parts used: whole flowering plant, fresh or dried in shade.

Related species: *T. fruticans* (tall germander): larger plant with white stems, blue-green leaves and large blue flowers.

T. scorodonia (wood sage, wood germander): pebbly sage-like leaves and yellow flowers, smelling faintly of garlic, prefers acid soils in shade; leaves used to heal and dry wounds, and in teas inhaled for throat and sinus problems.

Thlaspi arvense (Cruciferae)
Field Pennycress

Description: strong-smelling annual with branched stem to 45 cm/18 in, oval leaves, often clasping the stem. Small white flowers in spikes appear in spring and summer, followed by pods containing black seeds. Grows wild in waste places, and sometimes a troublesome 'weed' of arable ground.

Uses: finely chopped leaves have a spicy flavour like watercress, and are used in salads and cooked dishes. Seeds were once ground and used as a mustard.

Cultivated: rarely necessary, but may be sown *in situ* in spring in fertile soil.

Parts used: leaves and young shoots before flowering; seeds dried in the sun and ground.

Related species: *T. alliaceum* (garlic pennycress): similar plant, with earlier flowers, narrow seedpods and scent of garlic, similar uses.

Thymus vulgaris (Labiatae)
Common Thyme
garden thyme

Description: variable aromatic perennial evergreen shrub with gnarled thin, square stems, woody at the base, prostrate or upright to 30 cm/12 in. Leaves small, elliptical and grey-green, paler beneath; small flowers in summer, lilac or white, fragrant and popular with bees. Found wild on warm, dry rocky banks and heaths; widely grown commercially for the leaves and essential oil; favourite culinary and hedging herb in gardens, with numerous decorative and variegated forms.

Uses: popular since classical times, thyme has a number of important uses. Leaves make a tonic and stimulating tea, used to treat digestive complaints and respiratory disorders, especially for loosening mucus. Antiseptic and vermifuge essential oil (thymol) added to disinfectants, toothpaste, perfumes, toiletries and liqueurs. A culinary herb with a powerful flavour, thyme is added sparingly to bouquets garnis, stuffings and savoury dishes.

common thyme

Cultivation: sow seeds or take cuttings in summer; divide plants in spring, or layer older bushes by mounding. Plant in very well drained soil in full sun. Clip after flowering and again in autumn; replace every 4-5 years, and in cold climates protect in winter, grow in containers or as a hedge.

lemon thyme

caraway thyme

wild thyme

Parts used: leaves and flowering tips, fresh or dried in sun.

Related species: T. capitatus (cone-head thyme): large-flowered species, grown commercially for essential oil production.

T. x *citriodora* (lemon thyme): light green species with pink flowers and strong lemon scent.

T. herba-barona (caraway thyme); arching stems rooting at tips, bronze-green leaves, strong caraway flavour.

T. mastichinus: grey-green leaves and pink flowers; widely grown in Spain for flavouring, marinades and as essential accompaniment to olives.

T. serpyllum (wild thyme, mother of thyme): very hardy, mat-forming species with late red-purple flowers and mild flavour; ideal for herb lawns; reputation as a herb for women's ailments.

Trifolium pratense (Leguminosae)
Red Clover

Description: short-lived perennial often grown as an annual, with branching roots, and arching stems, up to 50 cm/20 in. Leaves long-stemmed and trefoil. Flowers pink-mauve in summer and autumn.

Uses: dried flowers produce a volatile oil and a soothing tea for promoting sleep; taken medicinally as an expectorant for respiratory disorders, and to treat skin problems such as eczema and psoriasis. Externally, an infusion soothes burns and sores. Flowers also make a good wine and yield a yellow dye.

Cultivation: sow in spring (rub the seeds with sandpaper to improve germination) in free-draining, slightly alkaline soil in rows or patches.

Parts used: flowerheads, fresh or dried in shade.

Related species: T. alexandrinum (berseem, Egyptian clover): very tall white fodder crop grown in Egypt and Middle East.

T. amabile (Aztec clover): Mexican and South American species, eaten as a pot herb mixed with cereals.

T. hybridum (alsike clover): small white-flowered hybrid grown as fodder and green manure in cold regions and on wet acid soils.

T. repens (white clover, Dutch clover): creeping, drought-resistant perennial with larger leaves and fragrant white or pinkish flowers liked by bees; numerous cultivated forms.

Tropaeolum majus
(Tropaeolaceae)
Nasturtium

Description: South American perennial grown in temperate climates as an annual, with creeping or climbing stems to 3 m/10 ft. Leaves bright green or blue-green. Flowers orange, sometimes red or yellow, in summer and autumn, followed by spherical fruits, first green and then brown, containing three large seeds.

Uses: antiseptic and digestive herb, also used to treat respiratory and urinary disorders; seeds are a vermifuge, and crushed for use in poultices for boils and sores. Leaves are edible and used in salads, the flowers as a garnish, and both seeds and flower buds are pickled for their pungent mustard-like flavour.

Cultivation: sow spring or early summer where plants are to grow, or in pots for transplanting after frosts cease. Grow in full sun with shelter from wind, in rich soil for leaf crops, poorer dry ground for flowers and seeds.

Parts used: leaves fresh or dried; flowers; seeds while green, or when ripe for grinding as seasoning.

Tussilago farfara (Compositae)
❧ **Coltsfoot**
coughwort, horse-hoof

Description: robust herbaceous perennial with white, scaly creeping stolons,
and pale red downy, scaly stems, up to
30 cm/12 in, bearing golden-yellow
dandelion-like flowers that open in
sun in early spring. Sturdy long-
stemmed fragrant leaves follow in late
spring from basal clumps, rounded or
heart-shaped, irregularly toothed and
up to 30 cm/12 in in diameter, pale
beneath with a network of clear veins.
A wild plant of ditches, moist banks,
waste places and loamy soils.

Uses: leaves are an important cough
remedy for bronchitis and laryngitis,
commonly added to herbal smoking
mixtures. Both leaves (after crushing
the veins) and flowers can be used in
poultices for sores and ulcers; root is
boiled to make coltsfoot rock or
candy. Flowers are made into wine,
and mature leaves can be dried and
burnt to an ash used as a salt substitute. **Caution:** roots contain similar
substances to comfrey, and may be
equally dangerous if taken internally.

Cultivation: usually gathered from the
wild, but seeds may be sown in moist
soil in summer, or plants divided in
autumn or used for root cuttings in
winter. Plant where exposed to sunlight for most of the day. In some soils
may become invasive.

Parts used: flowers before fully open,
fresh or dried in shade; leaves in summer, fresh or cut up and dried in
shade.

Urtica dioica (Urticaceae)
❧ **Stinging Nettle**

Description: stinging perennial with
branching roots, and bristly stems
sprawling or erect up to 1.8 m/6 ft.
Leaves covered in stinging hairs; tiny
yellow-green flowers, females hanging
like catkins, males in spikes in summer and autumn.

Uses: young shoots and leaves widely
used in spring soups and as a green
vegetable, and added to beer. Older
leaves laxative in infusion, expectorant and styptic. Made into hair restor-
ers and used homeopathically to treat
skin ailments. Stems fibres are strong
enough for linen weaving, papermak-
ing and spining into ropes. Foliage
is a commercial source of chlorophyll
and an effective compost activator.
Caution: handle with care, as the
formic acid injected by serious stings
may cause recurrent 'nettle rash'.

Cultivation: rarely necessary, but seeds
may be sown in summer in fertile soil,
or roots can be divided in spring.

Parts used: leaves gathered before
flowering, fresh or dried in sun.

Related species: *U. breweri, U. thunber-
giana:* North American and Japanese
species respectively.

U. urens (annual nettle, burning
nettle): smaller plant with reddish
stems and small oval deep green
leaves; similar uses.

Valeriana officinalis
(Valerianaceae)
❧ **Valerian**
garden heliotrope, cat's valerian

Description: deciduous perennial with
strong-smelling branching roots, and
stout tubular furrowed stems, up to
1.2 m/4 ft. Leaves bright green and
pinnate, with 2-10 pairs of shiny oval
leaflets, pointed and toothed. Small
white or pink flowers in branching terminal clusters in summer. Grows wild
in ditches, woods and fertile grassland.

Uses: mildly sedative and antispasmod-
ic, used to treat tension, anxiety,
insomnia, migraine and nervous ailments, as well as colic and cramp;
externally in infusion for eye problems. Attractive to cats. An occasional
culinary flavouring. **Caution:** large
doses or extended use may lead to
addiction.

Cultivation: sow in spring where plants
are to grow, or separate stolons in
autumn and plant in moist borders or
beside pools. Tolerates full sun or
deep shade; plants benefit from an
annual dressing of manure.

Parts used: roots at least 2 years old
and gathered after leaves fall, used
fresh or dried in shade.

Related species: *V. celtica* (nard,
spike): prostrate plant with brown-
ish-yellow flowers, grown in rock
gardens.

V. edulis: North American species
with large tapering roots, occasionally cooked as a root vegetable.

V. phu (Cretan spikenard): white-
flowered species with ornamental
golden garden form; similar uses.

Veratrum viride (Liliaceae)

Green False Hellebore

American white hellebore, itchweed, Indian poke

Description: statuesque clump-forming perennial with strong, thick roots, rosette of broad elliptical pleated or ribbed leaves. Hairy, robust stems up to 1.5 m/5 ft bear branched spikes of pale green or greenish-white 6-petalled star-like flowers in summer. A wild plant of moist grassy places on hills and mountain pastures (not to be confused with *Helleborus viridis*, green hellebore).

Uses: handsome flowering plant for a prominent position, anti-parasitic; used by North American Indians as an arrow poison, and by the pharmaceutical industry in preparations for reducing blood pressure. **Caution:** highly toxic and not for home preparation.

Cultivation: divide roots in autumn or spring, or sow seeds in trays of peaty soil in a cool greenhouse in spring (seeds take several months to germinate). Grow in moist semi-shade.

Parts used: roots dug in autumn, cut in pieces and dried in sun or warmth.

Related species: *V. album* (white hellebore, langwort, false helleborine): similar plant with yellowish-green flowers with similar uses; roots dried and ground into 'hellebore powder', an insecticide.

Verbena officinalis (Verbenaceae)

Vervain

Description: hairy branching perennial with woody rootstock, and slender rough angular stems up to 90 cm/3 ft, bearing long sparse 3-lobed leaves, dull greyish-green and toothed. Small lilac flowers in thin stiff spikes in late summer. Found wild in hedges, waysides and dry barren places; commonly cultivated in France and other European countries.

Uses: ancient herb popular with druids as a panacea, and used in the Middle Ages to ward off plague. Used homeopathically for dropsy; medicinally to treat rheumatism, and stomach and liver disorders. Tea is a stimulant, and relieves fevers and nervous tension. Externally used for sores and skin problems, and for eye complaints.

Cultivation: sow in spring or autumn on the surface of well-drained soil in full sun; press or water in the seeds and thin seedlings to 30 cm/12 in apart.

Parts used: green flowering plant, fresh or dried in sun or warmth.

Veronica officinalis (Scrophulariaceae)

(Heath) Speedwell

fluellen

Description: hairy prostrate mat-forming perennial, with stems creeping and rooting at nodes or erect to 30 cm/12 in. Small rough leaves in opposite pairs, oval and finely toothed; flowering shoots from leaf axils, in summer bearing bright lilac-blue flowers with a white eye, in clusters. Grows wild in pastures and woods, and on dry slopes and heaths on acid soils.

Uses: a medieval healing herb, still used in a tonic tea ('Swiss tea') for liver, digestive and general intestinal complaints. Fresh juice used for skin ailments, for which there is also a homeopathic preparation. Cultivated as an ornamental ground-cover plant in the garden.

Cultivation: sow in spring or divide plants in early summer, and grow in rich, fertile soil in full sun. Water freely in dry weather, and replace plants every 4-5 years.

Parts used: whole green flowering plant, fresh or dried in shade or a warm room.

Related species: *V. beccabunga* (brooklime, water pimpernel): fleshy aquatic perennial with small, bright blue flowers found beside streams and in other wet places; popular salad plant high in vitamin C, and a very mild purgative.

Veronicastrum virginicum, syn. *Veronica virginica* (culver's root, bowman's root): very tall slender blue- or white-flowered perennial, once used by Shakers as a digestive. **Caution:** highly purgative.

Vinca minor (Apocynaceae)

ᘓ Lesser Periwinkle

Description: evergreen perennial, with stems prostrate and rooting at leaf nodes, and leafy flowering stems erect to 60 cm/2 ft. Leaves glossy and oval, flowers pale blue with lighter centres, or white, on hollow stalks in early summer.

Uses: used as a gargle for sore throats, as a styptic and astringent for wounds, sores and ulcers, and in a tea to reduce blood pressure and hypertension. **Caution:** large amounts may be toxic, leading to circulatory disorders.

Cultivation: divide in spring or take stem cuttings in autumn, and grow in fertile moist soils with a little lime.

Parts used: green flowering plant in spring, fresh or dried.

Related species: *Vinca major* (greater periwinkle, blue buttons): longer-stalked leaves and stems rooting only at the tips.

Viola tricolor (Violaceae)

ᘓ Wild Pansy

heartsease, field pansy, johnny jump-up

Description: variable annual or short-lived perennial, almost evergreen, with hollow stems sprawling or erect to 20 cm/8 in. Leaves oval and indented. Flowers yellow with purple and white markings, from spring to autumn, followed by capsules filled with shiny, light brown seeds, splitting into three segments when ripe.

Uses: renowned mild heart tonic, used to treat high blood pressure, indigestion and colds; cleanses blood and induces perspiration. Also used to treat dropsy and rheumatic conditions, and for skin disorders such as acne and eczema.

Cultivation: sow spring or summer where plants are to grow; press seeds into soil but leave uncovered. Surplus seedlings may be transplanted to any position in semi-shade. Plants self-seed freely. Cut back leggy plants to induce bushy growth and further flowers.

Parts used: green flowering herb and root, fresh or dried in shade.

Related species: *V. odorata* (sweet violet): trailing stoloniferous perennial with sweet-scented purple, white or pink flowers; ancient strewing herb and commercial crop for perfume industry; leaves and flowers used to treat coughs, catarrh and respiratory disorders; flowers crystallized.

V. sororia, syn. *V. papilionacea*: North American purple-flowered wild species with several cultivated forms; used by Indians for colds and headaches.

Vitex agnus-castus (Verbenaceae)

ᘓ Chaste Berry

Indian spice, monk's pepper, chaste tree

Description: aromatic shrub or small tree up to 6 m/20 ft, with palmate leaves divided into narrow leaflets on grey, downy shoots. Small violet fragrant flowers in dense trusses up to 30 cm/12 in long in autumn, followed in warm climates by purple-black berries. Found wild on light, stony soils in southern Europe; cultivated as a garden ornamental, sometimes with white flowers.

Uses: an ancient Greek herb thought to guarantee chastity, now used to regulate female hormonal activity. Also reputed to be a male anaphrodisiac; used as symbolic strewing herb in Italian monasteries. Seeds are used as a peppery condiment, slender branches in basketwork.

Cultivation: sow seeds in spring, layer in summer, or take cuttings under glass in autumn. Grow in well-drained, light soil, in full sun, and against a warm sheltered wall in temperate regions.

Parts used: fruits picked in autumn, fresh or dried in shade.

Related species: *Vitex negundo* (Chinese chaste tree): medium shrub with square stems and lavender flowers in late summer.

Right: *A fruitful, healthy herb garden – the results of only a little research and planning.*

BEE AND BUTTERFLY HERBS

- anise
- betony
- chicory
- comfrey
- evening primrose
- hyssop
- lemon balm
- mint
- sage
- thyme
- yarrow
- bergamot
- broom
- chives
- coltsfoot
- fennel
- lavender
- meadowsweet
- rosemary
- self-heal
- valerian

AN ESSENTIAL HERB COLLECTION

- basil – a tender annual
- bay – grown as a small trained specimen
- chives – for edging
- dill – an annual
- fennel – bulky and tall
- French tarragon – tall, best in a container
- lemon balm – a herbaceous perennial
- marjoram – shrubby
- mint – best in a pot
- parsley – ideal for edging
- rosemary – a bushy shrub
- sweet cicely – American (*Osmorrhiza longistylis*) or European (*Myrrhis odorata*)
- thyme – mats of evergreen foliage
- winter savory – short evergreen shrub

HERBS FOR FIRST AID

Part of the herb garden can be reserved for a selection of plants to provide help in emergencies; most can be used fresh in teas, compresses and infusions.

- aloe vera – grow as a pot plant and use a broken leaf to relieve sunburn
- lavender – use as an infusion for coughs, colds and headaches
- pot marigold – make a poultice from the flowers for burns and stings
- witch hazel – use in compresses for bruises and bleeding
- German chamomile – can be taken as a tea for insomnia
- lemon balm – infuse for digestive and menstrual upsets
- St John's wort – use as a compress for cuts and small wounds

PLANTS FOR FORMAL OUTDOOR TOPIARY

- box
- cephalotaxus
- *Cupressus sempervirens*
- holly
- *Ligustrum japonicum*
- *Thuja occidentalis*

- cassinia
- *Cryptomeria japonica*
- *Eugenia myrtifolia*
- ivy – on a wire frame
- *Phillyrea angustifolia*
- yew

PLANTS FOR A GREY AND WHITE HERB BORDER

- *Acorus calamus* 'Variegatus'
- *Artemisia* 'Powis Castle'
- *Buxus sempervirens* 'Elegantissima'
- *Chrysanthemum balsamita*
- *Iris pallida* 'Variegata Argentea'
- *Mentha suaveolens* 'Variegata'
- *Nepeta cataria*
- *Ruta graveolens* 'Variegata'
- *Sambucus nigra* 'Albovariegata'
- *Thymus* 'Silver Posy'

- *Althaea officinalis*
- *Artemisia absinthium* 'Lambrook Silver'
- *Chamaemelum nobile* 'Flore Pleno'
- *Colchicum autumnale* 'Alboplenum'
- *Marrubium vulgare*
- *Myrtus communis* 'Variegata'
- *Primula vulgaris* 'Alba Plena'
- *Salvia sclarea*
- *Symphytum* x *uplandicum* 'Variegatum'
- *Vinca major* 'Variegata'

MARY FLOWERS

These are just a few of the numerous plants suitable for inclusion in a traditional St Mary Garden.

- *Alchemilla mollis*, lady's mantle
- *Cardamine pratensis*, lady's smock
- *Galium verum*, lady's bedstraw
- *Primula veris*, cowslip (Our Lady's keys)
- *Tanacetum balsamita*, costmary

- *Calendula officinalis*, marigold
- *Convallaria majalis*, lily of the valley (Our Lady's tears)
- *Lilium candidum*, Madonna lily
- *Silybum marianum*, Our Lady's milk thistle

Add to these any flowers that are white (for purity) and blue (the colour of the Virgin Mary's robe), together with the monastic strewing herbs hyssop, tansy and meadowsweet as symbols of purity.

COOKING WITH HERBS

Herb and Chilli Gazpacho

Gazpacho is a lovely soup set off perfectly by the addition of a few herbs.

SERVES 6

1.2 kg/2½ lb ripe tomatoes

225 g/8 oz onions

2 green peppers

1 green chilli

1 large cucumber

2 tbsp red wine vinegar

1 tbsp balsamic vinegar

2 tbsp olive oil

1 clove of garlic, peeled and crushed

300 ml/½ pint/1¼ cups tomato juice

2 tbsp tomato purée

salt and pepper

2 tbsp finely chopped mixed fresh
  herbs, plus some extra to garnish

1 Keep back about a quarter of all the fresh vegetables, except the green chilli, and place all the remaining ingredients in a food processor and season to taste. Process finely and chill in the refrigerator.

2 Chop all the remaining vegetables, and serve in a separate bowl to sprinkle over the soup. Crush some ice cubes and add to the centre of each bowl and garnish with fresh herbs. Serve with bread rolls.

Pear and Watercress Soup with Stilton Croûtons

Pears and Stilton taste very good when you eat them together after the main course – here, for a change, they are served as a starter.

<u>Serves</u> 6

1 bunch watercress

4 medium pears, sliced

900 ml/1½ pints/3¾ cups chicken stock, preferably home-made

salt and pepper

120 ml/4 fl oz/½ cup double cream

juice of 1 lime

<u>Croutons</u>

25 g/1 oz butter

1 tbsp olive oil

200 g/7 oz/3 cups cubed stale bread

140 g/5 oz/1 cup chopped Stilton cheese

1 Keep back about a third of the watercress leaves. Place all the rest of the watercress leaves and stalks in a pan with the pears, stock and a little seasoning. Simmer for about 15-20 minutes. Reserving some watercress leaves for garnishing, add the rest of the leaves and immediately blend in a food processor until smooth.

2 Put the mixture into a bowl and stir in the cream and the lime juice to mix the flavours thoroughly. Season again to taste. Pour all the soup back into a pan and reheat, stirring gently until warmed through.

3 To make the croûtons, melt the butter and oil and fry the bread cubes until golden brown. Drain on kitchen paper. Put the cheese on top and heat under a hot grill until bubbling. Reheat the soup and pour into bowls. Divide the croûtons and remaining watercress between the bowls.

Warm Chicken Salad with Sesame and Coriander Dressing

This salad needs to be served warm to make the most of the wonderful sesame and coriander flavourings. It makes a simple starter or a delicious light lunch dish.

SERVES 6

4 medium chicken breasts, boned and skinned

225 g/8 oz mange-tout

2 heads decorative lettuce such as lollo rosso or feuille de chêne

3 carrots, peeled and cut into small matchsticks

170 g/6 oz button mushrooms, sliced

6 rashers of bacon, fried and chopped

DRESSING

115 ml/4 fl oz/½ cup lemon juice

2 tbsp wholegrain mustard

250 ml/8 fl oz/1 cup olive oil

65 ml/2½ fl oz/⅓ cup sesame oil

1 tsp coriander seeds, crushed

1 tbsp fresh coriander leaves chopped, to garnish

1 Mix all the dressing ingredients in a bowl. Place the chicken breasts in a shallow dish and pour on half the dressing. Refrigerate overnight, and store the remaining dressing here.

2 Cook the mange-tout for 2 minutes in boiling water, then cool under running cold water to stop them cooking any further. Tear the lettuces into small pieces and mix all the other salad ingredients and the bacon together. Arrange all these in individual serving dishes.

3 Grill the chicken breasts until cooked through, then slice them on the diagonal into quite thin pieces. Divide between the bowls of salad, and add some dressing to each dish. Combine quickly and scatter some fresh coriander over each bowl.

Spinach and Roquefort Pancakes with Walnuts and Chervil

Pancakes make a good starter or buffet dish as you can prepare them in advance. The pancakes can be frozen, but not the filling.

16 PANCAKES

115 g/4 oz/1 cup plain flour

2 eggs

5 tbsp sunflower oil

a little salt

250 ml/8 fl oz/1 cup milk

45 g/1½ oz/3 tbsp butter for frying

FILLING

1 kg/2 lb frozen spinach, thawed

225 g/8 oz/1 cup cream cheese

225 g/8 oz/1 packed cup Roquefort cheese

2 tbsp chopped walnuts

2 tsp chopped chervil

SAUCE

50 g/2 oz/4 tbsp butter

50 g/2 oz/½ cup flour

600 ml/1 pint/2½ cups milk

1 tsp wholegrain mustard

170 g/6 oz/¾ packed cup Roquefort cheese

1 tbsp finely chopped walnuts

1 tbsp fresh chopped chervil, to garnish

1 Process the flour, eggs, oil and salt, slowly adding milk until the mixture has the consistency of single cream. (You may not need to add all the milk.) Let the batter rest in the refrigerator for 1 hour. Put 1 tsp of the butter into a frying pan, and once it has melted swirl it around to coat the surface of the pan.

2 Drop a large tablespoonful of batter into the pan and tilt to spread it around evenly. Cook until golden brown on the bottom, then turn and cook briefly on the other side. Lay the pancake on a wire rack. Cook the others in the same way.

From top: *Spinach and Roquefort Pancakes; Warm Chicken Salad with Sesame and Coriander Dressing*

3 Cook the spinach over a low heat for about 15 minutes. Strain off the water and let the spinach cool. Process in a food processor with the cream cheese and Roquefort until smooth. Turn into a bowl and add half the walnuts and chervil.

4 Preheat the oven to 190°C/375°F/gas 5. Fill all the pancakes and place in a shallow ovenproof dish, rolled tightly and in rows. Make the sauce by melting the butter, adding the flour and cooking for a minute or two. Add the milk and stir constantly until the sauce comes to the boil. Stir in all the other ingredients except the chervil. Pour the sauce over the pancakes and bake for 20 minutes. Serve immediately, sprinkled with chopped chervil and the remaining walnuts.

Spinach, Cognac, Garlic and Chicken Pâté

Pâté is an easy starter, as it can be made well in advance. This smooth version is delicious with warm brown rolls and butter or garlic bread.

12 SERVINGS

12 slices streaky bacon
2 tbsp butter
1 onion, peeled and chopped
1 clove garlic, peeled and crushed
285 g/10 oz frozen spinach, thawed
50 g/2 oz/¾ cup wholemeal bread crumbs
2 tbsp Cognac
500 g/1 lb minced chicken (dark and light meat)
500 g/1 lb minced pork
2 eggs, beaten
2 tbsp chopped mixed fresh herbs, such as parsley, sage and dill
salt and pepper

1 Fry the bacon in a pan until it is only just done, then arrange it round the sides of a 900 ml/1½ pint/1 US quart dish, if possible leaving a couple of slices to garnish.

2 Melt the butter in a pan. Fry the onion and garlic until soft. Squeeze the spinach to remove as much water as possible, then add to the pan, stirring until the spinach is dry.

3 Preheat the oven to 180°C/350°F/gas 4. Combine all the remaining ingredients, apart from any remaining bacon strips, in a bowl and mix well to blend. Spoon the pâté into the loaf tin and cover with any remaining bacon.

4 Cover the tin with a double thickness of foil and set it in a baking pan. Pour 2.5 cm/1 in boiling water into the baking pan. Bake for about 1¼ hours. Remove the pâté and let it cool. Place a heavy weight on top of the pâté and refrigerate overnight.

Beef, Celeriac and Horseradish Pâté

This strongly flavoured pâté would make a good lunch dish as well as a starter.

SERVES 4

500 g/1 lb topside of beef, cubed
350 ml/12 fl oz/1½ cups red wine
85 ml/3 fl oz/⅓ cup Madeira
250 ml/8 fl oz/1 cup beef or chicken stock
2 tbsp finely chopped celeriac
1 tbsp horseradish cream
salt and pepper
2 bay leaves
2 tbsp brandy
170 g/6 oz/¾ cup butter, melted

1 Preheat the oven to 130°C/250°F/gas ½. Place the beef in a casserole. Mix all the other ingredients together except the brandy and butter, and pour them over the beef. Cover tightly and cook for 2 hours.

2 Remove and drain. Strain the liquid and reduce to about 45 ml/3 tbsp. Slice and roughly chop the meat and put it with the reduced liquid in the food processor. Blend until fairly smooth. Add the brandy and a third of the butter. Turn into a pâté dish and leave to cool.

3 Melt the remaining butter, skim any foam off the top and pour over the top of the beef, leaving any residue at the bottom of the pan. Cover the pâté and refrigerate overnight.

Smoked Trout with Minted Grapefruit

Trout and grapefruit make a magical combination, especially with a slight hint of mint.

SERVES 4

1 lollo rosso lettuce

1 tbsp lemon juice

2 tbsp chopped fresh mint, and a few whole leaves for garnish

500 g/1 lb smoked trout skinned, boned and sliced

2 grapefruit, peeled and segmented

120 ml/4 fl oz/½ cup good bottled mayonnaise

1 Toss the lettuce with the lemon juice and half the mint. Arrange on a plate and place the smoked trout among the leaves. Add the grapefruit segments as a decoration.

2 Mix the other half of the chopped mint with the mayonnaise and serve separately in a small bowl, garnished with a mint leaf or two.

Potted Salmon with Lemon and Dill

This sophisticated starter would be ideal for a dinner party. Preparation is done well in advance, so you can concentrate on the main course.

350 g/12 oz/1¾ cups cooked salmon, skinned
140 g/5 oz/⅔ cup butter, softened
rind and juice of 1 large lemon
2 tsp chopped fresh dill
salt and pepper
75 g/3 oz/¾ cup flaked almonds, roughly chopped

1 Flake the salmon into a bowl and then place in a food processor together with two-thirds of the butter, the lemon rind and juice, half the dill, and the salt and pepper. Blend until quite smooth.

2 Mix in the flaked almonds. Check for seasoning and pack the mixture into small ramekins.

3 Scatter the other half of the dill over the top of each ramekin. Clarify the remaining butter, and pour over each ramekin to make a seal. Refrigerate before serving. Serve with crudités.

Herbed Halibut Mille-Feuille

The crisp puff pastry balances the creamy fish, and the herbs add their own special flavours.

<u>SERVES 2</u>
250 g/9 oz puff pastry
butter for baking sheet
1 egg, beaten
1 small onion
1 tsp fresh ginger, grated
½ tbsp oil
150 ml/¼ pint/⅔ cup fish stock
1 tbsp dry sherry
350 g/12 oz halibut, cooked and flaked
225 g/8 oz crab meat
salt and pepper
1 avocado
juice of 1 lime
1 mango
1 tablespoon chopped mixed
  parsley, thyme and chives, to garnish

1 Roll the pastry out into a square 25 x 25 cm/10 x 10 in, trim the edges and place on a buttered baking sheet. Prick with a fork, then rest it in the refrigerator for at least 30 minutes. Preheat the oven to 230°C/450°F/gas 8. Brush the top with beaten egg, and bake for 10-15 minutes or until golden.

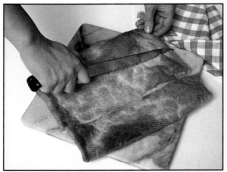

2 Let the pastry cool for a few minutes, then cut it twice across in one direction and once in the other to make six pieces. Leave to cool completely.

3 Fry the onion and ginger in the oil until tender. Add the fish stock and sherry, and simmer for 5 minutes. Add the halibut and crab meat, and season to taste. Peel and chop the avocado and toss in the lime juice. Peel and chop the mango reserving a few slices for garnishing. Add both to the fish.

4 Build up alternate layers of fish and pastry, starting and finishing with a piece of pastry. Serve garnished with herbs and mango slices.

Salmon and Ginger Pie, with Lemon Thyme and Lime

This exceptional pie is highly recommended. This recipe uses salmon's special flavour to the full.

<u>SERVES 4-6</u>
800 g/1¾ lb middle cut of salmon
3 tbsp walnut oil
1 tbsp lime juice
2 tsp chopped fresh lemon thyme
2 tbsp white wine
salt and pepper
400 g/14 oz puff pastry
50 g/2 oz/½ cup flaked almonds
3-4 pieces stem ginger in syrup, chopped

1 Split the salmon in half, remove all the bones and skin, and divide into 4 fillets. Mix the oil, lime juice, thyme, wine and pepper, and pour over the fish. Leave to marinate overnight in the refrigerator.

2 Divide the pastry into two pieces, one slightly larger than the other, and roll out – the smaller piece should be large enough to take two of the salmon fillets and the second piece about 5 cm/2 in larger all round. Drain the fillets. Discard the marinade.

3 Preheat the oven to 190°C/350°F/gas 5. Place two of the fillets on the smaller piece of pastry, and season. Add the almonds and ginger and cover with the other two fillets.

4 Season again, cover with the second piece of pastry and seal well. Brush with beaten egg and decorate with any leftover pastry. Bake for 40 minutes.

From top: *Herbed Halibut Mille-Feuille; Salmon and Ginger Pie*

Cod, Basil and Tomato with a Potato Thatch

With a green salad, it makes an ideal dish for lunch or a family supper.

SERVES 8

1 kg/2 lb smoked cod
1 kg/2 lb white cod
600 ml/1 pint/2½ cups milk
2 sprigs basil
1 sprig lemon thyme
75 g/3 oz/⅓ cup butter
1 onion, peeled and chopped
75 g/3 oz/¾ cup flour
2 tbsp tomato purée
2 tbsp chopped basil
12 medium-sized old potatoes
50 g/2 oz/¼ cup butter
300 ml/½ pint/1¼ cups milk
salt and pepper
1 tbsp chopped parsley

1 Place both kinds of fish in a roasting pan with the milk, 1.2 litres/2 pints/5 cups water and herbs. Simmer for about 3-4 minutes. Leave to cool in the liquid for about 20 minutes. Drain the fish, reserving the liquid for use in the sauce. Flake the fish, taking care to remove any skin and bone.

2 Melt the butter in a pan, add the onion and cook for about 5 minutes until tender but not browned. Add the flour, tomato purée and half the basil. Gradually add the reserved fish stock, adding a little more milk if necessary to make a fairly thin sauce. Bring this to the boil, season with salt and pepper, and add the remaining basil. Add the fish carefully and stir gently. Pour into an ovenproof dish.

3 Preheat the oven to 180°C/350°F/gas 4. Boil the potatoes until tender. Add the butter and milk, and mash well. Add salt and pepper to taste and cover the fish, forking to create a pattern. If you like, you can freeze the pie at this stage. Bake for 30 minutes. Serve with the chopped parsley.

Tiger Prawns in Filo with Mint, Dill and Lime

Another wonderful combination – the mint, dill and lime blend together to make a magical concoction that will delight everyone who tries it.

SERVES 4

4 large sheets filo pastry

75 g/3 oz/¹/₃ cup butter

16 large tiger prawns, cooked and shelled

1 tbsp chopped fresh mint, plus a little more to garnish

1 tbsp chopped fresh dill

juice of 1 lime, plus another lime cut into wedges

1 Keep the sheets of filo pastry covered with a dry, clean cloth to keep them moist. Cut one sheet of filo pastry in half widthways and brush both halves with melted butter. Place one half on top of the other.

2 Preheat the oven to 230°C/450°F/gas 8. Cut eight of the tiger prawns in half down the back of the prawn and remove any black parts.

3 Place four prawns in the centre of the filo pastry and sprinkle a quarter of the mint, dill and lime juice over the top. Fold over the sides, brush with butter and roll up to make a parcel.

4 Repeat with the other ingredients and place the parcels join side down, on a greased baking sheet. Bake for 10 minutes or until golden. Serve with lime wedges, tiger prawns and mint.

Camembert, Chervil and Plum Profiteroles

Most people are familiar with chocolate profiteroles, but this savoury version is just as delicious and makes an attractive starter.

S ERVES 8

300 ml/½ pint/1¼ cups water
140 g/5 oz/⅔ cup butter, cubed
170 g/6 oz/1½ cups plain flour
2 tsp mustard powder
1 tsp powdered cinnamon
4 eggs
75 g/3 oz/¾ cup grated Cheddar
F ILLING
225 g/8 oz/1 packed cup Camembert
a little milk
1 tsp fresh chervil, chopped
6 fresh plums, stoned and finely
  chopped
S AUCE
1 x 285 g/10 oz can red plums
½ tsp powdered cinnamon
1 tsp chopped fresh chervil, plus a
  few sprigs to garnish

1 To make the profiteroles, put the water into a saucepan and add the butter. Gently melt the butter, then bring to the boil. As soon as this happens, sieve in the flour, mustard powder and cinnamon. Beat hard with a wooden spoon until the mixture comes away from the sides of the pan.

2 Leave to cool for 10 minutes, then beat in the eggs, one at a time. Add the grated Cheddar, and beat until glossy. Use a large nozzle to pipe blobs about 2.5 cm/1 in across on a greased baking sheet. Bake at 200°C/400°F/ gas 6 for 20 minutes. Cool on a wire rack.

3 Chop the Camembert in small pieces and put in a food processor. Add a little milk and the chervil, and blend to a smooth paste. Remove from the food processor and add the fresh plums.

4 Also make the sauce while the pastries are cooling. Drain the canned plums and stone if necessary. Add them to the cinnamon and chervil in the food processor and blend to a fairly smooth purée.

5 Assemble the profiteroles by halving them and placing some of the Camembert mixture inside. Place the profiteroles on individual plates and dust with a little cinnamon. Serve the sauce separately.

Pork, Thyme and Water Chestnut Filo Parcels

Filo pastry is easy to use and delicious – the light, crisp wrapping makes a simple recipe into a celebration.

M AKES 8

1 tbsp sunflower oil, plus more for
  frying
1 tsp fresh grated ginger
285 g/10 oz pork fillet, finely
  chopped
6 spring onions, chopped
115 g/4 oz/1 cup chopped mushrooms
75 g/3 oz/½ cup chopped bamboo
  shoots
12 water chestnuts, finely chopped
2 tsp cornflour
1 tbsp soy sauce
2 tsp anchovy essence
2 tsp fresh thyme, chopped
salt and pepper
8 large sheets filo pastry
25 g/1 oz/scant 2 tbsp butter, melted

1 Heat the oil and fry the ginger for a few seconds and then add the pork. Stir well and cook until colour changes. Add the spring onions and mushrooms and cook until tender. Add the bamboo shoots and water chestnuts.

2 In a small bowl, mix the cornflour with the soy sauce and anchovy essence. Add to the pan and stir well. Add the chopped thyme, season with salt and pepper, and cook until thickened.

3 Take a sheet of filo pastry and fold in half to make a square. Place two tablespoonfuls of filling across one corner and fold the corner over, then fold in the sides. Brush the folded sides lightly with a little melted butter to help the pastry stick. Complete the roll, and place it join side down on a cloth, then fold the cloth over the top to cover it. Finish all the rolls, putting each one in the cloth as it is made.

4 Heat some oil for semi-deep frying, and fry 2-3 rolls at a time until evenly browned. Drain on absorbent paper and serve hot.

From top: *Camembert, Chervil and Plum Profiteroles; Pork, Thyme and Water Chestnut Filo Parcels*

Lamb Pie, with Pear, Ginger and Mint Sauce

Cooking lamb with fruit is an idea taken from traditional Persian cuisine. The ginger and mint add bite to the mild flavours.

S ERVES 6

1 boned mid-loin of lamb, 1 kg/2 lb after boning

salt and pepper

8 large sheets filo pastry

25 g/1 oz/scant 2 tbsp butter

S TUFFING

1 tbsp butter

1 small onion, chopped

115 g/4 oz/1 cup wholemeal bread-crumbs

grated rind of 1 lemon

170 g/6 oz/³⁄₄ cup drained canned pears from a 400 g/14 oz can (rest of can, and juice, used for sauce)

¹⁄₄ tsp ground ginger

1 small egg, beaten

skewers, string and large needle to make roll

S AUCE

rest of can of pears, including juice

2 tsp finely chopped fresh mint

1 Prepare the stuffing: melt the butter in a pan and add the onion, cooking until soft. Preheat the oven to 180°C/ 350°F/gas 4. Put the butter and onion into a mixing bowl and add the breadcrumbs, lemon rind, pears and ginger. Season lightly and add enough beaten egg to bind.

2 Spread the loin out flat, fat side down, and season. Place the stuffing along the middle of the loin and roll carefully, holding with skewers while you sew it together with string. Heat a large baking pan in the oven and brown the loin slowly on all sides. This will take 20-30 minutes. Leave to cool, and store in the refrigerator until needed.

3 Preheat the oven to 200°C/ 400°F/gas 6. Take two sheets of filo pastry and brush with melted butter. Overlap by about 13 cm/5 in to make a square. Place the next two sheets on top and brush with butter. Continue until all the pastry has been used.

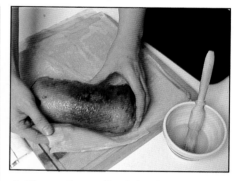

4 Place the roll of lamb diagonally across one corner of the pastry, without overlapping the sides. Fold the corner over the lamb, fold in the sides, and brush the pastry well with melted butter. Roll to the far corner of the sheet. Place join side down on a buttered baking sheet and brush all over with the rest of the melted butter. Bake for about 30 minutes or until golden brown.

5 Blend the remaining pears with their juice and the mint, and serve with the lamb.

Steak and Kidney Pie, with Mustard and Bay Gravy

This is a sharpened-up, bay-flavoured version of a traditional favourite. The fragrant mustard, bay and parsley perfectly complement the flavour of the beef.

SERVES 4

450 g/1 lb puff pastry
2½ tbsp flour
salt and pepper
750 g/1½ lb rump steak, cubed
170 g/6 oz pig's or lamb's kidney
25 g/1 oz/scant 2 tbsp butter
1 medium onion, chopped
1 tbsp made English mustard
2 bay leaves
1 tbsp chopped parsley
150 ml/5 fl oz/²/³ cup beef stock
1 egg, beaten

1 Roll out two-thirds of the pastry on a floured surface to about 3 mm/⅛ in thick. Line a 1.5 litre/2½ pint/1½ US quart pie dish. Place a pie funnel in the middle.

2 Put the flour, salt and pepper in a bowl and toss the cubes of steak in the mixture. Remove all fat and skin from the kidneys, and slice thickly. Add to the steak cubes and toss well. Melt the butter in a pan and fry the onion until soft, then add the mustard, bay leaves, parsley and stock and stir well.

3 Preheat the oven to 190°C/375°F/gas 5. Place the steak and kidney in the pie and add the stock mixture. Roll out the remaining pastry to a thickness of 3 mm/⅛ in. Brush the edges of the pastry forming the lower half of the pie with beaten egg and cover with the second piece of pastry. Press the pieces of pastry together to seal the edge, then trim. Use the trimmings to decorate the top in a leaf pattern.

4 Brush the whole pie with beaten egg and make a small hole over the top of the funnel. Bake for about 1 hour until the pastry is golden brown.

Turkey with Apples, Bay and Madeira

This casserole will win you many compliments without the worry of a complicated menu. The unusual apple garnish looks very attractive.

<small>SERVES 4</small>

750 g/1½ lb turkey breast fillets, cut into 2 cm/¾ in slices

salt and pepper

50 g/2 oz/4 tbsp butter, plus another 15 g/½ oz/1 tbsp for the apple garnish

4 tart apples, peeled and sliced

60 ml/2 fl oz/4 tbsp Madeira, plus another 30 ml/1 fl oz/2 tbsp for the apple garnish

150 ml/¼ pint/⅔ cup chicken stock

3 bay leaves

2 tsp cornflour

150 ml/¼ pint/⅔ cup double cream

1 Season the turkey, melt 25 g/1 oz/ 2 tbsp the butter in a pan and fry the meat to seal it. Transfer to a casserole. Preheat the oven to 180°C/ 350°F/gas 4. Add the remaining butter to the pan with two sliced apples, and cook gently for 1-2 minutes.

2 Add the Madeira, stock and bay leaves to the turkey and stir in. Simmer for another couple of minutes. Cover the casserole and bake for about 40 minutes.

3 Blend the cornflour with a little of the cream, then add the rest of the cream. Add this mixture to the casserole and return to the oven for 10 minutes to allow the sauce to thicken.

4 To make the garnish, melt 25 g/ 1 oz/2 tbsp butter in a pan and gently fry the apple slices. Add the Madeira and set it alight. Once the flames have died down continue to fry the apple until it is lightly browned, and garnish the casserole with it.

Beef with Orange Herbal Mustard

The orange herbal mustard is delicious with many different dishes, including cold ham and pork pies. It gives beef a fantastic flavour. This will become a firm favourite.

SERVES 4

45 ml/3 tbsp oil

750 g/1½ lb braising steak cubed

225 g/8 oz/2 cups chopped onion

1 clove garlic, peeled and crushed

2 tbsp flour

300 ml/½ pint/1¼ cups beef stock

2 oranges, plus 1 more for garnish
  and herbal mustard

15 ml/1 tbsp tomato purée

45 ml/3 tbsp Grand Marnier

15 ml/1 tbsp maple syrup

salt and pepper

100 g/4 oz/1 cup sliced mushrooms

HERBAL MUSTARD

2 tbsp mixed fresh herbs, finely
  chopped, such as thyme and chives

juice and grated rind of half an
  orange

3 tbsp Dijon mustard

1 Heat the oil and fry the beef to seal it. Transfer to a casserole. Fry the onion and garlic, drain and add to the casserole. Add the flour to the pan and cook for 1 minute, then add the stock and bring to the boil.

2 Finely slice off the coloured part of the rind of two oranges and chop into small pieces. Squeeze both oranges, and add the juice and the rind to the casserole. Add the tomato purée, Grand Marnier and maple syrup, and season. Preheat the oven to 180°C/350°F/gas 4.

3 Cover the casserole and cook in the oven for at least 1½ hours. Add the mushrooms and return to the oven for another 30 minutes. Serve garnished with slices from half the remaining orange and the herbal mustard described below (remember to grate the orange before cutting it up).

4 To make the herbal mustard, grate the orange rind and mix with the chopped fresh herbs. Then mix in the orange juice and the Dijon mustard. Serve with the beef in a separate dish.

Chicken Stew with Blackberries and Lemon Balm

This delicious stew combines some wonderful flavours, and the combination of red wine and blackberries gives it a dramatic appearance.

SERVES 4

4 chicken breasts, partly boned
salt and pepper
25 g/1 oz/scant 2 tbsp butter
1 tbsp sunflower oil
25 g/1 oz/4 tbsp flour
150 ml/¼ pint/⅔ cup red wine
150 ml/¼ pint/⅔ cup chicken stock
grated rind of half an orange plus
    15 ml (1 tbsp) juice
3 sprigs lemon balm, finely chopped,
    plus 1 sprig to garnish
150 ml/¼ pint/⅔ cup double cream
1 egg yolk
100 g/4 oz/⅔ cup fresh blackberries,
    plus 50 g/2 oz/⅓ cup to garnish

1 Remove any skin from the chicken, and season the meat. Heat the butter and oil in a pan, fry the chicken to seal it, then transfer to a casserole dish. Stir the flour into the pan, then add wine and stock and bring to the boil. Add the orange rind and juice, and also the chopped lemon balm. Pour over the chicken.

2 Preheat the oven to 180°C/350°F/ gas 4. Cover the casserole and cook in the oven for about 40 minutes.

3 Blend the cream with the egg yolk, add some of the liquid from the casserole and stir back into the dish with the blackberries (reserving those for the garnish). Cover and cook for another 10-15 minutes. Serve garnished with the rest of the blackberries and lemon balm.

Pork and Mushrooms with Sage and Mango Chutney

The mango chutney and sage leaves add a special flavour to this traditional dish.

SERVES 4

25 g/1 oz/scant 2 tbsp butter
1 tbsp sunflower oil
750 g/1½ lb cubed pork
175 g/6 oz onion, peeled and
    chopped
2 tbsp flour
450 ml/¾ pint/1⅞ cups stock
4 tbsp white wine
salt and pepper
225 g/8 oz mushrooms, sliced
6 fresh sage leaves, finely chopped
2 tbsp mango chutney
1 fresh mango, peeled and sliced, to
    garnish

1 Heat the butter and oil and fry the pork in a pan to seal it. Transfer to a casserole. Fry the onion in the pan, stir in the flour and cook for 1 minute.

2 Preheat the oven to 180°C/350°F/ gas 4. Gradually add the stock and white wine to the onion and bring to the boil. Season well and add the mushrooms, sage leaves and mango chutney.

3 Pour the sauce mixture over the pork and cover the casserole. Cook in the oven for about 1 hour, depending on the cut of pork, until tender. Check the seasoning, garnish with mango slices, and serve with rice.

From top: *Pork and Mushrooms with Sage and Mango Chutney; Chicken Stew with Blackberries and Lemon Balm*

Leek and Monkfish with Thyme Sauce

Monkfish is a well known fish now, thanks to its excellent flavour and firm texture.

SERVES 4

1 kg/2 lb monkfish, cubed

salt and pepper

75 g/3 oz/generous ⅓ cup butter

4 leeks, sliced

1 tbsp flour

150 ml/¼ pint/⅔ cup fish or
  vegetable stock

2 tsp finely chopped fresh thyme,
  plus more to garnish

juice of 1 lemon

150 ml/¼ pint/⅔ cup single cream

radicchio, to garnish

1 Season the fish to taste. Melt about a third of the butter in a pan, and fry the fish for a short time. Put to one side. Fry the leeks in the pan with another third of the butter until they have softened. Put these to one side with the fish.

2 In a saucepan, melt the rest of the butter, add the remaining butter from the pan, stir in the flour, and add the stock. As the sauce begins to thicken, add the thyme and lemon juice.

3 Return the leeks and monkfish to the pan and cook gently for a few minutes. Add the cream and season to taste. Do not let the mixture boil again, or the cream will separate. Serve immediately garnished with thyme and radicchio leaves.

Fish Stew with Calvados, Parsley and Dill

This rustic stew harbours all sorts of interesting flavours and will please and intrigue. Many varieties of fish can be used, just choose the freshest and best.

SERVES 4

1 kg/2 lb assorted white fish

1 tbsp chopped parsley, plus a few leaves to garnish

225 g/8 oz mushrooms

225 g/8 oz can of tomatoes

salt and pepper

2 tsp flour

15 g/½ oz/1 tbsp butter

450 ml/¾ pint/1⅞ cups cider

3 tbsp Calvados

1 large bunch fresh dill sprigs, reserving 4 fronds to garnish

1 Chop the fish roughly and place it in a casserole or stewing pot with the parsley, mushrooms, tomatoes and salt and pepper to taste.

2 Preheat the oven to 180°C/350°F/ gas 4. Work the flour into the butter. Heat the cider and stir in the flour and butter mixture a little at a time. Cook, stirring, until it has thickened slightly.

3 Add the cider mixture and the remaining ingredients to the fish and mix gently. Cover and bake for about 30 minutes. Serve garnished with sprigs of dill and parsley leaves.

Lamb and Leeks with Mint and Spring Onions

This is especially good with new season's lamb and organically grown leeks – best of all with leeks from your garden. If you have some home-made chicken stock it boosts the flavour tremendously; if not, use a good quality ready-made stock rather than a stock cube.

SERVES 6

2 tbsp sunflower oil

2 kg/4 lb lamb (fillet or boned leg), cubed

10 spring onions, thickly sliced

3 leeks, thickly sliced

1 tbsp flour

150 ml/¼ pint/⅔ cup white wine

300 ml/½ pint/1¼ cups chicken stock

1 tbsp tomato purée

1 tbsp sugar

salt and pepper

2 tbsp fresh mint leaves, finely chopped, plus a few more to garnish

115 g/4 oz/⅔ cup dried pears, chopped

1 kg/2 lb potatoes, peeled and sliced

30 g/1¼ oz/2 tbsp melted butter

1 Heat the oil and fry the lamb to seal it. Transfer to a casserole. Preheat the oven to 180°C/350°F/gas 4.

2 Fry the onions and leeks for 1 minute, stir in the flour and cook for another minute. Add the wine and stock and bring to the boil. Add the tomato purée, sugar, salt and pepper with the mint and pears and pour into the casserole. Stir the mixture. Arrange the sliced potatoes on top and brush with the melted butter.

3 Cover and bake for 1½ hours. Then increase the temperature to 200°C/400°F/gas 6, cook for a further 30 minutes, uncovered, to brown the potatoes. Garnish with mint leaves.

Stuffed Parsleyed Onions

Although devised as a vegetarian dish, these stuffed onions make a wonderful accompaniment to meat dishes, or an appetizing supper dish with crusty bread and a salad.

SERVES 4

4 large onions

4 tbsp cooked rice

4 tsp finely chopped fresh parsley,
  plus extra to garnish

4 tbsp strong Cheddar cheese,
  finely grated

salt and pepper

2 tbsp olive oil

1 tbsp white wine, to moisten

1 Cut a slice from the top of each onion and scoop out the centre to leave a fairly thick shell. Combine all the remaining ingredients, moistening with enough wine to mix well. Preheat the oven to 180°C/350°F/gas 4.

2 Fill the onions and bake in the oven for 45 minutes. Serve garnished with the extra parsley.

Herbed Chicken with Apricot and Pecan Potato Baskets

The potato baskets make a pretty addition to the chicken and could easily have different fillings when you feel the need for a change.

SERVES 8

8 chicken breast fillets

2 tbsp butter

6 mushrooms, chopped

1 tbsp chopped pecan nuts

115 g/4 oz/½ cup chopped, cooked ham

50 g/2 oz/½ cup wholemeal breadcrumbs

1 tbsp chopped parsley, plus some whole leaves to garnish

salt and pepper

cocktail sticks to secure rolls

SAUCE

2 tsp cornflour

120 ml/4 fl oz/½ cup white wine

50 g/2 oz/¼ cup butter

50 g/2 oz/¼ cup apricot chutney

POTATO BASKETS

4 large baking potatoes

170 g/6 oz pork sausage meat

1 x 225 g/8 oz can apricots in natural juice, drained and quartered

¼ tsp cinnamon

½ tsp grated orange peel

2 tbsp maple syrup

2 tbsp butter

35 g/1¼ oz/¼ cup chopped pecan nuts, plus some pecan halves to garnish

1 Place the chicken breasts between two sheets of greaseproof paper and flatten with a rolling pin or mallet. Melt the butter in a pan and sauté the mushrooms, pecans and ham. Stir in the breadcrumbs and parsley, and season to taste. Divide this mixture between the chicken breasts and roll up and secure each one with a cocktail stick. Refrigerate while making the sauce.

2 Put the potatoes in the oven to bake at 160°C/325°F/gas 3 while you prepare the sauce. Mix the cornflour with a little of the wine to make a smooth paste. Put the remaining wine in a pan and add this paste. Simmer until smooth, and add the butter and apricot chutney and cook for about 5 minutes, stirring constantly.

3 Place the chicken breasts in a shallow ovenproof dish and pour over the sauce. Bake in the oven (do not adjust the temperature) for 20 minutes, basting several times.

4 When the potatoes are cooked through, cut them in half and scoop out the inside, leaving a reasonable layer within the shell. Mash the potato and place in a mixing bowl.

5 Fry the sausage meat and remove some of the fat that comes off. Add the remaining ingredients and cook for 1 minute. Add the sausage meat mixture to the potato and blend gently. Fill the potato shells. Sprinkle the pecan halves over the top, put in the oven with the chicken and bake for another 30 minutes.

6 Remove the chicken breasts from the oven and then drain the sauce into a separate container. Slice the breasts, put on to individual plates and pour the sauce over the top. Serve with the potato baskets and garnish with parsley leaves.

Venison Steaks with Elderberry and Orange

Farmed venison is now widely available. The strong flavour of the meat is well matched by the sweet sauce.

SERVES 4

4 venison steaks, 170-225 g/6-8 oz each

olive oil for basting

black pepper

salt

2 tbsp red wine

4 tbsp orange juice, plus slices of orange to garnish

2 tbsp elderberry jelly

sprigs of parsley, to garnish

1 Pound the venison steaks a little with a meat mallet to make the meat more tender.

2 Brush with olive oil and season with freshly ground black pepper. Grill under a high heat until done to your taste. Sprinkle with a little salt.

3 In a pan, reduce the red wine, then add the orange juice and elderberry jelly and simmer for 10 minutes. Pour over the steaks and garnish with slices of orange and parsley sprigs.

From top: *Venison Steaks with Elderberry and Orange; Herbed Chicken with Apricot and Pecan Potato Baskets*

Chicken with Sloe Gin and Juniper

 Juniper is used in the manufacture of gin, and the reinforcement of the flavour by using both sloe gin and juniper is delicious. Sloe gin is easy to make, but can also be bought ready-made.

SERVES 8

2 tbsp butter

2 tbsp sunflower oil

8 chicken breast fillets

350 g/12 oz carrots, cooked

1 clove garlic, peeled and crushed

1 tbsp finely chopped parsley

60 ml/2 fl oz/¼ cup chicken stock

60 ml/2 fl oz/¼ cup red wine

60 ml/2 fl oz/¼ cup sloe gin

1 tsp crushed juniper berries

salt and pepper

1 bunch basil, to garnish

1 Melt the butter with the oil in a pan, and sauté the chicken until browned on all sides.

2 In a food processor, combine all the remaining ingredients except the watercress, and blend to a smooth purée. If the mixture seems too thick add a little more red wine or water until a thinner consistency is reached.

3 Put the chicken breasts in a pan, pour the sauce over the top and cook until the chicken is cooked through – about 15 minutes. Adjust the seasoning and serve garnished with chopped fresh basil.

Duck Breasts with Red Plums, Cinnamon and Coriander

Duck breasts can be bought separately, which makes this dish very easy to prepare.

SERVES 4

4 duck breasts, 175 g/6 oz each, skinned

salt

2 tsp stick cinnamon, crushed

50 g/2 oz/¼ cup butter

1 tbsp plum brandy (or Cognac)

250 ml/8 fl oz/1 cup chicken stock

250 ml/8 fl oz/1 cup double cream

pepper

6 fresh red plums, stoned and sliced

6 sprigs coriander leaves, plus some extra to garnish

1 Preheat the oven to 190°C/375°F/ gas 5. Score the duck breasts and sprinkle with salt. Press the crushed cinnamon on to both sides of the duck breasts. Melt half the butter in a pan and fry them on both sides to seal, then place in an ovenproof dish with the butter and bake for 6-7 minutes.

2 Remove the dish from the oven and return the contents to the pan. Add the brandy and set it alight. When the flames have died down, remove from the pan and keep warm. Add the stock and cream to the pan and simmer gently until reduced and thick. Adjust the seasoning.

3 Reserve a few plum slices for garnishing. In a pan, melt the other half of the butter and fry the plums and coriander, just enough to cook the fruit through. Slice the duck breasts and pour some sauce around each one, then garnish with slices of plum and chopped coriander.

Turkey with Fig, Orange and Mint Marmalade

Turkey is a low-fat meat that should be used all the year round, not just at Christmas. This unusual sauce gives its rather bland flavour a tremendous lift.

SERVES 4

500 g/1 lb dried figs

½ bottle sweet, fruity white wine

4 turkey fillets, 170-225 g/6-8 oz each

1 tbsp butter

2 tbsp dark orange marmalade

10 mint leaves, finely chopped, plus a few more to garnish

juice of ½ lemon

salt and pepper

1 Place the figs in a pan with the wine and bring to the boil, then simmer very gently for about 1 hour. Leave to cool and refrigerate overnight.

2 Melt the butter in a pan and fry the turkey fillets until they are cooked through. Remove from the pan and keep warm. Drain any fat from the pan and pour in the juice from the figs. Bring to the boil and reduce until about 150 ml/¼ pint/⅔ cup remains.

3 Add the marmalade, mint leaves and lemon juice, and simmer for a few minutes. Season to taste. When the sauce is thick and shiny, pour it over the meat and garnish with the figs and mint leaves.

Lamb with Mint and Lemon

Lamb has been served with mint for many years – rightly, because it is a great combination.

SERVES 8

8 lamb steaks, 225 g/8 oz each

grated rind and juice of 1 lemon

2 cloves garlic, peeled and crushed

2 spring onions, finely chopped

2 tsp finely chopped fresh mint leaves, plus some leaves for garnishing

4 tbsp extra virgin olive oil

salt and black pepper

1 Make a marinade for the lamb by mixing all the other ingredients and seasoning to taste. Place the lamb steaks in a shallow dish and cover with the marinade. Refrigerate overnight.

2 Grill the lamb under a high heat until just cooked, basting with the marinade occasionally during cooking. Turn once during cooking. Garnish with mint leaves.

Sirloin Steaks with Bloody Mary Sauce and Coriander

This cocktail of ingredients is just as successful as the well-known drink, but the alcohol evaporates in cooking, so you need not worry about a hangover.

SERVES 4

4 sirloin steaks, 225 g/8 oz each
MARINADE
2 tbsp soy sauce
4 tbsp balsamic vinegar
2 tbsp olive oil
SAUCE
1 kg/2 lb very ripe tomatoes, peeled and chopped
tomato purée, if required
50 g/2 oz/½ cup chopped onions
2 spring onions
1 tsp chopped fresh coriander
1 tsp ground cumin
1 tsp salt
1 tbsp fresh lime juice
120 ml/4 fl oz/½ cup beef consommé
60 ml/2 fl oz/¼ cup vodka
1 tbsp Worcester sauce

1 Lay the steaks in a shallow dish, mix the marinade ingredients together in a bowl, pour over the steaks and leave for at least a couple of hours in the refrigerator, turning once or twice.

2 If the tomatoes are not quite ripe, add a little tomato purée. Place all the sauce ingredients in a food processor and blend to a fairly smooth texture. Put in a pan, bring to the boil and simmer for about 5 minutes.

3 Remove the steaks from the marinade and place under a hot grill. Discard the marinade. Grill the steaks under a high heat until cooked. Serve with the sauce.

Roast Pork with Sage, Marjoram and Celery Leaves

Pork is an inexpensive choice which is equally suitable for a family dinner or a celebration meal. The fruity purée makes a delicious change from the more usual plain apple sauce.

SERVES 8

2.75 kg/6 lb joint of pork
3 tbsp fresh sage
1 tbsp fresh marjoram
3 tbsp chopped celery leaves
salt and pepper
50 ml/2 fl oz/¼ cup cider
PURÉE
15 ml/1 tbsp butter
2 eating apples
2 bananas
1 tbsp Calvados

1 Preheat the oven to 165°C/315°F/gas 2½. Cut a large piece of foil and place the pork in the centre. In a bowl mix the sage, marjoram and celery leaves together. Cover the fatty part of the pork with the herb mixture, season to taste and wrap tightly. Roast for about 1 hour.

2 Fold back the foil and baste the joint with the cider. Continue cooking for another hour until a sharp knife pressed into the thickest part produces clear juices.

3 To make the purée, peel and slice the apples and bananas, put the butter in a pan and sauté the fruit. Add the Calvados and set it alight. When the flames have died down remove the mixture from the heat, put it in the food processor and purée. Serve the pork with the purée on the side.

From top: *Sirloin Steaks with Bloody Mary Sauce and Coriander; Roast Pork with Sage, Marjoram and Celery Leaves*

Sweetcorn in a Garlic Butter Crust

Whether you are catering for vegetarians or serving this with other meat dishes, it will disappear in a flash. Even people who are not usually keen on corn on the cob have been won over by this recipe.

SERVES 6

6 ripe cobs of corn

225 g/8 oz/1 cup butter

2 tbsp olive oil

2 cloves garlic, peeled and crushed

2 tsp freshly ground black pepper

115 g/4 oz/1 cup wholemeal breadcrumbs

1 tbsp chopped parsley

1 Boil the corn cobs in salted water until tender, then leave to cool.

2 Melt the butter, and add the oil, garlic and black pepper. Pour the mixture into a shallow dish. Mix the breadcrumbs and parsley in another shallow dish. Roll the corn cobs in the melted butter mixture and then in the breadcrumbs.

3 Grill the cobs under a high grill until the breadcrumbs are golden.

OTHER GARLIC BUTTER IDEAS

• Partially cut through a French loaf at regular intervals. Spread the garlic butter mixture between the slices and bake in a moderate oven for 30 minutes.

• To make garlic croutons, melt the garlic butter in a pan and add cubes of bread. Toss frequently over a medium heat. When golden brown add to soups or salads.

• Drizzle over chicken breasts before roasting.

Vegetable and Herb Kebabs with Green Peppercorn Sauce

Other vegetables can be included in these kebabs, depending on what is available at the time. The green peppercorn sauce is also an excellent accompaniment to many other dishes.

<u>SERVES 4</u>

**8 bamboo skewers soaked in water
  for 1 hour**
24 mushrooms
16 cherry tomatoes
16 large basil leaves
16 thick slices of courgette
16 large mint leaves
16 squares of red sweet pepper

TO BASTE
120 ml/4 fl oz/½ cup melted butter
1 clove garlic, peeled and crushed
1 tbsp crushed green peppercorns
salt
GREEN PEPPERCORN SAUCE
50 g/2 oz/¼ cup butter
3 tbsp brandy
250 ml/8 fl oz/1 cup double cream
1 tsp crushed green peppercorns

1 Thread the vegetables on to the bamboo skewers. Place the basil leaves immediately next to the tomatoes, and the mint leaves wrapped around the courgette slices.

2 Mix the basting ingredients and baste the kebabs thoroughly. Place the skewers on a barbecue or under the grill, turning and basting regularly until the vegetables are just cooked – about 5-7 minutes.

3 Heat the butter for the sauce in a frying pan, then add the brandy and light it. When the flames have died down, stir in the cream and the peppercorns. Cook for approximately 2 minutes, stirring all the time. Serve the kebabs with the green peppercorn sauce.

161

Garlic and Marjoram Mushrooms with Pumpkin Seed and Tomato Bread

Garlic mushrooms are always popular, and this unusual Italian-style bread makes a delicious accompaniment.

SERVES 6
GARLIC MUSHROOMS
350 g/12 oz mushrooms
3 tbsp olive oil
1 tbsp water
2 cloves garlic, peeled and crushed
4 tbsp chopped fresh marjoram
juice of 1 lemon
salt and pepper
TOMATO BREAD
50 g/2 oz/¹⁄₃ cup sun-dried tomatoes in olive oil
200 ml/7 fl oz/scant 1 cup boiling water
1 tsp chopped fresh basil
1 tsp chopped fresh marjoram
1 tsp chopped fresh rosemary
50 g/2 oz/generous 3 tbsp butter
1 tsp salt
500 g/1 lb/4 cups plain flour
1 sachet (7 g/¹⁄₄ oz) dried yeast
3 tbsp olive oil
1 egg
1 tbsp pumpkin seeds

1 To cook the mushrooms, put all the ingredients in a saucepan and bring the liquid to the boil, then turn down the heat and simmer for 10 minutes. Tip the mushrooms and liquid into a bowl. Refrigerate overnight.

From top: *Chicken Drumsticks in a Honey and Coriander Crust; Garlic and Marjoram Mushrooms with Tomato Bread*

2 To make the bread, drain the tomatoes and chop roughly. Put them in a bowl and pour on the boiling water. Add the herbs and leave to soak for 20-25 minutes.

3 Place the butter, salt and flour in a mixing bowl and rub the fat into the flour until the mixture resembles breadcrumbs. Stir in the yeast. Drain the liquid from the tomatoes, reserving the liquid, and heat this until lukewarm. Add the drained tomatoes.

4 Mix the tomato and herb liquid with the olive oil and egg. Make a well in the centre of the flour mixture and pour in most of the liquid mixture. Mix well to form a fairly stiff dough. If it is too stiff, add more liquid.

5 Knead the dough until smooth, in the bowl or on a floured board or surface. Form into a round loaf shape and put this on a greased baking sheet. Cover with a clean cloth and leave in a warm room until slightly risen – this will take about 30 minutes. Preheat the oven to 220°C/425°F/gas 7.

6 Brush the loaf with a little water and gently press the pumpkin seeds into the top and sides. Bake for 15-20 minutes. Turn the loaf out on to a wire rack. Tap the upturned bottom. If the loaf is done it will sound hollow – if not, put it back in the oven for a few more minutes. Let it cool before slicing.

Chicken Drumsticks in a Honey and Coriander Crust

This delicious crunchy coating will be a hit with guests and family alike.

MAKES 8 DRUMSTICKS
8 chicken drumsticks
170 g/6 oz/³⁄₄ cup butter
2 tbsp sunflower oil
5 tbsp clear honey
1 tbsp French mustard
1 tsp roughly crushed coriander seeds
1 tsp freshly ground black pepper
450 g/1 lb/4 cups breadcrumbs
coriander sprigs, to garnish

1 Grill the chicken drumsticks for 6 minutes, turning several times. Place the butter, oil and honey in a small pan and warm until all three ingredients are combined.

2 Preheat the oven to 180°C/350°F/gas 4. Add the mustard, coriander and pepper to the mixture. Stir well and brush on to the chicken. Roll in the breadcrumbs.

3 Bake in the oven for 20-25 minutes until fully cooked through. When cooked, the juices should run clear. Serve garnished with a sprig of coriander.

Lamb Steaks Marinated in Mint and Sherry

The marinade is the key to the success of this recipe. The sherry imparts a wonderful tang.

SERVES 6

6 large lamb steaks or 12 smaller chops

MARINADE

2 tbsp chopped fresh mint leaves

1 tbsp black peppercorns

1 medium onion, chopped

120 ml/4 fl oz/½ cup sherry

60 ml/2 fl oz/¼ cup extra virgin olive oil

2 cloves garlic

1 Place the mint leaves and peppercorns in a food processor and blend until very finely chopped. Add the chopped onion and process again until smooth. Add the rest of the marinade ingredients and process until completely mixed. The marinade should be of a fairly thick consistency.

2 Place the steaks or chops in a shallow dish and pour on the marinade. Cover with non-PVC clear film and refrigerate overnight.

3 Grill or barbecue the steaks on a very high heat until cooked, basting occasionally with the marinade.

Salmon Steaks with Oregano Salsa

This combination of salmon with piquant tomato works incredibly well. An ideal dish for a summer lunch.

Serves 4

1 tbsp butter

4 salmon steaks, 225 g/8 oz each

120 ml/4 fl oz/¹⁄₂ cup white wine

¹⁄₂ tsp freshly ground black pepper

fresh oregano, to make 2 tsp chopped, plus sprigs to garnish

4 spring onions, trimmed

225 g/8 oz ripe tomatoes, peeled

2 tbsp extra virgin olive oil

¹⁄₂ tsp caster sugar

1 tbsp tomato purée

1 Preheat the oven to 140°C/275°F/gas 1. Butter an ovenproof dish, put in the salmon steaks, and add the wine and black pepper. Cover with silver foil and bake for 15 minutes, until the fish is just cooked. Leave to cool.

2 Put the oregano in a food processor and chop it very finely. Add the spring onions, tomatoes and all the remaining ingredients. Process in bursts until chopped but not a smooth purée.

3 Serve the salmon cold with the salsa, garnished with a sprig of fresh oregano.

Guacamole, Basil and Tomato Pitta Breads

This is a favourite family recipe – the fresh basil and tomato are perfect partners for each other and for the spicy guacamole.

SERVES 6

6 large pitta breads
1-2 large beef tomatoes, sliced
12 basil leaves
2 large ripe avocados
1 tomato
½ red onion
1 clove garlic, peeled and crushed
1 tbsp lime juice
¼ tsp chilli powder
2 tbsp chopped fresh dill

1 Open the ends of the pitta breads to make pockets and place a couple of slices of tomato and two basil leaves in each one.

2 Roughly chop the avocados, the remaining tomato and the red onion. Mix all the remaining ingredients briefly in a food processor.

3 Add the mixture from the food processor to the roughly chopped avocado, tomato and onions, and stir gently. Fill the pockets with the avocado mixture and serve immediately.

Brie and Grape Sandwiches with Mint

A slightly unusual sandwich combination, which works well judging by the speed with which the sandwiches disappear at family picnics or summer tea parties.

SERVES 4

8 thick slices Granary bread
butter for spreading
350 g/12 oz ripe Brie cheese
30-40 large grapes
16 fresh mint leaves

1 Butter the bread. Slice the Brie into thick slices, to be divided between the sandwiches.

2 Place the Brie slices on four slices of bread. Peel, halve and seed the grapes and put on top of the Brie. Chop the mint finely by hand or in a food processor, and sprinkle the mint over the Brie and grapes. Place the other four slices of bread over the top and cut each sandwich in half.

OTHER HERB SANDWICH IDEAS

- Feta cheese, black olives, lettuce, tomato and freshly chopped mint in pitta bread
- Italian salami, cream cheese, tomato and fresh basil on ciabatta bread
- Sliced chicken breast, mayonnaise and dill sprigs on granary bread
- Grilled mozzarella and sundried tomato foccacia bread sandwich, with black olives, fresh rocket and basil leaves
- Hummus, lettuce and freshly chopped coriander on French bread
- Dry cured Parma ham, green olives and rocket leaves on poppy-seeded white bread

From top: *Brie and Grape Sandwiches with Mint; Guacamole, Basil and Tomato Pitta Breads*

Broccoli and Cauliflower with a Cider and Apple Mint Sauce

The cider sauce made here is also ideal for other vegetables, such as celery or beans. It is flavoured using tamari, a Japanese soy sauce and apple mint.

SERVES 4

1 large onion, chopped

2 large carrots, chopped

1 large clove garlic

1 tbsp dill seed

4 large sprigs apple mint

2 tbsp olive oil

2 tbsp plain flour

300 ml/½ pint/1¼ cups dry cider

500 g/1 lb broccoli florets

500 g/1 lb cauliflower florets

2 tbsp tamari

2 tsp mint jelly

1 Sauté the onions, carrots, garlic, dill seeds and apple mint leaves in the olive oil until nearly cooked. Stir in the flour and cook for half a minute or so. Pour in the cider and simmer until the sauce looks glossy.

2 Boil the broccoli and cauliflower in separate pans until tender.

3 Pour the sauce into a food processor and add the tamari and the mint jelly. Blend until finely puréed. Pour over the broccoli and cauliflower.

Courgette and Carrot Ribbons with Brie, Black Pepper and Parsley

This recipe produces a delicious vegetarian meal, or simply a new way of presenting colourful vegetables as an accompaniment to a main course.

SERVES 4

1 large green pepper, diced

1 tbsp sunflower oil

225 g/8 oz Brie cheese

2 tbsp crème fraîche

1 tsp lemon juice

4 tbsp milk

2 tsp freshly ground black pepper

2 tbsp parsley, very finely chopped, plus extra to garnish

salt and pepper

6 large courgettes

6 large carrots

1 Sauté the green pepper in the sunflower oil until just tender. Place the remaining ingredients, apart from the carrots and courgettes, in a food processor and blend well. Place the mixture in a saucepan and add the green pepper.

2 Peel the courgettes. Use a potato peeler to slice them into long, thin strips. Do the same thing with the carrots. Put the courgettes and carrots in separate saucepans, cover with just enough water to cover, then simmer for 3 minutes until barely cooked.

3 Heat the sauce and pour into a shallow vegetable dish. Toss the courgette and carrot strips together and arrange them in the sauce. Garnish with a little finely chopped parsley.

Smoked Salmon and Dill Pasta

This has been tried and tested as both a main-dish salad and a starter, and the only preference stated was that as a main dish you got a larger portion, so that made it better.

SERVES 2 AS A MAIN COURSE OR 4 AS A STARTER
salt
350 g/12 oz/3 cups pasta twists
6 large sprigs fresh dill, chopped, plus more sprigs to garnish
2 tbsp extra virgin olive oil
1 tbsp white wine vinegar
300 ml/½ pint/1¼ cups double cream
pepper
170 g/6 oz smoked salmon

1 Boil the pasta in salted water until it is just cooked. Drain and run under the cold tap until completely cooled.

2 Make the dressing by combining all the remaining ingredients, apart from the smoked salmon and reserved dill, in the bowl of a food processor and blend well. Season to taste.

3 Slice the salmon into small strips. Place the cooled pasta and the smoked salmon, in a mixing bowl. Pour on the dressing and toss carefully. Transfer to a serving bowl and garnish with the dill sprigs.

Avocado and Pasta Salad with Coriander

Served as one of a variety of salads or alone, this tasty combination is sure to please. The dressing is fairly sharp, yet tastes wonderfully fresh.

SERVES 4
115 g/4 oz/1¼ cups pasta shells or bows
900 ml/1½ pints/3¾ cups chicken stock
4 sticks celery, finely chopped
2 avocados, chopped
1 clove garlic, peeled and chopped
1 tbsp finely chopped fresh coriander, plus some whole leaves to garnish
115 g/4 oz/1 cup grated mature Cheddar cheese
DRESSING
150 ml/¼ pint/⅔ cup extra virgin olive oil
1 tbsp cider vinegar
2 tbsp lemon juice
grated rind of 1 lemon
1 tsp French mustard
1 tbsp chopped fresh coriander
salt and pepper

1 Bring the chicken stock to the boil, add the pasta, and simmer for about 10 minutes until just cooked. Drain and cool under cold running water.

2 Mix the celery, avocados, garlic and chopped coriander in a bowl and add the cooled pasta. Sprinkle with the grated Cheddar.

3 To make the dressing place all the ingredients in a food processor and process until the coriander is finely chopped. Serve separately, or pour over the salad and toss before serving. Garnish with coriander leaves.

From top: *Smoked Salmon, Lemon and Dill Pasta; Avocado and Pasta Salad with Coriander*

Stuffed Tomatoes, with Wild Rice, Corn and Coriander

These tomatoes could be served as a light meal with crusty bread and a salad, or as an accompaniment to most meats or fish.

SERVES 4

8 medium tomatoes

50 g/2 oz/⅓ cup sweetcorn kernels

2 tbsp white wine

50 g/2 oz/¼ cup cooked wild rice

1 clove garlic

50 g/2 oz/½ cup grated Cheddar cheese

1 tbsp chopped fresh coriander

salt and pepper

1 tbsp olive oil

1 Cut the tops off the tomatoes and remove the seeds with a small teaspoon. Scoop out all the flesh and chop finely – also chop the tops.

2 Preheat the oven to 180°C/350°F/gas 4. Put the chopped tomato in a pan. Add the sweetcorn and the white wine. Cover with a close-fitting lid and simmer until tender. Drain.

3 Mix together all the remaining ingredients except the olive oil, adding salt and pepper to taste. Carefully spoon the mixture into the tomatoes, piling it higher in the centre. Sprinkle the oil over the top, arrange the tomatoes in an ovenproof dish, and bake at 180°C/350°F/gas 4 for 15-20 minutes until cooked through.

Spinach, Walnut and Gruyère Lasagne with Basil

This nutty lasagne is a delicious combination of flavours which easily equals the traditional meat and tomato version.

<u>Serves 8</u>

350 g/12 oz spinach lasagne (quick cooking)

Walnut and tomato sauce

3 tbsp walnut oil

1 large onion, chopped

225 g/8 oz celeriac, finely chopped

1 x 400 g/14 oz can chopped tomatoes

1 large clove garlic, finely chopped

½ tsp sugar

115 g/4 oz/²/₃ cup chopped walnuts

150 ml/¼ pint/²/₃ cup Dubonnet

Spinach and gruyere sauce

75 g/3 oz/¹/₃ cup butter

2 tbsp walnut oil

1 medium onion, chopped

75 g/3 oz/²/₃ cup flour

1 tsp mustard powder

1.2 litres/2 pints/5 cups milk

225 g/8 oz/2 cups grated Gruyère cheese

salt and pepper

ground nutmeg

500 g/1 lb frozen spinach, thawed and puréed

2 tbsp basil, chopped

1 First make the walnut and tomato sauce. Heat the walnut oil and sauté the onion and celeriac. Cook for about 8-10 minutes. Meanwhile purée the tomatoes in a food processor. Add the garlic to the pan and cook for about 1 minute, then add the sugar, walnuts, tomatoes and Dubonnet. Season to taste. Simmer, uncovered, for 25 minutes.

2 To make the spinach and Gruyère sauce, melt the butter with the walnut oil and add the onion. Cook for 5 minutes, then stir in the flour. Cook for another minute and add the mustard powder and milk, stirring vigorously. When the sauce has come to the boil, take off the heat and add three-quarters of the grated Gruyère. Season to taste with salt, pepper and nutmeg. Finally add the puréed spinach.

3 Preheat the oven to 180°C/350°F/gas 4. Layer the lasagne in an oven-proof dish. Start with a layer of the spinach and Gruyère sauce, then add a little walnut and tomato sauce, then a layer of lasagne, and continue until the dish is full, ending with layer of either sauce.

4 Sprinkle the remaining Gruyère over the top of the dish, followed by the basil. Bake for 45 minutes.

Potato Salad with Curry Plant Mayonnaise

Potato salad can be made well in advance and is therefore a useful buffet dish. Its popularity means that there are very rarely any leftovers.

<u>SERVES 6</u>

salt

1 kg/2 lb new potatoes, in skins

300 ml/½ pint/1¼ cups shop-bought mayonnaise

6 curry plant leaves, roughly chopped

black pepper

mixed lettuce or other salad greens, to serve

1 Place the potatoes in a pan of salted water and boil for 15 minutes or until tender. Drain and place in a large bowl to cool slightly.

2 Mix the mayonnaise with the curry plant leaves and black pepper. Stir these into the potatoes while they are still warm. Leave to cool, then serve on a bed of mixed lettuce or other assorted salad leaves.

Tomato, Savory and French Bean Salad

Savory and beans must have been invented for each other. This salad mixes them with ripe tomatoes, making a superb accompaniment for all cold meats or vegetable salads.

SERVES 4

500 g/1 lb French beans

1 kg/2 lb ripe tomatoes

3 spring onions, roughly sliced

1 tbsp pine nuts

4 sprigs fresh savory

FOR THE DRESSING

2 tbsp extra virgin olive oil

juice of 1 lime

75 g/3 oz Dolcelatte cheese

1 clove garlic, peeled and crushed

salt and pepper

1 Prepare the dressing first so that it can stand a while before using. Place all the dressing ingredients in the bowl of a food processor, season to taste and blend until all the cheese has been finely chopped and you have a smooth dressing. Pour it into a jug.

2 Top and tail the beans, and boil in salted water until they are just cooked. Drain them and run cold water over them until they have completely cooled. Slice the tomatoes, or, if they are fairly small, quarter them.

3 Toss the salad ingredients together, except for the pine nuts and savory. Pour on the salad dressing. Sprinkle the pine nuts over the top, followed by the savory.

Summer Fruit Gâteau with Heartsease

No one could resist the appeal of little heartsease pansies. This cake would be lovely for a sentimental summer occasion in the garden.

SERVES 6-8

100 g/3¾ oz/scant ½ cup soft margarine, plus more to grease mould

100 g/3¾ oz/scant ½ cup sugar

2 tsp clear honey

150 g/5 oz/1¼ cups self-raising flour

½ tsp baking powder

2 tbsp milk

2 eggs, plus white of one more for crystallizing

1 tbsp rosewater

1 tbsp Cointreau

16 heartsease pansy flowers

caster sugar, as required, to crystallize

icing sugar, to decorate

500 g/1 lb strawberries

strawberry leaves, to decorate

1 Preheat the oven to 190°C/375°F/gas 5. Grease and lightly flour a ring mould. Take a large mixing bowl and add the soft margarine, sugar, honey, flour, baking powder, milk and 2 eggs to the mixing bowl and beat well for 1 minute. Add the rosewater and the Cointreau and mix well.

2 Pour the mixture into the tin and bake for 40 minutes. Allow to stand for a few minutes and then turn out onto the plate that you wish to serve it on.

3 Crystallize the heartsease pansies, by painting them with lightly beaten egg white and sprinkling with caster sugar. Leave to dry.

4 Sift icing sugar over the cake. Fill the centre of the ring with strawberries – if they will not all fit, place some around the edge. Decorate with crystallized heartsease flowers and some strawberry leaves.

Borage, Mint and Lemon Balm Sorbet

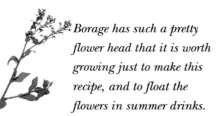

Borage has such a pretty flower head that it is worth growing just to make this recipe, and to float the flowers in summer drinks. The sorbet itself has a very refreshing, delicate taste, perfect for a hot afternoon.

SERVES 6-8

500 g/1 lb/2⅛ cups sugar

500 ml/17 fl oz/2⅛ cups water

6 sprigs mint, plus more to decorate

6 lemon balm leaves

250 ml/8 fl oz/1 cup white wine

2 tbsp lemon juice

borage sprigs, to decorate

1 Place the sugar and water in a saucepan with the washed herbs. Bring to the boil. Remove from the heat and add the wine. Cover and cool. Chill for several hours, then add the lemon juice. Freeze in a suitable container. As soon as the mixture begins to freeze, stir it briskly and replace in the freezer. Repeat every 15 minutes for at least 3 hours or until ready to serve.

2 To make the small ice bowls, pour about 1 cm/½ in cold, boiled water into small freezer-proof bowls, about 600 ml/1 pint/1¼ US pints in capacity, and arrange some herbs in the water. Place in the freezer. Once this has frozen add a little more water to cover the herbs and freeze.

3 Place a smaller freezer-proof bowl inside the larger bowl and put a heavy weight inside such as a metal weight from some scales. Fill with more cooled boiled water, float more herbs in this and freeze.

4 To release the ice bowls, warm the inner bowl with a small amount of very hot water and twist it out. Warm the outer bowl by standing it in very hot water for a few seconds, then tip out the ice bowl. Spoon the sorbet into the ice bowls, decorate with sprigs of mint and borage and serve.

From top: *Summer Fruit Gateau; Borage, Mint and Lemon Balm Sorbet*

Lemon Meringue Bombe with Mint Chocolate

This easy ice cream will cause a sensation at a dinner party – it is unusual but quite the most delicious combination of tastes that you can imagine.

SERVES 6-8

2 large lemons

150 g/5 oz/²⁄₃ cup granulated sugar

3 small sprigs fresh mint

150 ml/¹⁄₄ pint/²⁄₃ cup whipping cream

600 ml/1 pint/2¹⁄₂ cups Greek natural yogurt

2 large meringues

225 g/8 oz good-quality mint chocolate, grated

1 Slice the rind off the lemons with a potato peeler, then squeeze them for juice. Place the lemon rind and sugar in a food processor and blend finely. Add the cream, yoghurt and lemon juice and process thoroughly. Pour the mixture into a mixing bowl and add the meringues, roughly crushed.

2 Reserve one of the mint sprigs and chop the rest finely. Add to the cream and lemon mixture. Pour into a 1.2 litre/2 pint/1¹⁄₄ US quart glass pudding basin and freeze for 4 hours.

3 When the ice cream has frozen, scoop out the middle and pour in the grated mint chocolate, reserving a little for the garnish. Replace the ice cream to cover the chocolate and refreeze.

4 To turn out, dip the basin in very hot water for a few seconds to loosen the ice cream, then turn the basin upside down over the serving plate. Decorate with grated chocolate and a sprig of mint.

Apple Mint and Pink Grapefruit Fool

Apple mint can easily run riot in the herb garden; this is an excellent way of using up an abundant crop.

SERVES 4-6

500 g/1 lb tart apples, peeled and sliced

225 g/8 oz pink grapefruit segments

3 tbsp clear honey

2 tbsp water

6 large sprigs apple mint, plus more to garnish

150 ml/¼ pint/⅔ cup double cream

300 ml/½ pint/1¼ cups custard

1 Place the apples, grapefruit, honey, water and apple mint in a pan, cover and simmer for 10 minutes until soft. Leave in the pan to cool, then discard the apple mint. Purée the mixture in a food processor.

2 Whip the double cream until it forms soft peaks, and fold into the custard, keeping 2 tablespoonfuls to decorate. Carefully fold the cream into the apple and grapefruit mixture. Serve in individual glasses, chilled and decorated with swirls of cream and small sprigs of apple mint.

Passion Fruit and Angelica Syllabub

Passion fruit have a unique fragrance and flavour which makes this syllabub quite irresistible.

Serves 6

6 passion fruit

1 tbsp chopped crystallized angelica, plus more to decorate

grated rind and juice of 2 limes

120 ml/4 fl oz/½ cup white wine

50 g/2 oz/⅓ cup icing sugar

300 ml/½ pint/1¼ cups double cream

150 ml/¼ pint/⅔ cup Greek natural yogurt

1 Scoop out the flesh, seeds and juice of the passion fruit and divide between 6 serving dishes. Place the crystallized angelica in a food processor with the lime rind and juice, and blend to a purée.

2 In a large bowl, mix the lime pureé with the wine and icing sugar. Stir until the sugar is dissolved.

3 Whip the double cream until it begins to form soft peaks and then gradually beat in the wine mixture – the cream should thicken slightly. Whisk in the yogurt.

4 Spoon the cream mixture over the passion fruit, and refrigerate until ready to serve. Decorate with more crystallized angelica before serving.

Japanese Fruit Salad with Mint and Coffee

This dessert was served in a Japanese department store. Although it sounds a little strange, it works very well – the coffee flavour is excellent with the fruit.

<u>SERVES 6</u>

12 canned lychees and the juice from the can

1 small fresh pineapple

2 large ripe pears

2 fresh peaches

12 strawberries

6 small sprigs of mint plus 12 extra sprigs to decorate

1 tbsp instant coffee granules

2 tbsp boiling water

150 ml/¼ pint/⅔ cup double cream

1 Peel the fruit as necessary and chop into equal-sized pieces. Place all the fruit in a large glass bowl and pour on the lychee juice.

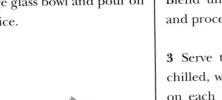

2 Put the mint, coffee granules and boiling water in a food processor. Blend until smooth. Add the cream and process again briefly.

3 Serve the fruit salad drained and chilled, with two small sprigs of mint on each plate, and the coffee sauce separately.

Clementines in Beaumes de Venise with Geranium

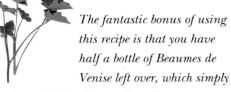

The fantastic bonus of using this recipe is that you have half a bottle of Beaumes de Venise left over, which simply has to be drunk as a digestif.

SERVES 6

10 whole clementines

12 scented geranium leaves

½ bottle Muscat de Beaumes de Venise

orange leaves, to decorate

1 Peel the clementines and remove the pith.

2 Place the clementines in a glass dish and pour over the wine. Add the scented geranium leaves and refrigerate overnight. Discard leaves, then serve chilled and decorated with orange leaves. Any juice left over from this dessert can be served as a *digestif*.

Chocolate Mint Truffle Filo Parcels

These exquisite little parcels are utterly irresistible. There will be no leftovers.

18 PARCELS

1 tbsp very finely chopped mint

75 g/3 oz/¾ cup ground almonds

50 g/2 oz plain chocolate, grated

2 dessert apples, peeled and grated

115 g/4 oz crème fraîche or fromage frais

9 large sheets filo pastry

75 g/3 oz/⅓ cup butter, melted

1 tbsp icing sugar, to dust

1 tbsp cocoa powder, to dust

1 Preheat the oven to 190°C/375°F/ gas 5. Mix the mint, almonds, chocolate, crème fraîche and grated apple in a bowl. Cut the filo pastry sheets into 7.5 cm/3 in squares, and cover with a cloth to prevent them from drying out.

2 Brush a square of filo with melted butter, lay on a second sheet, brush again, and place a spoonful of filling in the middle of the top sheet. Bring in all four corners and twist to form a purse shape. Repeat to make 18 parcels.

3 Place the filo parcels on a baking sheet, well brushed with melted butter. Bake for approximately 10 minutes. Leave to cool and then dust with the icing sugar, and then with the cocoa powder.

From left to right: *Clementines in Beaumes de Venise with Geranium; Chocolate Mint Truffle Filo Parcels*

Rosemary Vinegar

Flavoured vinegars make a huge difference to the taste of a salad dressing. They are very simple to make, and the jars are a pretty window-sill decoration. Try the same recipe with nasturtium flowers, if you like.

ABOUT 600 ML/1 PINT/2½ CUPS

rosemary sprigs, to fill a 600 ml/1 pint/2½ cup measure, plus more to decorate

600 ml/1 pint/2½ cups white distilled vinegar

1 Fill a sterilized wide-necked bottle or jar with the sprigs of rosemary. Fill to the top with vinegar. Cover tightly and place in a sunny spot for around 4-6 weeks.

2 Filter the vinegar mixture through a coffee filter paper. Discard the rosemary. Heat the vinegar until it begins to simmer, but do not boil.

3 Wash the bottle or jar and its lid well in hot, soapy water, rinse thoroughly, and dry in a warm oven. Pour the vinegar back into it or other sterilized decorative bottles. You can add a fresh sprig or two of rosemary for decorative purposes if you wish, then seal. Store in a dark place. Use within one year.

Herb Garden Dressing

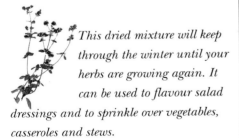

This dried mixture will keep through the winter until your herbs are growing again. It can be used to flavour salad dressings and to sprinkle over vegetables, casseroles and stews.

115 g/4 oz/1 cup dried oregano

115 g/4 oz/1 cup dried basil

50 g/2 oz/½ cup dried marjoram

50 g/2 oz/½ cup dried dill weed

50 g/2 oz/½ cup dried mint leaves

50 g/2 oz/½ cup onion powder

2 tbsp dry mustard

2 tsp salt

1 tbsp freshly ground black pepper

1 Mix the ingredients together and keep in a sealed jar to use as needed.

2 When making a batch of salad dressing, take 2 tbsp of the herb mixture and add it to 350 ml/ 12 fl oz/1½ cups of extra virgin olive oil and 120 ml/4 fl oz/½ cup cider vinegar. Mix thoroughly and allow to stand for 1 hour or so. Mix again before using.

Dill Pickles

A good pickle to have in your store cupboard. It is excellent sliced into hamburger, served with cold meats, and in canapés and snacks. If you like, try varying the type of cucumbers used. The French are fond of tiny 'cornichons', while the traditional Northern and Eastern European gherkins are much larger.

ABOUT 2.5 LITRES/4 PINTS/2½ US QUARTS

6 small cucumbers

400 ml/16 fl oz/2 cups water

1 litre/1¾ pints/4 cups white wine vinegar

115 g/4 oz/½ cup salt

3 bay leaves

3 tbsp dill seed

2 cloves garlic, slivered

dill flowerheads, to garnish

1 Slice the cucumbers into medium-thick slices. Put the water, vinegar and salt in a saucepan and boil, then remove immediately from the heat.

2 Layer the herbs and garlic between slices of cucumber in sterilized preserving jars until the jars are full, then cover with the warm salt and vinegar mixture. Leave on a sunny window sill for at least a week before using.

Parsley, Sage and Thyme Oil

Herb oils are an excellent ingredient for use in stir-fry cooking as well as salad dressings. This mixed herb combination is a good basic choice, but you can also be adventurous and try other, more exotic ingredients. Adding garlic and chillis to a herb oil produces a fiery condiment: try dribbling a tiny amount on to pasta for extra flavour.

<u>600 ML/1 PINT/2½ CUPS</u>

600 ml/1 pint/2½ cups sunflower oil

50 g/2 oz/½ cup chopped fresh parsley

25 g/1 oz/⅛ cup chopped fresh sage

50 g/2 oz/¼ cup chopped fresh thyme

1 Pour the oil into a sterilized jar and add all the herbs. Cover and allow to stand at room temperature for about a week, no longer. Stir or shake occasionally during that time.

2 Then strain off the oil into a sterilized bottle and discard the used herbs. Add a fresh sprig or two for decorative purposes if you wish. Seal the jar carefully. Store, preferably in a cool place, for 6 months at the most.

Cranberry and Port Sauce with Lemon Thyme

Cranberry and port sauce is delicious served with turkey, chicken, pork or ham. Lemon thyme really sets off its unique flavour.

<u>ABOUT 600 ML/1 PINT/2½ CUPS</u>

4 tbsp port
4 tbsp orange juice
115 g/4 oz/½ cup sugar
225 g/8 oz fresh cranberries
1 tbsp finely grated orange rind
1 tbsp very finely chopped lemon thyme

1 Pour the port and orange juice into a saucepan and add the sugar. Place the pan over a low heat and stir frequently with a metal spoon to dissolve the sugar.

2 Transfer the mixture to a larger pan. Increase the heat a little and add the cranberries. Bring the mixture to the boil and simmer for 5 minutes, stirring occasionally, until the cranberries are just tender and the skins begin to burst.

3 Remove the pan from the heat and carefully mix in the orange rind and lemon thyme.

4 Leave the sauce to cool, then pour into sterilized glass jars and seal with waxed paper circles and cellophane lids secured with rubber bands. Add a label and decorate with short lengths of string tied around the top if you like.

Lemon and Mint Curd

Home-made lemon curd is infinitely tastier than the commercial variety. The addition of mint gives this version an interesting extra tang. Try experimenting with different types of mint. Lemon curd is best made using the freshest of ingredients. Buy fresh eggs, and try to find unwaxed lemons.

<u>ABOUT 1.5 KG/3 LB</u>

6 fresh mint leaves
2 lb/900 g/4 cups caster sugar
350 g/12 oz/1½ cups butter, cut into chunks
rind of 6 lemons, thinly pared, in large pieces, and their juice
8 eggs, beaten

1 Place the mint leaves and sugar in a food processor, and blend until the mint leaves are very finely chopped and combined with the sugar.

2 Put the mint sugar and all the other ingredients into a bowl and mix together.

3 Set the bowl over a pan of simmering water. Cook, whisking gently, until all the butter has melted and the sugar has dissolved. Remove the lemon rind.

4 Continue to cook in this way, stirring frequently, for 35-40 minutes or until the mixture thickens. Pour into sterilized glass jars, filling them up to the rim. Seal with waxed paper circles and cellophane lids secured with rubber bands. Add a label and tie short lengths of string around the top of the jars to decorate. This lemon curd should be used within 3 months.

From top: *Lemon and Mint Curd; Cranberry and Port Sauce with Lemon Thyme*

Rhubarb and Ginger Mint Preserve

Ginger mint is easily grown in the garden, and is just the thing to boost the flavour of rhubarb jam. Stewed rhubarb also tastes good with a little ginger mint added to the pan.

ABOUT 2.75 KG/6 LB

2 kg/4 lb rhubarb

250 ml/8 fl oz/1 cup water

juice of 1 lemon

5 cm/2 in piece fresh root ginger, peeled

1.5 kg/3 lb/6 cups sugar

115 g/4 oz/²/₃ cup preserved stem ginger, chopped

2-3 tbsp very finely chopped ginger mint leaves

1 Wash and trim the rhubarb, cutting it into small pieces about 2.5 cm/1 in long. Place the rhubarb, water and lemon juice in a preserving pan and bring to the boil. Peel and bruise the piece of fresh root ginger and add it to the pan. Simmer, stirring frequently, until the rhubarb is soft and then remove the ginger.

2 Add the sugar and stir until it has dissolved. Bring the mixture to the boil and boil rapidly for 10-15 minutes, or until setting point is reached. With a metal slotted spoon, remove any scum from the surface of the jam.

3 Add the stem ginger and ginger mint leaves. Pour into sterilized glass jars, seal with waxed paper circles and cover with cellophane lids secured with rubber bands. Decorate with brown paper raffia.

Rose Petal Jelly

This subtle jelly is ideal for polite afternoon teas with thinly sliced pieces of bread and butter – it adds a real summer afternoon flavour to the bread.

ABOUT 900 G/2 LB

600 ml/1 pint/2½ cups red or pink rose petals

450 ml/¾ pint/1⅞ cups water

700 g/1 lb 9 oz/generous 3 cups caster sugar

100 ml/3½ fl oz/scant ½ cup white grape juice

100 ml/3½ fl oz/scant ½ cup red grape juice

50 g/2 oz packet powdered fruit pectin

2 tbsp rosewater

1 Trim all the rose petals at the base to remove the white tips. Place the petals, water and about one-eighth of the sugar in a saucepan and bring to the boil. Reduce the heat and simmer for 5 minutes. Remove from the heat and leave to stand overnight for the rose fragrance to infuse.

2 Strain the flowers from the syrup, and put the syrup in a preserving pan or suitable saucepan. Add the grape juices and pectin. Boil hard for 1 minute. Add the rest of the sugar and stir well. Boil the mixture hard for 1 minute more. Remove from the heat.

3 Test for setting – it should make a soft jelly, not a thick jam. Do this by placing a teaspoonful of the hot mixture on a saucer. Leave it to cool: the surface should wrinkle when pushed with a finger. If it is still runny, return the pan to the heat and continue boiling and testing until the jelly sets.

4 Finally add the rosewater. Ladle the jelly into sterilized glass jars and seal with waxed paper circles and cellophane lids secured with rubber bands. Decorate the tops of the jars with circles of fabric held in place with lengths of ribbon.

Cheese and Marjoram Scones

A great success for a hearty tea. With savoury toppings, these scones can make a good basis for a light lunch, served with a crunchy, green salad.

ABOUT 18 SCONES

115 g/4 oz/1 cup wholemeal flour
115 g/4 oz/1 cup self-raising flour
pinch salt
40 g/1½ oz/scant 3 tbsp butter
¼ tsp dry mustard
2 tsp dried marjoram
50-75 g/2-3 oz/½-⅔ cup finely grated Cheddar cheese
1 tsp sunflower oil (optional)
120 ml/4 fl oz/½ cup milk, or as required
50 g/2 oz/⅓ cup pecan nuts or walnuts, chopped

1 Gently sift the two kinds of flour into a bowl and add the salt. Cut the butter into small pieces, and rub these into the flour until it resembles fine breadcrumbs.

2 Add the mustard, marjoram and grated cheese, and mix in sufficient milk to make a soft dough. Knead the dough lightly.

3 Preheat the oven to 220°C/425°F/gas 7. Roll out the dough on a floured surface to about 2 cm/¾ in thickness and cut it out with a 5 cm/2 in square cutter. Grease some baking trays with the paper from the butter (or use a little sunflower oil), and place the scones on the trays.

4 Brush the scones with a little milk and sprinkle the chopped pecans or walnuts over the top. Bake for 12 minutes. Serve warm.

Dill and Potato Cakes

Potato cakes are quite scrumptious and should be more widely made. Try this spendid combination and you are sure to be converted.

ABOUT 10 CAKES

225 g/8 oz/2 cups self-raising flour

3 tbsp butter, softened

pinch of salt

1 tbsp finely chopped fresh dill

170 g/6 oz/scant 1 cup mashed potato, freshly made

2-3 tbsp milk, as required

1 Preheat the oven to 230°C/450°F/gas 8. Sift the flour into a bowl, and add the butter, salt and dill. Mix in the mashed potato and enough milk to make a soft, pliable dough.

2 Roll out the dough on a well-floured surface until it is fairly thin. Cut into neat rounds with a 7.5 cm/3 in cutter.

3 Grease a baking tray, place the cakes on it, and bake for 20-25 minutes until risen and golden.

Rosemary Bread

Sliced thinly, this herb bread is delicious with cheese or soup for a light meal.

1 LOAF

1 packet (7 g/¼ oz) dried fast-action yeast

170 g/6 oz/1½ cups wholemeal flour

170 g/6 oz/1½ cups self-raising flour

2 tbsp butter, plus more to grease bowl and tin

60 ml/2 fl oz/¼ cup warm water (45°C/110°F)

250 ml/8 fl oz/1 cup milk (room temperature)

1 tbsp sugar

1 tsp salt

1 tbsp sesame seeds

1 tbsp dried chopped onion

1 tbsp fresh rosemary leaves, plus more to decorate

115 g/4 oz/1 cup cubed Cheddar cheese

coarse salt, to decorate

1 Mix the fast-action yeast with the flours in a large mixing bowl. Melt the butter. Stir in the warm water, milk, sugar, butter, salt, sesame seeds, onion and rosemary. Knead thoroughly until quite smooth.

2 Flatten the dough, then add the cheese cubes. Quickly knead them in until they have been well combined.

3 Place the dough into a clean bowl greased with a little butter, turning it so that it becomes greased on all sides. Cover with a clean, dry cloth. Put the greased bowl and dough in a warm place for about 1½ hours, or until the dough has risen and doubled in size.

4 Grease a 23 x 13 cm/9 x 5 in loaf tin with the remaining butter. Knock down the dough to remove some of the air, and shape it into a loaf. Put the loaf into the tin, cover with the clean cloth used earlier and leave for about 1 hour until doubled in size once again. Preheat the oven to 190°C/ 375°F/gas 5.

5 Bake for 30 minutes. During the last 5-10 minutes of baking, cover the loaf with silver foil to prevent it from becoming too dark. Remove from the loaf tin and leave to cool on a wire rack. Decorate with rosemary leaves and coarse salt scattered on top.

Blackberry, Sloe Gin and Rosewater Muffins

Other berries can be substituted for the blackberries, such as elderberries or blueberries.

<u>ABOUT 12 MUFFINS</u>

300 g/11 oz/2½ cups plain white flour

50 g/2 oz/generous ¼ cup light brown sugar

4 tsp baking powder

pinch of salt

60 g/2¼ oz/generous ½ cup chopped blanched almonds

90 g/3½ oz/generous ½ cup fresh blackberries

2 eggs

200 ml/7 fl oz/⅞ cup milk

4 tbsp melted butter, plus a little more to grease cups, if using

1 tbsp sloe gin

1 tbsp rosewater

1 Mix the flour, sugar, baking powder and salt in a bowl and stir in the almonds and blackberries, mixing them well to coat with the flour mixture. Preheat the oven to 200°C/400°F/gas 6.

2 In another bowl, mix the eggs with the milk, then gradually add the butter, sloe gin and rosewater. Make a well in the centre of the bowl of dry ingredients and add the egg and milk mixture. Stir well.

3 Spoon the mixture into greased muffin cups or cases. Bake for 20-25 minutes or until browned. Turn out the muffins on to a wire rack to cool. Serve with butter.

195

Chocolate and Mint Fudge Cake

Chocolate and mint are popular partners and they blend well in this unusual recipe. The French have been using potato flour in cakes for years. Mashed potato works just as well.

1 CAKE

6-10 fresh mint leaves
170 g/6 oz/³⁄₄ cup caster sugar
115 g/4 oz/¹⁄₂ cup butter, plus extra to grease tin
75 g/3 oz/¹⁄₂ cup freshly made mashed potato
50 g/2 oz plain chocolate, melted
170 g/6 oz/1¹⁄₂ cups self-raising flour
pinch of salt
2 eggs, beaten
FILLING
4 fresh mint leaves
115 g/4 oz/¹⁄₂ cup butter
115 g/4 oz/⁷⁄₈ cup icing sugar
2 tbsp chocolate mint liqueur
TOPPING
225 g/8 oz/1 cup butter
50 g/2 oz/¹⁄₄ cup granulated sugar
2 tbsp chocolate mint liqueur
2 tbsp water
170 g/6 oz/1¹⁄₂ cups icing sugar
25 g/1 oz/¹⁄₄ cup cocoa powder
pecan halves, to decorate

1 Tear the mint leaves into small pieces and mix with the caster sugar. Leave overnight. When you use the flavoured sugar, remove the leaves and discard them.

Opposite: *Chocolate and Mint Fudge Cake; Strawberry Mint Sponge*

2 Preheat the oven to 200°C/400°F/gas 6. Cream the butter and sugar with the mashed potato, then add the melted chocolate. Sift in half the flour with a pinch of salt and add half of the beaten eggs. Mix well, then add the remaining flour and eggs.

3 Grease and line a 20 cm/8 in tin and pile in the mixture. Bake for 25-30 minutes or until a skewer or pointed knife stuck into the centre comes away clean. Turn out on to a wire rack to cool. When cool, split into two layers.

4 Chop the mint leaves in a food processor, then add the butter and sugar. Once the cake is cool, sprinkle the chocolate mint liqueur over both halves and sandwich together with the filling.

5 Put the butter, granulated sugar, liqueur and water into a small pan. Melt the butter and sugar, then boil for 5 minutes. Sieve the icing sugar and cocoa together and add the butter and liqueur mixture. Beat until cool and thick. Cover the cake with this mixture, and decorate with the pecan halves.

Strawberry Mint Sponge

This combination of fruit, mint and ice cream is a real winner.

1 CAKE

6-10 fresh mint leaves, plus more to decorate
170 g/6 oz/³⁄₄ cup caster sugar
170 g/6 oz/³⁄₄ cup butter, plus extra to grease tin
3 eggs
170 g/6 oz/1¹⁄₂ cups self-raising flour
1.2 litres/2 pints/2¹⁄₂ US pints strawberry ice cream
600 ml/1 pint/2¹⁄₂ cups double cream
2 tbsp mint liqueur
350 g/12 oz/2 cups fresh strawberries

1 Tear the mint into pieces and mix with the caster sugar. Leave overnight.

2 Grease and line a deep springform cake tin. Preheat the oven to 190°C/375°F/gas 5. Remove the mint from the sugar. Mix the butter and sugar and add the flour, then the eggs. Pile the mixture into the tin.

3 Bake for 20-25 minutes, or until a skewer or pointed knife inserted in the middle comes away clean. Turn out on to a wire rack to cool. When cool, carefully split horizontally into two equal halves.

4 Clean the cake tin and line it with clear non-PVC film. Put the bottom half of the cake back in the tin. Spread on the ice cream mixture and level the top. Put on the top half of the cake and freeze for 3-4 hours.

5 Whip the cream with the mint liqueur. Remove the cake from the freezer and quickly spread a layer of whipped cream all over it, leaving a rough finish. Put the cake back into the freezer until about 10 minutes before serving. Decorate the cake with the strawberries and place fresh mint leaves on the plate around the cake.

Carrot Cake with Geranium Cheese

At a pinch you can justify carrot cake as being good for you – at least this is an excuse for taking a good many calories on board. But the flavour is worth it.

1 CAKE

2-3 scented geranium leaves
  (preferably with a lemon scent)
225 g/8 oz/2 cups icing sugar
115 g/4 oz/1 cup self-raising flour
1 tsp bicarbonate of soda
¹/₂ tsp ground cinnamon
¹/₂ tsp ground cloves
200 g/7 oz/1 cup soft brown sugar
225 g/8 oz/1¹/₂ cups grated carrot
150 g/5 oz/¹/₂ cup sultanas
150 g/5 oz/¹/₂ cup finely chopped
  preserved stem ginger
150 g/5 oz/¹/₂ cup pecan nuts
150 ml/¹/₄ pint/²/₃ cup sunflower oil
2 eggs, lightly beaten
butter to grease tin
CREAM CHEESE TOPPING
60 g/2¹/₄ oz/generous ¹/₄ cup
  cream cheese
30 g/1¹/₄ oz/2 tbsp softened butter
1 tsp grated lemon rind

1 Put the geranium leaves, torn into small- to medium-sized pieces, in a small bowl and mix with the icing sugar. Leave in a warm place overnight for the sugar to take up the scent of the leaves.

From left: *Lavender Cookies; Carrot Cake with Geranium Cheese*

2 Sift the flour, soda and spices together. Add the soft brown sugar, carrots, sultanas, ginger and pecans. Stir well then add the oil and beaten eggs. Mix with an electric beater for about 5 minutes, or 10-15 minutes longer by hand.

3 Preheat the oven to 180°C/350°F/ gas 4. Grease a 13 x 23 cm/5 x 9 in loaf tin, line the base with greaseproof paper, and then grease the paper. Pour the mixture into the pan and bake for about 1 hour. Remove the cake from the oven, leave to stand for a few minutes, and then turn it out on to a wire rack to cool.

4 While the cake is cooling, make the cream cheese topping. Remove the pieces of geranium leaf from the icing sugar and discard them. Place the cream cheese, butter and lemon rind in a bowl. Using an electric beater or a wire whisk, gradually add the icing sugar, beating well until smooth.

5 Once the cake has cooled, cover the top with the cream cheese mixture.

Lavender Cookies

Instead of lavender you can use any other flavouring, such as cinnamon, lemon, orange or mint.

ABOUT 30 BISCUITS

150 g/5 oz/⁵/₈ cup butter, plus more
  to grease baking sheets
115 g/4 oz/¹/₂ cup granulated sugar
1 egg, beaten
1 tbsp dried lavender flowers
170 g/6 oz/1¹/₂ cups self-raising
  flour
leaves and flowers, to decorate

1 Preheat the oven to 180°C/350°F/ gas 4. Cream the butter and sugar together, then stir in the egg. Mix in the lavender flowers and the flour.

2 Grease two baking sheets and drop spoonfuls of the mixture on them. Bake for about 15-20 minutes, until the biscuits are golden. Serve with some fresh leaves and flowers to decorate.

Herbal Punch

A good party drink that will have people coming back for more, and a delightful non-alcoholic choice for drivers.

SERVES 30 PLUS

450 ml/³⁄₄ pint/2 cups honey

4 litres/7 pints/8¹⁄₂ US pints water

450 ml/³⁄₄ pint/2 cups freshly squeezed lemon juice

3 tbsp fresh rosemary leaves, plus more to decorate

1.5 kg/3¹⁄₂ lb/8 cups sliced strawberries

450 ml/³⁄₄ pint/2 cups freshly squeezed lime juice

1.75 litres/3 pints/4 US pints sparkling mineral water

ice cubes

3-4 scented geranium leaves

1 Combine the honey, 1 litre/ 1³⁄₄ pints/4¹⁄₂ cups water, one-eighth of the lemon juice, and the rosemary leaves in a saucepan. Bring to the boil, stirring until all the honey is dissolved. Remove from the heat and allow to stand for about 5 minutes. Strain into a large punch bowl.

2 Press the strawberries through a fine sieve into the punch bowl, add the rest of the water and lemon juice, and the lime juice and sparkling water. Stir gently. Add the ice cubes 5 minutes before serving, and float the geranium and rosemary leaves on the surface.

Angelica Liqueur

This should be drunk in tiny glasses after a large meal. Not only will it help the digestive system, it tastes superb.

ABOUT 1 LITRE

1 tsp fennel seeds

1 tsp aniseed

20 coriander seeds

2-3 cloves

2 tbsp crystallized angelica stems

225 g/8 oz/1 cup caster sugar

1 bottle vodka

1 Crush the fennel, aniseed and coriander seeds and cloves a little, and chop the crystallized angelica stems.

2 Put the seeds and angelica stems into a large preserving jar.

3 Add the sugar. Pour on the vodka and leave by a sunny window for 2 weeks, swirling the mixture daily.

4 Strain through fine muslin into a sterilized bottle and seal. Leave in a dark cupboard for at least 4 months. Drink in small quantities with a piece of angelica in each glass.

Strawberry and Mint Champagne

This is a simple concoction that makes a bottle of champagne go a lot further. It tastes very special on a hot summer's evening.

S<small>ERVES</small> 4-6

500 g/1 lb strawberries
6-8 fresh mint leaves
1 bottle champagne or sparkling
  white wine

1 Purée the strawberries and mint leaves in a food processor.

2 Strain through a fine sieve into a bowl. Half fill a glass with the mixture and top up with champagne. Decorate with a sprig of mint.

Melon, Ginger and Borage Cup

Melon and ginger complement each other magnificently. If you prefer, you can leave out the powdered ginger – the result is milder but equally delicious.

S<small>ERVES</small> 6-8

½ large honeydew melon
1 litre/1¾ pints/1 quart ginger beer
1 tsp powdered ginger (or to taste)
borage sprigs with flowers, to decorate

1 Discard the seeds from the half melon and scoop the flesh into a food processor. Blend to a thin purée.

2 Pour the purée into a large jug and top up with ginger beer. Add powdered ginger to taste. Pour into glasses and decorate with borage.

From left: *Melon, Ginger and Borage Cup; Strawberry and Mint Champagne*

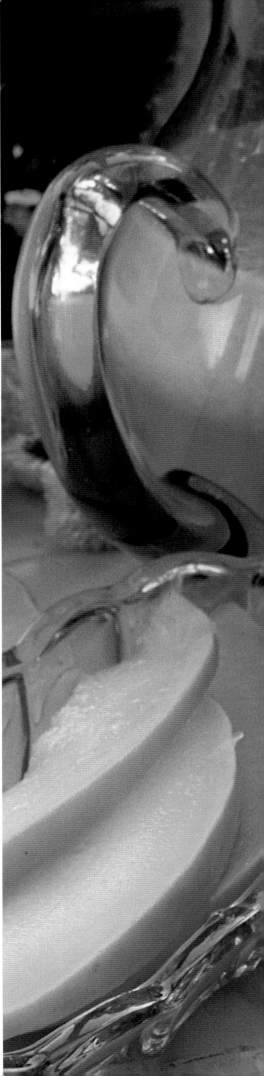

Mint Cup

Mint is a perennially popular flavour and this delicate cup is a wonderful mixture with an intriguing taste.

SERVES 1

4 sprigs fresh mint

½ tsp sugar

crushed ice

½ tsp lemon juice

2 tbsp grapefruit juice

120 ml/4 fl oz/½ cup chilled tonic water

lemon slices, to decorate

1 Crush two of the sprigs of mint with the sugar and put these into a glass. Fill the glass with crushed ice.

2 Add the lemon juice, grapefruit juice and tonic water. Stir gently and decorate with the remaining mint sprigs and slices of lemon.

Elderflower Sparkler

The flavour of elderflowers is becoming popular once again. This recipe produces one of the most delicious drinks ever concocted. Many prefer it to real French champagne because of its light and refreshing taste.

ABOUT 5 LITRES/8½ PINTS/ 10 US PINTS

750 g/1¾ lb/3½ cups caster sugar

475 ml/16 fl oz/2 cups hot water

4 large fresh elderflower heads

2 tbsp white wine vinegar

juice and pared rind of 1 lemon

4 litres/7 pints/8½ US pints water

1 Mix the sugar with the hot water. Pour the mixture into a large glass or plastic container. Add all the remaining ingredients. Stir well, cover and leave for about 5 days.

2 Strain off the liquid into sterilized screw-top bottles (glass or plastic). Leave for a further week or so. Serve very cold with slivers of lemon rind.

Chamomile Tea

The pretty yellow flowers that are used for brewing this tea give the infusion a delicate colour.

<u>Serves 4</u>

600 ml/1 pint/2½ cups boiling water
1 tbsp dried chamomile flower heads
caster sugar or honey (optional)

1 Put the chamomile flowers into a teapot or directly into a cup or mug. Pour on the boiling water and leave to infuse for about 5 minutes, or longer if you prefer a stronger flavour.

2 Strain the tea and, if you wish, add a small amount of caster sugar or honey and stir to dissolve.

OTHER HERBAL TEAS

- Iced mint tea with fresh lemon verbena.
- Mint and lavender flower tea, serve iced in summer.
- Marigold and lemon balm.

Blackcurrant and Lemon Verbena Tisane

 A warm, comforting fruity drink that will revive you on a cold winter's night. It is also excellent served chilled on a hot summer's day.

<u>Serves</u> 4

600 ml/1 pint/2½ cups boiling water
1 tbsp fresh or frozen blackcurrants
10 lemon verbena leaves
brown sugar (optional)

1 Pour the boiling water over the blackcurrants and lemon verbena leaves and leave to infuse for about 5 minutes, or longer to taste.

2 Strain the liquid into cups or tall glasses and decorate with a sprig of lemon verbena. If you prefer a sweeter drink, stir in 1 tsp of brown sugar.

HERBS IN THE HOME

Fresh Herbal Wreath

This ring looks very attractive hanging in the kitchen. If you choose culinary herbs to include in the design, it can act as a dried herb store as well, and you can snip pieces off the ring to include in recipes as they are needed. The example is purely decorative, as the herbs are not usually needed for cooking.

hot glue gun
silver rose wire
'twiggy' wreath ring, approximately
  25 cm/10 in diameter
small bunches of whichever herbs are
  handy – this example includes leaves
  and sprigs of golden sage,
  chamomile, lavender, santolina,
  scented geranium
scissors
2 m/2 yd co-ordinating ribbon,
  2 cm/¾ in wide

1 Use the hot glue gun or wire to attach a good covering of golden sage and anthemis leaves to the wreath ring.

2 Make small bunches of the lavender and santolina, binding them with wire on to the wreath ring.

3 Choose the point where you want to attach the ribbons, and put three medium-sized scented geranium leaves here to act as a backing for the ribbon. Make double loops and streamers with the ribbon of your choice, bind them with wire and glue or wire them on to the ring. Other small flowers or herbs could also be fixed on as an extra. Once the herbs start to dry, keep adding more so that the ring becomes fuller and fuller. It will then eventually dry to a beautiful decoration.

Lavender Nosegay Pot

Lavender smells wonderful in any room, and if you can use a deep blue variety it looks even better. Another suggestion is to use a selection of lavenders, perhaps pink, white and pale blue, together to make a different arrangement. It is better to use ready dried lavender than fresh, as the fresh wilts.

terracotta pot

1 block grey florist's foam for dried flowers

4-5 large bunches lavender

scissors

1 m/1 yd ribbon

thin florist's wire (optional)

1 Press the foam into the pot. Decide on the height you would like the lavender and trim the stalks to that length, plus about 4 cm/2 in to go into the foam. Insert a small bunch into the centre of the pot.

2 Continue filling the pot tightly with lavender. It takes quite a few bunches to fill even a small pot, so have plenty to hand.

3 Once the pot is completely full and you cannot get another stem into the arrangement, wrap the ribbon around the top of the pot and tie a large bow. The ribbon used here was wired with thin florist's wire, which makes it easier to produce an attractive bow.

Tussie-Mussie

This delightful herbal posy is easily made and would make a delightful alternative to a bottle of wine as a gift to take to a dinner party.

6 Minuet roses
1 bunch southernwood
florist's wire
hellebore leaves
few stems of asparagus fern
posy frill
florist's tape
scissors
ribbon, as preferred

1 Take one of the roses and wrap some southernwood around it. Bind well with wire. Make up and add small bunches of hellebore leaves.

2 Add small wired bunches of southernwood and asparagus fern.

3 Continue to bind in more roses and greenery, until you are happy with the size and composition of the posy. Push the flowers through the centre of the posy frill, secure with florist's tape and tie ribbons around it to decorate.

Rose and Herb Basket

Fresh flowers and herbs make a perfect partnership. The scent of the roses and herbs together is subtle but wonderful, especially if you hang the arrangement so that you brush lightly against it as you pass – but do not place it so that the roses are likely to be crushed. If you do not have the herbs listed here, there are many alternatives, for example sage and rosemary, and the leaves of any evergreen shrub.

1 block green florist's foam
small flower basket with handle
plastic sheet
florist's tape
scissors
hellebore leaves
scented geranium leaves
12 small sprays golden oregano
12 cream roses

1 Soak the florist's foam well. Line the basket with the plastic sheet so that no water will seep through the basketwork. Put the foam brick inside the liner and hold it in with tape. Cover the foam completely with a mixture of hellebore leaves and scented geranium leaves.

2 Add the sprays of golden oregano, placing them so that there will be room between them for the roses. Place the roses evenly throughout the arrangement, putting six on each side of the handle so that the arrangement looks well balanced, but not too symmetrical. Top up the foam with water each day to prolong the life of the arrangement.

Front to back: *Tussie-Mussie; Rose and Herb Basket*

Herbal Tablepiece

Extremely strong-smelling herbs should be avoided for table centres, as their fragrance may overpower the flavour of the meal. However, gently scented herbs make a delightful table decoration.

shallow basket without handle

2 blocks grey florist's foam for dried flowers

florist's wire

florist's tape

scissors

2 bunches cardoon thistles

3 large ivory candles

bunches of dried herbs, where possible in flower, including oregano, lavender, marjoram, fennel

1 Fill the basket with foam, wedging it into position. Group the cardoon heads into three positions in the foam. Make hairpins from wires, and tape three hairpins around the base of each candle. Place the candles into the foam.

2 Wire small bunches of lavender and marjoram, and spread evenly around the arrangement.

3 Place the fennel flower heads in the arrangement singly or wired together in groups, depending upon the space you wish to fill.

Caution: make sure that this arrangement is never left unattended with the candles alight.

Dried Herbal Topiary Tree

Topiary trees are an attractive way of displaying flowers and natural objects. This design includes small terracotta pots, which add to the textural interest in the top of the tree.

1 large terracotta pot for the base
cement or plaster of paris
piece of tree branch for the trunk
13 cm/5 in ball of grey florist's foam
  for dried flowers
small pieces of similar foam
2 large bunches of glycerined copper
  beech foliage or other preserved
  foliage
scissors
heavy-gauge florist's wire
wire cutters
12 miniature terracotta pots
2 bunches golden rod
light florist's wire
hot glue gun, if necessary
2 bunches poppy heads

1 Cover the hole in the large terracotta pot and half fill with wet cement or plaster of paris. As the cement begins to harden, stand the branch in the pot to form the trunk. Leave to dry for at least 48 hours before proceeding to next step.

2 Press the foam ball on to the trunk, making sure it is firmly in place, but not so far down that the trunk comes out the other side of the ball. Cover the cement in the base with pieces of foam.

3 Cover the ball and the base with pieces of copper beech or other preserved foliage. Thread heavy-gauge wire through the holes in the small pots and twist to make a stem so that they can be attached to the tree and pressed into the foam at the base.

4 Arrange the pots throughout the tree and base, and fill with small wired bunches of golden rod, trimming with scissors where needed. These can be glued into position if necessary, using the hot glue gun. Finally, add the poppy heads.

215

Herbal Christmas Wreath

Orange slices can be dried on a wire rack in an oven at the lowest possible setting for several hours until crisp. They should then be carefully varnished to prevent reabsorption of moisture.

a few stems fresh holly

2 sprays fresh conifer

scissors

hot glue gun

wreath ring, approximately 23 cm/ 9 in diameter

gold spray paint

5 cm/2 in terracotta pot

broken pieces of terracotta pot

7 ears of wheat, sprayed gold

1 small bunch dried sage

1 small bunch oregano

florist's wire

3 dried orange slices

1 Attach the holly and conifer to the ring using the hot glue gun. Cover approximately half the ring.

2 In a well-ventilated area, spray a little gold paint on to the pot and pieces of pot and glue them to the design. Add the ears of wheat. Make small bunches of sage and tuck those among the pieces of broken pot.

3 Make a chunky bunch of the dried oregano, wiring it together. Glue into the main pot in the centre of the design. Cut the orange slices into quarters and glue those into the arrangement. The fresh ingredients will dry on the wreath and look most attractive.

Dried Herbal Posy

This pretty posy could be given as a present or to say 'thank you'. It would also make a very pretty dressing table decoration. The ingredients are dried, so it can be made well in advance, or make a few to have to hand as gifts.

1 small bunch dried red roses
florist's wire
1 small bunch alchemilla
1 small bunch marjoram
cotton posy frill, deep pink
3 sprays dried bay
hot glue gun
florist's tape
scissors
ribbon, as preferred

1 Start with a small cluster of red roses, binding them with wire to form a centre. Add some alchemilla, binding gently but firmly in the same spot.

2 Bind in some marjoram and then more red roses and alchemilla, until you are happy with the size of the posy. Push the stems of the posy through the centre of the posy frill.

3 Separate the bay leaves from the stems and glue them in one at a time, through the arrangement and around the edge as a border.

4 Push the posy frill up towards the flowers and fasten with tape. Tie a length of ribbon around the stem of the posy and make a bow.

Scented and Decorated Candles

Candlelight is always a beautiful way of illuminating a room or dining table. Perfume can easily be added to candles by dropping a single drop of essential oil to the puddle of melted candle wax near the wick. These candles have been decorated with pressed herbs; the matching essential oil can be added later.

tall preserving jar, or other tall
container
boiling water
large candles
pressed herbs, including geranium,
lemon verbena, ivy, fennel flowers
essential oils of the herbs, as
preferred

1 Fill the jar with boiling water. Decorating the candles one by one, dip a candle into the water, holding it by the wick, and keep it submerged for about one and a half minutes. Using tweezers, quickly press the leaves on to the softened wax.

2 Once the design is finished or the wax is no longer soft enough for the leaves to stick, immerse the candle in the boiling water again. This leaves a layer of wax over the design – the more you dip the candle, the further inwards the pressed leaves will move.

3 Make a set of several designs and display them in a group. Add one or more essential oils to the candles.

Herbal Pot-Pourri

Pot-pourri made at home bears no resemblance to the commercially manufactured variety. Using dried herbs you can quickly produce a mixture that smells wonderful and which will scent the room delightfully. Give it an occasional stir to release more fragrance.

1 handful dried mint leaves
2 handfuls dried marigold flowers
1 handful any other dried herbs, such
as thyme, sage, marjoram
10 slices dried orange
6 cinnamon sticks
a few dried chillies
4 nutmegs
1 tsp mint essential oil
1 tbsp sweet orange
essential oil
1 tbsp orris root
large metal or glass bowl
plastic bag

1 Mix all the ingredients, except for the orris root, together in the bowl – do not use a wooden or plastic one, as this will absorb the essential oils and will smell for a long time. Make sure the oils are well mixed with all the other ingredients.

2 Tip the mixture into a large plastic bag, add the orris root and shake well. Leave to mature for a week or two, shaking occasionally. Then tip the mixture into a suitable display bowl or dish. Remember that essential oils can damage a polished surface, so keep away from wooden table tops.

Front to back: *Herbal Pot-Pourri; Scented and Decorated Candles*

Herbal Moth Bags

Moths dislike any pungent herbal fragrance. Herbs such as tansy and southernwood work very effectively, but lavender is perhaps the most irritating to them, and the most pleasing to us.

2 cups dried lavender flowers
1 cup dried tansy leaves
2 cups dried southernwood
2 crushed cinnamon sticks
1 tsp orris root
small hessian bags
small rubber bands
ribbon or cord, as preferred

1 Mix all the ingredients together and bag them up in small hessian bags. Secure the necks with small rubber bands.

2 Decorate with cord or ribbons, and hang in wardrobes or place in drawers.

Herb Pillows and Cushions

Hop pillows have long been known for their sleep-inducing properties, but herbal mixtures are just as effective and can also be used to give a general fragrance to a room. This mixture is a useful basic recipe, but any dried herbs of your choice can be used.

1 cup dried mint
1 cup dried lavender
1 cup dried lemon verbena
1 cup dried lemon thyme
3 cups dried lemon scented geranium
  leaves
calico or muslin bags
rubber bands, or needle and thread
1 tsp orris root (optional)
1 tsp herbal essential oil (optional)
plastic bag

1 Mix all the ingredients together. Put them in the bags, and secure tightly with rubber bands or draw strings, or by sewing up the ends. Slip these herbal bags into pillows or cushions to give a gentle fragrance.

2 For a stronger smell, add 1 tsp of orris root and the same amount of any herbal essential oil. Leave the mixture to mature in a plastic bag for a week or two before using.

Lavender Sachets

Lavender sachets are always a welcome gift, and several sachets kept among the linen in the airing cupboard will impart a fragrance that makes clean sheets even more inviting.

small calico or muslin bags
lavender flowers
rubber bands
ribbon, as preferred
selection of dried flowers
hot glue gun
sprigs of dried herbs (optional)

1 Fill the bags with the dried lavender flowers, and secure with a rubber band. Do not overfill the bags, or they will be difficult to secure.

2 Tie the neck of the bag with a ribbon and decorate with a selection of dried flowers, attached with a hot glue gun. One of the most effective ways to decorate the bags is to use a couple of dried roses and perhaps a sprig of lavender or other herb.

Rosebud and Cardamom Pomander

These rosebud pomanders are fun to make and add a pretty touch to any room. They can be hung on a wall, or over a dressing-table mirror. When the colour has faded they can be sprayed gold as a Christmas ornament.

ribbon or cord for hanging
medium florist's wire
7.5 cm/3 in ball grey florist's foam for dried flowers
scissors
small rosebuds
general-purpose adhesive
green cardamom pods

1 Make a long loop with the ribbon or cord. Bind the base of the loop with wire. Leave a long end of wire, and push this through the centre of the ball and out through the other side. Trim the wire to about 2.5 cm/1 in long, and bend the end over to lose the end in the foam ball.

2 Stick the rosebuds into the foam by their stems. If they have no stems, use a little glue. Cover the entire ball with roses, pressing them close together to make sure that none of the foam is visible. Once the ball is completely covered, glue some green cardamom pods between the rosebuds to give a contrast in colour and texture.

223

Scented Wooden Brushes

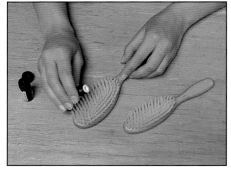

Wooden brushes and accessories can be given a delightful fragrance with a very tiny amount of essential oil. Varnish is damaged by essential oils, so do not get any oil on the shiny back of the brush.

wooden hairbrush, unvarnished
essential oil, such as lavender
wooden hair clip, unvarnished

1 Take the wooden hairbrush and sprinkle two or three drops of your favourite essential oil on to the bristle side. The oil will be absorbed by the bristles and the wood, and will impart a fragrance for quite some time. When the scent fades, add a little more oil. As you brush your hair it will leave a lingering fragrance. Do not use too much oil, as this is messy and may also damage a polished surface.

2 To add more fragrance to your hair, sprinkle a couple of drops of essential oil on the wooden hair clip. This should be an unvarnished one, which will absorb the oil and will not be damaged by it.

Herb Corsages

Making your own buttonhole or corsage is easy. Tiny posy frills are obtainable from specialist floral suppliers, or you could use the centre of a paper doyley.

1 medium-sized flower

1 sprig any herb with attractive leaves

thin florist's wire

miniature posy frill, or cut-down doyley

florist's tape

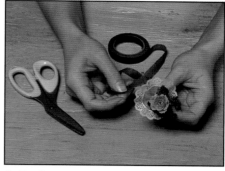

1 For a centrepiece, you could use a rose or small spray carnation. Wrap some herb foliage around it – parsley would look good – and bind tightly with thin wire.

2 Push the stems through the centre of the frill and tape them together, covering the stems all the way down. Other combinations could include rosemary, sage, lavender or box.

Rosemary Hair Tonic

Rosemary is an excellent substitute for mildly medicated shampoos, and this tonic also helps control greasy hair and enhances the shine and natural colour.

250 ml/8 fl oz/1 cup fresh rosemary tips

1.2 litres/2 pints/5 cups bottled water

1 Put the ingredients in a saucepan and bring to the boil. Simmer for approximately 20 minutes, then allow to cool in the pan.

2 Strain the mixture and store it in a clean bottle. Use after shampooing the hair.

Herbal Bath Bags

*These are much more fun
than putting commercial
bubble bath into the water.
Tie them over the taps and
make sure the hot running water is going
through them – this will release lovely
herbal scents that relax and comfort you.*

**3 x 23 cm/9 in diameter circles of
 muslin**

6 tbsp bran

1 tbsp lavender flowers

1 tbsp chamomile flowers

1 tbsp rosemary tips

3 small rubber bands

3 m/3 yd narrow ribbon or twine

1 Place 2 tbsp bran in the centre of
each circle of muslin. Add the lavender to one bag, the chamomile to a
second and the rosemary to the third.

2 Gather each circle of material up
and close with a rubber band. Then
tie a reasonable length of ribbon or
twine around each bag to make a loop
so that the bag can be hung from the
hot tap in the stream of water.

Rose Hand Cream

This is an excellent scented hand cream which softens and moisturizes.

1 tsp beeswax

¼ tsp honey

4 tbsp almond oil

4 tbsp rosewater

1 Put the beeswax, honey and almond oil in a glass jar standing in a small pan of hot water. Stir until melted and blended.

2 Stir vigorously while pouring in the rosewater. Take the jar out of the water, and continue to stir gently until the mixture has cooled.

Dill Aftershave

Most recipes are for fragrances for women, so here is one for men. It is best kept in the refrigerator so that the cool liquid has a bracing effect as well as smelling good.

50 g/2 oz/¼ cup dill seed

1 tbsp honey

600 ml/1 pint/2½ cups bottled water

1 tbsp distilled witch hazel

1 Place the dill seed, honey and water in a small saucepan and bring to the boil. Simmer for about 20 minutes.

2 Allow to cool in the pan, then add the witch hazel. Strain the cooled mixture into a bottle and refrigerate.

Lavender Bubble Bath

There is no need to buy commercially made bubble baths again. This fragrance is quite delicious and so simple to make that you can make some spares as gifts for friends and family – you will be in great demand!

1 bunch lavender
clean wide-necked jar, with screw top
1 large bottle clear organic shampoo
5 drops oil of lavender

1 Place the bunch of lavender head downwards in the jar. If the stalks are longer than the jar cut them down, as it is the flowers that do the work. Add the shampoo and the lavender oil.

2 Close the jar and place on a sunny window sill for 2-3 weeks, shaking occasionally.

3 Strain the liquid and re-bottle. Use about 1 tbsp in a bath.

Dandelion Tea

Most warm herbal teas have a comforting effect. Dandelions are a diuretic, and can help to reduce water retention and bloated feelings. Many people find that this is a useful treatment for rheumatism. This tea also acts as a mild laxative so should not be drunk in large quantities.

5-6 dandelion leaves
boiling water
1 tsp honey (optional)

1 Remove any stems from the dandelion leaves. Break them into strips and place in the bottom of a mug. Pour on enough boiling water to fill the mug and leave to stand for 5-10 minutes.

2 Strain, discard most of the dandelion leaves, and drink. If you prefer a sweeter brew, add a small teaspoonful of honey.

DANDELIONS

- Dandelion roots when dried can be used as a coffee substitute; they can also be added to beer and wine.
- Dandelion leaves are eaten as a salad vegetable in Mediterranean countries; they can also be blanched and served as a cooked accompaniment.

Thyme Tea

Thyme is excellent for treating chest infections and coughs. This tea is a comforting extra treatment, but do not rely on it to cure. However, it will help to combat sleeplessness and irritating coughs.

25g/1 oz fresh thyme
600 ml/1 pint/2½ cups boiling water
honey

1 Take the fresh thyme and cover with the boiling water. Allow to infuse for at least 5-10 minutes, to taste.

2 Add a little honey, and drink while still piping hot.

DECORATIVE THYME

- Collect and air-dry bunches of thyme when in flower. The flowers can be used in dried floral arrangements.
- Alternatively, when the flowers are dry, crumble them between your fingertips and add to pot-pourri mixtures.

Lavender and Marjoram Bath

A long warm bath is an excellent way of relieving the stresses and strains of a busy day. This bath mixture has the added bonus of moisturizing the skin while it gently soothes away cares and troubles. The essential oils induce sleep. To enhance the effect, you could add a bath bag containing fresh lavender and marjoram to the water.

2 tbsp almond oil
7 drops lavender oil
3 drops marjoram oil

1 Measure out all the ingredients into a small dish or bowl.

2 Mix all the ingredients together and pour them into the bath while the water is running, then have a long, soothing soak.

Lemon Grass, Coriander and Clove Bath

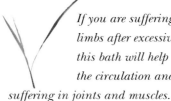

If you are suffering from stiff limbs after excessive exercise, this bath will help stimulate the circulation and relieve suffering in joints and muscles.

2 tbsp almond oil
2 drops lemon grass oil
2 drops coriander oil
2 drops clove oil

1 Carefully measure the almond oil into a small dish.

2 Slowly drop in all the essential oils. Mix all the ingredients and pour into the bath while the water is running. Rinse the dish under the running tap to make sure all the oils have gone into the bath water. Take a long, relaxing bath.

Lavender Oil

Lavender oil is the most useful of all the essential oils, and perhaps the safest. Allergic reaction is virtually unknown and, unlike many of the other essential oils, it is safe to apply it directly to the skin.

It can help to promote sleep – sprinkle a few drops on to the pillow, or on to a handkerchief placed on the pillow, for adults and children to enjoy untroubled rest.

It is also excellent for treating burns, stings, scalds and minor wounds. Deter flying insects by rubbing the essential oil into uncovered parts of the body, such as hands and feet, on a warm evening when sitting outside.

Lavender oil can be added to bottled water (about 6 drops to 600 ml/1 pint/2½ cups) and sprinkled on to dry pillow cases or any other linen before ironing to leave a lingering fragrance.

From left: *Lemon Grass, Coriander and Clove Bath; Lavender and Marjoram Bath*

Comfrey Infusion

This is a useful lotion to make up to treat minor cuts and scrapes. It should be used at room temperature when not too cold, as it is more soothing warm.

2 tsp fresh comfrey leaves (or 1 tsp dried comfrey)
300 ml/½ pint/1¼ cups boiling water

1 Shred the fresh comfrey leaves into small pieces and cover with the boiling water. Allow to steep for 10 minutes. Leave to cool.

2 Gently bathe cuts and abrasions with this lotion on a lint pad. It is also good for minor burns, scalds and sunburn.

Mint Footbath and Massage Oil

After a long day on your feet, try soaking them in this soothing footbath. Then rub the mint oil into your feet to smooth and soften before you go to bed. The mint essential oil also has a refreshing scent.

MINT BATH
12 large sprigs mint
120 ml/4 fl oz/½ cup cold water
2.4 litres/4 pints/10 cups boiling water
MASSAGE OIL
1 tbsp almond oil
1 drop mint essential oil

1 Place the mint in a food processor and add the cold water. Process well until it becomes a green purée. Pour this into a large bowl and add the boiling water. Once the mixture has cooled to a bearable temperature, soak both feet at once until the water is too cool to be comforting.

2 Gently rub your feet dry with a soft towel. Mix the almond oil and the mint essential oil and rub well into both feet.

Basil Water

This is a delicious herbal brew – some herbal teas are a little unpalatable, but this is very good. Basil relieves nausea and is thought to have mild antiseptic properties, but these should not be relied upon and the brew should only be used as an extra treatment for infections.

1 large sprig basil
300 ml/½ pint/1¼ cups boiling water
1 tsp fresh orange juice

1 Pour the boiling water over the sprig of basil, leave to infuse for about 5 minutes and then remove the basil.

2 Add the orange juice and stir. Drink while hot.

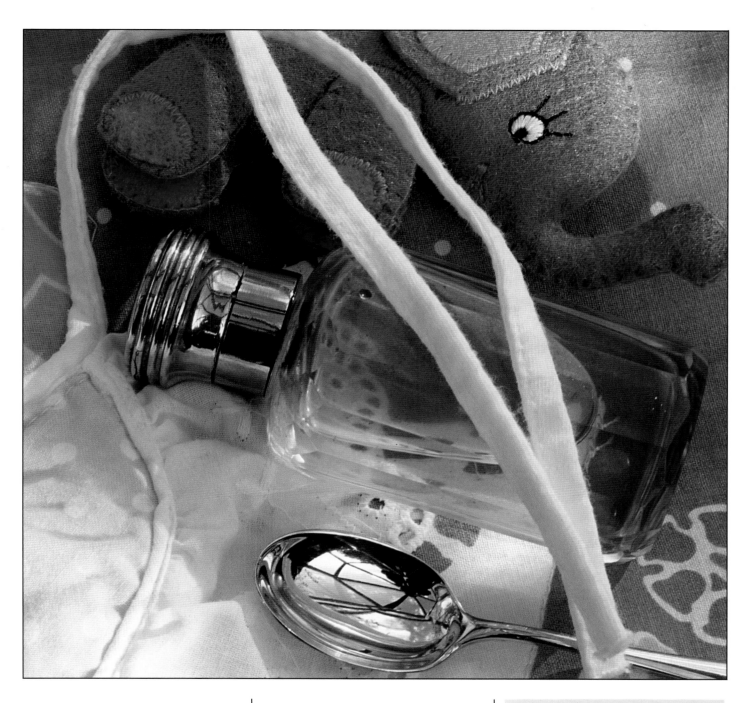

Fennel Gripe Water

Used occasionally to help digestion and to soothe colic, this gripe water can be gently effective. Although gripe water is usually associated with babies, it can also be useful for adults and children. Use 1 tsp fennel seeds to 1¼ cups water. For a small baby, after making, dilute the infusion with 2 parts water to 1 part gripe water. It may be drunk warm or cold.

1 tsp fennel seeds

300 ml/½ pint/1¼ cups boiling water

1 Crush the fennel seeds, cover with the boiling water and leave to steep for about 20 minutes.

2 Strain the brew, discarding the fennel seeds.

HERBAL PROJECTS FOR CHILDREN

• Lavender bags trimmed with sprigs of chamomile and bright ribbons.

• Pressed herb flower and leaf cards and stationery.

• Creating miniature dried gardens from lavender, marigolds and roses.

Index

Stockists and Suppliers

The Chelsea Gardener
125 Sydney Street
London SW3 6NR
(0171) 352 5656
UK
(*Specialists in potted herbs*)

Gardiners Herbs
35 Victoria Road
London SW14 8EX
(0181) 878 7981
UK
(*Herb plants, herb garden design*)

Hollington Nurseries
Woolton Hill
Newbury
Berkshire RG15 9XT
(01635) 253908
UK
(*Herb garden and nurseries; mail order*)

Idencraft Herbs
Frittenden Road
Staplehurst
Kent TN12 0DH
UK
(01580) 891432
(*Herb garden and nurseries*)

Lakeland Plastics
Alexandra Buildings
Windermere
Cumbria LA23 1BQ
UK
(015394) 88100
(*Specialist culinary supplies*)

R & G Stevens
Lucas Green Nurseries
Lucas Green Road
West End
Woking GU24 9LY
UK
(01483) 474041
(*Culinary herb nurseries*)

Sherringhams Nurseries
299a Lane Cove Road
North Ryde
NSW 2113
Australia
(*Plants and garden supplies*)

Distinctive Gardens Nursery
160 Russell Street
Morley
WA 6062
Australia
(091) 370 5141
(*Herb plants and general nursery*)

Ploughmans Lavender Nursery
Duff Road
RD 2 Waiuku
New Zealand
(*Lavender specialists*)

Picture Acknowledgements
All photographs in this book were taken by John Freeman and Michelle Garrett, apart from those on pages 36 (left) and 37, 54 and 55 and pages 36 (right), 75 (hollyhocks), 77 (sea thrift), 81 (knapweed), 82 (chamomile), 87 (rocket), 90 (herb robert), 93 (woad), 95 (lavender), 98 (mallow), 107 (greater plantain), 113 (savory) and 117 (variegated Russian comfrey) which were kindly lent by Jenny Balfour-Paul, Jacqui Hurst and the Garden Picture Library respectively. The pictures on pages 7 (bottom), 8 (top and bottom left) and 9 (right) were lent by Visual Arts Library.